# ENDORSEMENTS

What a powerful testimony! Neil Leary's life story presents numerous proofs that our great Savior, the Lord Jesus Christ, has the power to totally transform lives—though in Neil's case it took years to deliver him completely from addiction to alcohol and drugs (such as LSD). I highly recommend it.

Kenneth L. Barker
General Editor, NIV Study Bible

I want to encourage you to read the story of Neil Leary and see the great work of God in his life. Neil has gone from the pit of addiction and death to a new life in Christ. His story is unique to his experience, but the God who rescued Neil can do a great work in your life as well. As his pastor, I have known Neil for over twenty years. I encourage you to read this book with an open heart, ready to be encouraged and filled with hope.

Dr. Brent Taylor
Senior Pastor, First Baptist Church at The Fields
Carrollton, Texas

I've known Neil Leary for years as a Christian man. His story of how God saved and turned his life around is a testimony to the great patience and love God that has for all of us, no matter what we have done to ourselves. It is uplifting to read of a life that was so lost and yet in Christ can be so wonderfully found.

Pastor Rick Coburn
Calvary Chapel Plano

# LOST BOY FOUND

## THE STORY OF A MODERN-DAY LAZARUS

*Neil Leary*

# FORWARD

I've known Neil for more than twenty-five years but as I turned the last page of LOST BOY FOUND, I realized that I never knew the LOST BOY, only the FOUND. My late wife Debbie and I were friends with Neil, a servant of the Lord who God saved to tell this amazing story.

What you are about to read, is real, sobering, heartbreaking, and ultimately triumphant. I applaud the courage it took to put down on pages such painful memories of this deeply personal story of bondage and torment. It will take you to dark places unknown to many. From coast to coast, on highways and back roads, in bars and bar ditches, Neil paints an ugly picture from inside too many jails and half-way houses, of what lost looks like. But like prophets whose lives were often parables, Neil danced with the devil and drank with demons until he was miraculously saved. More than once spared from certain death, he lives today to spread a beautiful message of hope to those who have none, and to encourage those who serve a risen Savior, that God never gives up on us. As I burned through this page-turner, I was reminded of Romans 8:18, "For I consider that the sufferings of this present time are not worthy to be compared with the glory which shall be revealed in us." Buckle up your seat belt and pray your air-bags are engaged as you now turn the pages. Be thankful you did not have to dwell in the Hell that he did in order to live the victorious life in Christ that Neil and his beautiful family now enjoy.

Ron Hall, author
#1 New York Times Bestseller
*Same Kind of Different as Me*

"It was right that we should make
merry and be glad, for your brother
was dead and is alive again, and was
lost and is found."

Luke 15:32

# PROLOGUE

As my wife Tsion and I sat in a mansion not far from the palatial estates of one of our former Presidents, a presidential candidate and some of the richest most privileged people on the planet, the melody flew exquisitely from the Stradivarius as I silently wondered at the miracle which had taken place. Had I been found in this house 27 years before, or even in the neighborhood, the police would have carted me off to jail on general principals. The music was like nothing I'd ever heard before. Though I'd listened to many hours of beautiful classical music in the past, both live and through various media, never had I sat fifteen feet away from the rare and amazing instrument while a virtuoso plied his bow so skillfully, making it sing the most extraordinary sounds. My spirit soared to the heavens with it. Just two days before I had listened as, just twenty yards away another master played the Petrus Guarnerius 1735 Venedig, the king of the violins in a similar manner. To think that a man who had dwelt among the living dead for so many years, a man so despicable that my very presence evoked disgust and suspicion among most who encountered me, could be elevated to such heights is beyond natural understanding … in fact it is entirely supernatural.

*Part One*

# BEFORE THE FALL

# CHAPTER I

Like the thunderously clanging bells of Notre-Dame which Quasimodo rang while cackling maniacally, my emotions swung wildly back and forth from thoughts of suicide to homicide as I clung tenuously to life beside the highway in the middle of the Arizona desert, in the middle of the night. It's hard to imagine how I could have arrived at that point by the tender age of twenty years given the storybook life I had lived in the beginning.

On Christmas Eve 1959 as we rounded the corner in our old red Ford station wagon heading for our family's first house, my world came in to focus. My Dad is a wonderful, loving, giving man and likes to give gifts, surprises or just tasty meals to his friends … always with a careful touch. My first memory of the house at 5 Jo Drive, his Christmas present to our family that year, was in keeping with the precious man that he is. While toddling around near the Christmas tree as we arranged our belongings, Mom, my older sister Pam and I began to put things in order in our new house. Dear Dad had to drive all the way back to White Plains to pick up the Christmas ornaments and lights that he'd forgotten to load the first time. Typical of Dad was his uncomplaining foray into the dark to accomplish whatever it took to meet his family's needs. There were many days in the years to come when Dad would leave long before we awoke and return long after dinner, not necessarily because he loved to work, but because it was what was required. When he returned later that night we decorated the Christmas tree, and as we drifted off to sleep on blankets on the floor, the first few hours of my conscious existence came to a blissful end.

On Christmas morning my peers around the world were waking up in thatched huts, stone houses with slate roofs hundreds of years old, humble adobe cottages and a myriad of other homes quite different from the pristine new house in Westchester County, New York that was to be our home for the next six years. This was post World War II America and I was blessed to be born into a family that would ride the crest of a booming nation at the height of its wealth, power and prestige. Mine is a uniquely American story, yet because of the incredible diversity of our country and the many paths down which life would take me, I've had the privilege of getting to know and love people from all over the world and all strata of society.

My precious Mom had begun a career as a banker working for a prestigious investment bank in New York City where she met, fell in love with and married my Dad. My sister Pam came along after a little while, and mom's plans to be an urban professional were put on hold indefinitely. Rather than taking the easier, more "self-fulfilling" path and handing us off to harried hirelings to oversee her children while she pursued her dreams, she made the sacrifice few women in the west make today. Mom traded a full scholarship to earn her Masters at Georgetown University and the challenge and glamour of Manhattan for a much more difficult and rewarding job, so that we children would have someone who loved us deeply at our side during our most tender and impressionistic years. She did a marvelous job loving and caring for us and managing our new home. It's been said that when a job is well done, you hardly notice the execution. Our house was always clean as a whistle, and our meals, tasty and wholesome, were served with satisfying regularity. The house was always bright and cheerful, and besides doing piles of laundry and ironing, Mom always had a nice flower garden in the yard which was a blessing to us all. Now that I am a parent myself, I understand how much hard work went into what we sometimes took for granted. She may have occasionally felt that her time and exceptional talent were being underutilized, but we will never forget the comfort it was to know that Mom was always there. There were not many latch key kids in America back in the 1960s and I take my hat off to the great moms both then and now, who sacrifice seemingly more gratifying, exciting and intellectually challenging jobs for that most important one of being a loving mother. As a result of the terrible tragedy of the divorce epidemic which has forced many women into the workforce when they would have preferred to stay with their darling little ones, that part of the American Dream will remain only a dream for most kids today.

Five Jo Drive, the second house to be occupied on our street in the new Fawn Ridge subdivision, was one of countless new houses that were sprouting up in hundreds of new developments all over the nation, as with God's blessing, America stretched and flexed its muscles. Situated on the gently rolling land just east of the Hudson River in Peekskill, New York (now Cortlandt Manor) it was a great stage for the idyllic life which I led for my first few years. Everything had been crisply cut out of what had been farmland, as much of our vast country had been prior to the twentieth century. Behind our house ran a fieldstone wall, an enduring testimony to the blood sweat and tears some hardscrabble Yankee farmer had spilled carving out tillable land for his family from this rocky and not so pliable terrain. It was one of the first of many enticing mysteries for me; I could not get near the wall without thinking of the people who had gone before me so many years ago … what it must have been like … what could have motivated them. As a toddler I could not even budge many of the stones, and when Dad occasionally had to heft one that had fallen into our yard, I could see that even for a giant like him it was not an effortless task. Who could have built such a wall? I never followed it to see if it had an end—that would have spoiled the mystery and wonder. Looking back over the years to when my children were little and I worked two jobs to support my precious family, it's clear now that it was love for their families that relentlessly spurred the early settlers on through their back breaking labors. This also no doubt inspired the dogged determination of my own beloved father as over the years he trudged back and forth to New York City, across the state, the country, and around the world pursuing the generous paycheck which would provide for his brood and gain him smashing success in his chosen profession of commercial finance.

Beyond the fieldstone wall were the woods which stretched seemingly forever. There were probably only a few hundred acres, but to a two and half foot tall kid they seemed boundless and ripe for exploration. The early sixties were a time when you could still hear an old wooden screen door slam shut across the street, and when the weather was nice that was the only door most people would close during the day. It was a time when a young boy and his friend could still go off into the woods exploring for several hours, and their moms would not be in fear that some maniac had carried them away. Eddie Hall, a dark haired, freckled faced kid with a giant smile, was my first friend outside of my family. He was easygoing, very laid back and had a gentle, open outlook on life. His parents, Ed and Bunny, were close friends with my folks, and he and I paired up quickly and set off to explore the exciting world around us. He was Tom Sawyer to my Huck Finn. We spent many delightful hours tramping through those woods, or riding our bikes up and down Jo Drive and occasionally venturing to adjoining streets. It always seemed more natural and inviting to strike out into the woods and fields that bordered our neighborhood than it did to venture very far on the pavement. The lush Hudson River Valley countryside was warm and inviting … people were an unknown quantity.

Most of our time together was spent passing joyful days pursuing the usual boyhood stuff … all under our beautiful deep blue New York sky. On a typical day, majestic oak, maple, elm and pine trees swayed in the breeze as the birds chirped and the occasional Piper Cub droned lazily overhead in the distance … it seemed like a terrific, endless holiday! The only time that Eddie and I ever disagreed about anything that I can remember, was the time I decided to throw rocks over a neighbor's house. Eddie wisely didn't think it was a good idea, but joined in when I coaxed him. When one of my rocks went through a window, I ducked behind a bush and urged him to join me, but Eddie did the right thing and stood up when the lady of the house called out to see who had broken her window. Feeling betrayed I scolded him and tried to get him to duck down again, yet knew he was right and didn't hold it against him for long.

Springtime came gently in Westchester County. The harsh edge of winter slowly, damply melted away, a few crocuses poked their brilliant heads through the last snow, then the forsythia would bloom and a daffodil or two shining brightly proclaimed the end of winter. The first warm afternoon breeze would come and then a hundred shades of green seemed to appear overnight and explode from every direction. Spring meant Easter—Resurrection Day—a special joy filled time of year! Although I couldn't put my finger on it, not old enough to quite understand it, Easter morning was a day that I awoke excited and filled with awe and expectation ... it was a very special day and it wasn't just the candy! Having had the privilege of living in many different regions of America which God so skillfully and wonderfully made, I cannot remember a spring season anywhere which excelled the beauty of those in my state of birth. As the earth continued to blossom and beckoned in anticipation to the summer, the Lord's great outdoors sang a siren song to me, engendering a lifelong love for His dazzling handiwork.

The Good Humor ice cream man was one of the many delights of summer for us. His white pickup truck had a built in freezer where the truck bed would usually be, and a neat row of bells which jingled in unison when he pulled the cord hung in the spot where there would have been a rear view mirror if the freezer wasn't there to obstruct the view. He always seemed to arrive in mid-afternoon between lunch and dinner—just when we kids who had been playing vigorously all day were in need of a cool break. Behind my house was a tall maple tree, and one of my self-assigned duties was to climb it and play "Indian scout" looking out for the first signs of his approach. As I climbed higher and higher, each limb took me closer to the top of the canopy of the forest which backed up to our yard, and closer to the brilliant Yankee sunshine. It was worth the climb just for the view, and as I gazed over the treetops the warm breeze blew through my hair and caused the boughs to sway back and forth. The leaves rustled with the breeze and the enchanting, lilting sounds of the song birds, the occasional buzz of a bee and the calls of other creatures serenaded me as I kept my post ... the whole scene made my job a delightful one. The beauty was so compelling that sometimes I became lost in the moment and forgot my mission! After a little while I'd hear the cheerful bells of the Good Humor man calling the kids in the neighborhood adjacent to ours. I'd yell the alarm, slip down the tree as quickly as I could and tell my sister Pam, then run up the street sounding the alert. All the kids would scamper home, collect some change from their moms and make it back to the spot on the curb where he was dispensing his goodies before he pulled away. A special treat was to stand right next to the door when he opened the freezer and feel the frigid air roll out chasing the summer heat from my face.

Another of our favorite summer pastimes was the bug man. Regularly each summer in the evening, a Jeep drove through our neighborhood spraying to control the mosquito population. He always came late in the evening during the rare opportunity only the long days of summer sunshine afforded—after dinner play time! In contrast to our paranoid, catastrophe focused, lawsuit crazy world of today, society was pretty relaxed in the early and mid-sixties. No one thought twice about allowing us kids to run back and forth weaving through the dense fog of chemicals following the bug man as he drove slowly up the street. As far as I know, to this day none of us has shown any ill effects from it, but I wouldn't put it on *your* list of play choices for the kiddos!

Summers in Peekskill meant a wading pool in our back yard, dashing through the lawn sprinkler with our friends and an occasional trip to Sprout Lake, Bear Mountain, West Point, the Catskill Game Farm or another splendid nearby spot in this ever so lovely part of the planet. We'd have nice barbecues in our back yard, feasting around our wooden picnic table. Mom made the most terrific potato salad and iced tea! Fresh corn on the cob from the fields surrounding Peekskill and "mmmmm" the chicken Dad barbecued rounded out a typical feast ... and don't forget the watermelon! It was usually almost dark by the time we finished, and we would sit for a while afterward talking quietly in the evening cool. There is something about the hush that falls upon the earth as the light fades which seems to incline us to lower our voices as if in deference to God's creation, that awesome, powerful and complex system, as it is winding down operations for the day.

Our summers almost always included a trip to the beach. The Atlantic seaboard of the United States is graced with hundreds of miles of fabulous beaches, and usually we'd spend a week or so there each year. The first one I recall was Rehoboth Beach in Delaware. A quaint beach cottage just big enough for the Leary and Hampton families was perched on the dunes just a few yards from the sun flooded miles of sand and the sparkling ocean. Hours of swimming, splashing, basking in the sun and body surfing usually ended with a nice clam bake, cook out, or a trip to a scrumptious smelling local seafood place ... and a deep restful sleep. Ever since those days the ocean has been an exotic and romantic place to me. It may be because my Irish ancestors were seafarers, but the smell of salt air always seems to stir something deep within me, something like the effect of catching a whiff of a grilling steak might have upon a particularly hungry person or that of catnip on a cat! Very few things are as restful or comforting to me as lying beside or walking along the ocean shore listening to the breakers and meditating upon the ever enthralling beauty of God's world. We vacationed at many beautiful spots along the coast, often in south Florida where my grandparents wintered. Ah, those were simple and carefree days! I've often said that most kids don't know how good they have it … dad and mom providing food, clothing and shelter, protection and comfort of all varieties … and fun and luxuries too! Not all children growing up in America before or after me, nor most of the children of the world have had it so good, but my blessing was great. My preschool years were especially good. No one expected much from a shrimp, just toddle along, play, explore and do your best to obey and be nice. Do you think there is a job posting on the Internet for a spot like that? How blessed we were!

Those early years were marked by plenty of happiness and adventure—it was a full, wonderful life! Everything was new and interesting. The pace of life was casual and relaxed and I rarely had a care in the world. Like a fascinating series of Currier and Ives paintings, life for me consisted of blissfully discovering the world around me with my friends, excitement filled family gatherings during the holidays, and the joys of growing up in a small town. My little sister Beth came along just as things were getting interesting. Upon her arrival I was unceremoniously evicted from my private bedroom in our three bedroom house, but that turned into a blessing as I got to bunk with my older sister Pam for a couple of years. That time cemented our friendship and among other things afforded me the opportunity to learn the art of whistling. She was willing to teach me and attempted to a couple of times, but I didn't catch on quickly. One night just before bed time I asked her again and she said, "Alright, but this is the last time!" Knowing that she meant it, I watched and listened intently as she instructed me, and puckering up, did my level best to mimic her but failed. Then, with one final instruction I managed a faint whistle! Thus began a lifelong hobby of mine and one which has given me much pleasure, and helped me pass many a lonely hour years later when I lived in a very different world.

# CHAPTER 2

Woofie the cat was my soul mate. Born exactly the same day and year, I always felt a special affinity for him—we had an exclusive club! He was a large brown point Siamese and was an interesting mix of indoor and outdoor cat. He was a great hunter, and unlike most cats he came when you called him. At night when it was time for him to come inside, I'd whistle for him and he'd come just like a dog. As much as cats like heights, quite uncharacteristically he obeyed and stayed off the furniture—that was good, because his stay with us would have been *mighty* short otherwise! Like many families we had some fun traditions which heralded upcoming holidays and the beginning of seasons each year. Every year around Thanksgiving and Christmas my two sisters and I would prepare for bed early and line up in our pajamas on our sleeper sofa to watch The Wizard of Oz, Laurel and Hardy's Babes in Toyland and a few other classics on television. Since my Dad worked in New York City during those years, we could also look forward to riding the train into the city and seeing the big Christmas tree at Rockefeller Center, the Christmas show at Radio City and the decorations along 5th Avenue. Of course, there was Atlas, who while holding up the world with his colossal muscles, seemed to be genuflecting to St. Patrick's Cathedral across the street.

There were only a few bumps in the road for me back then. Occasionally while making one of my short solo trips exploring, I would cut through a small section of woods between some houses down the hill from ours. Apparently a kid who lived at one of the houses took it as a personal affront, because twice he came out and started swinging at me without even saying a word. The first time was quite a shock—nothing like that had ever happened to me before. Either because he was smaller or just a lousy fighter, I dispatched him pretty quickly each time. After the first incident I kept using the shortcut, but kept a wary eye out for him. After all I thought, I wasn't doing any harm and he didn't even offer an explanation as to my trespass! Another unanswered question was related to some kids from an adjacent neighborhood who often played baseball in the circle where two roads met at the bottom of Jo Drive. They would never let me play. If Eddie and I asked to join they'd say, "He can play but you can't!" It was years later that I realized that one these kids must have been the little guy's brother. I never did get a good look at him.

Another time a different harsh reality which broke the water of my otherwise peaceful pond was when I telephoned Eddie one day and we planned to rendezvous in the big woods behind our houses to catch a bunny rabbit, Elmer Fudd style (a box propped up by a stick with a long string attached to it and a carrot for bait). I brought the box and string, picked up an appropriate sized stick along the way, and waited for Eddie to bring the carrot for bait. After waiting an inordinate amount of time, I made my way down the path to his house to see what the delay was. Eddie was ashen faced when I met him, and there was an air of great heaviness, even a sense of evil when I arrived at their house … his infant brother had died. We later learned it was Sudden Infant Death Syndrome or crib death as they called it then. After Eddie left me in the basement and didn't return, I hung around for a long while, alternately contemplating what had happened and examining the swordfish mounted on the wall to stave off boredom. With some fear, I half expected the cops to come and haul someone off. Neither Eddie nor anyone else came back to check on me, so I wandered back home as the gravity of death sank in. A strange day ... something quite different. Later that night our whole family went up to their house, and as Eddie and his brothers Michael, Chris and I attempted to play, my Mom and Dad sat with his folks in their living room talking. I heard Eddie's mom crying and my own heart ached with hers.

As autumn approached and the days grew shorter, it seemed to hurry everything up. We needed to get our playing in before dark! As the leaves gradually changed to an incredible, seemingly incandescent array of different shades of red, orange, gold and yellow, the nights grew crisper and the sun took on a rustic burnt gold color as it sank closer to the horizon, you could sense the changing of the guard. The cold northern wind would rattle the drying leaves and usher in banks of dark gray clouds bringing sheets of chilling rain. One of the things I have missed the most spending all these years away from New York is that the year is sharply delineated there—nature itself clicks off milestones as if to prepare us for the inevitable changes of life. There is a sameness of the seasons in California and the Deep South of the United States that hides the passage of time. In the Hudson River Valley, autumn means one of the most beautiful displays of the Lord's artistry as He paints each day new with a kaleidoscope of fabulous colors: the leaves, the sunsets and the harvest moons all reflect the flair of His brush dabbed with an incredible spectrum of hues from His vast pallet. The annual migration of birds spelled change too. The valley is a major flyway for many avian creatures, the Canada goose being one of the most prominent. I'll never forget one cold gray afternoon years later as I stood along the banks of the Hudson and watched as hundreds upon hundreds of the regal geese approached. One wave after another and they flew directly overhead, slowly flapping their massive wings and honking their haunting calls to each other and to anyone who cared to listen. Transfixed, I lost track of time as rank after rank of the massive fowl surrealistically floated past on their trek to warmer lands.

The smell of burning leaves, frosty mornings and the lengthening shadows all meant that Thanksgiving was not far away. Thanksgiving has always been a very special time for me, rich in its own right but also in foreshadowing Christmas and New Years as well. The holiday brought to mind our Pilgrim forefathers who, after surviving a desperate winter in the untamed new world and then being blessed with a bountiful harvest, invited the local natives who had helped them to survive that devastating first year to a great feast. Contrary to the distorted version of the story that revisionist historians often tell, and that is retold in many of our nations our public schools today, the purpose of the feast was to give thanks and glory to God, the giver of all good things and not simply to thank the kind natives.

As the leaves continued to fall and eventually became ankle deep in some places, the biting cold of the north wind brought the first snow. Winters in the Peekskill in those days meant lots of snow—a paradise for kids! If we weren't in school or on some other mundane mission it was out the door and into the snow. Sledding and snowball fights were a blast, and one of my favorite winter adventures was building tunnels and "forts" in the snow alongside the road where the plow had piled it, often three or four feet high.

There is nothing quite so beautiful as new fallen snow … nothing quite so silent as a night when there is already a foot or more on the ground and the snow is falling so thickly that you can barely see the neighbor's house across the street. A certain hushed reverence and awe of the majesty of God's creation seems to descend. When we were really little, Dad would take the sleigh out and after Pam and I climbed on he'd pull us along, sometimes running to make it even more thrilling! Even today I can almost feel the thrill as the big frozen flakes bounced off my face. After my sister Beth arrived Dad bought a toboggan and we'd motor up to Ward Pound Ridge Reservation where all five of us would pile on and race down a big hill!

When I think of snow, I always think of Kinderhook. Further up the valley, just south of Albany and deep in dairy country, there was even more snow and cold and an even greater sense of the profound depth of the winter. By an order of magnitude, the seasons were brought into even bolder contrast there. Being well over a hundred miles north of metropolitan New York, things were much more wild and untamed there as well. Though men had been attempting to harness it for over 300 years, since they were fewer in number than in the land to the south, nature had its way there more often and everything outdoors was more intense it seemed. Further inland than Pleasantville, when the snow fell there, it fell more earnestly, more quickly, more thickly. Although my Dad had lived most of his life in snow country and was skilled driving on it, more than once we had to extend our stay in Kinderhook a day or so because of a heavy snowfall. Kinderhook was the home of my Dad's sister Cornelia, her husband Roy and their five children. They chose the lovely village as their home after he served meritoriously with Patton's 5th Armored Division during the Second World War.

23

One of three doctors in the county when they first arrived, once his practice started to pay off, he moved his growing family from a smaller house to a much larger, though then dilapidated house, and began restoring it to its earlier splendor. A Renaissance man, besides being a physician Uncle Roy was a skilled carpenter and electrician and oversaw renovation of the house as well as helping to build and managing the construction of the cottage on the east lawn where our grandparents lived.

The house my country cousins lived in was a large, stately house from another time. Almost as old as our nation itself, the house held a fascination for me that has lived on all these years, and I still dream about it occasionally today. There was something intriguing about the old house, almost magical—much more than just a building or a place. Growing up in the cradle of the American Revolution and given the fact that my Dad is a great history buff, I've always had a feeling of awe about the past, and the old house accentuated my fascination. With its two-by-twelve-inch hand hewn wooden floor planks (you could see into the basement through a knothole in one of them) and striking front entryway replete with a crystal chandelier, marble bust and handsome staircase with a hardwood banister leading to the second floor, it was distinctly different from any other place I'd seen. The musty labyrinth of the basement, the age, and the sheer size of the place made visiting there an adventure. Add to that the buzz and hum of the house on a holiday and the great fun to be had with my sisters and cousins, and it was always a time which we anticipated with joy.

The ceilings seemed to be twelve feet high, and the windows were probably six or seven feet high and three and a half feet wide. The lower half of the walls throughout the house were Prussian Blue, a beautiful light color something like a robin's egg but slightly darker, and was separated from the white upper half of the walls by a chair rail. The color was refreshing and in keeping with the Colonial Revival style popular during the time when my aunt and uncle restored the house, and added to the charm of the place.

The main house sat like a king in his court with the cottage, barn, and servant's quarters squatting neatly at its side. This was a house on a grand scale, and the massive oak, maple, chestnut, pine and other trees which had been growing for untold years graced the well-kept lawn surrounding the house, towered over it and complemented it well. The rich, green front lawn stretched out from the small forest on the east, past the cottage and in front of the main house. A semi-circular driveway in front of the house gave way to a large side lawn, really an extension of the front lawn, which extended west and wrapped around towards the back of the house. A hedgerow separated the side lawn from a little cottage, the servant's quarters, and next to that was a sunning area, again enclosed by hedges for modesty sake. The spacious back lawn was replete with a swing set and a concrete wading pool for the children. Another hedgerow shielded it from the main driveway which ended at the barn, with our grandparent's cottage across the way and the small forest on the left of and behind the barn.

The driveway onto the property in Kinderhook split, and one part swung into a semi-circle in front of the main house and returned to the street, while the other branched to the left sweeping past a huge broadleaf tree almost four feet in diameter, which sat right in the middle of a small plaza to the east of the main house and covered it like an umbrella. There was a towering pine on the left side of the driveway, which came replete with a really cool tree house (hand made by Uncle Roy) and which shaded the cottage where my grandparents lived. As the driveway turned to the left, a tunnel of shade was formed by the trees, which broke just in front of the barn where the drive ended. The big dark green two story barn right next to our grandparent's cottage was another place on the property that intrigued me. Originally a carriage house and used to stable horses, it became a garage for the family cars. Cars that is, while our grandparents still lived there. Since Aunt Cornelia never drove, my aunt and uncle only used one space for themselves. Later my cousin Mary kept a horse in part of the barn, and at one point Uncle Roy started to build an apartment into the second story, though for some reason never finished the project. There it stood, still smelling like a barn—dark and musty, and the big thick hand hewn planks made me think of the generations of earlier Americans who had lived and loved, laughed and died in this quaint, beautiful spot. I would go there sometimes and drink in all of the sights, sounds and smells, imagining and speculating about the human drama that had played out in and around it over the years.

A pathway to the right of the barn led past an old style outhouse (the kind only found in books or in the wilderness today) then into the courtyard behind Mr. Finkle's store. Like the sound of his name, the store belonged to another time. Facing one of the two main streets of town, it had been a "general store" and must have been bustling fifty, seventy five, and a hundred years before then. The warehouse next to the store was graced with a fading but still discernible cornucopia, emblazoned over the winch to the second story loft, long out of use. As the local dry goods merchant, Finkle's undoubtedly had at one time supplied the small town and surrounding farms with everything from seed to lumber to sugar to shirts. Every time we could, we kids would make a beeline down the path to visit his candy counter. Like something out of a classic movie, dozens of penny candy jars were lined up at kid level in front of, and behind the tall glass cases which ran almost the whole length of the north wall of the store. Although the candy counter was our goal, I always wanted to wander around and look at everything, though Mr. Finkle (seemingly as old as the building) discouraged such activity by children. The store was poorly lit and there was no telling what might be off in the dark recesses of it. The ancient the wooden floor was quite warped and there were all kinds of fascinating smells and curious looking articles of usage unknown to me—some probably farm implements and other artifacts of the days before power tools and other modern devices. My sisters, cousins and I would choose our favorites candy (mine was usually Tootsie Rolls) and we'd be off.

My generation was one of the last to see the remnants of the old world except in pictures or preserved in, or as museums. The store and the old house were here long before cars, computers and automated, motorized, plastic everything. The buildings were silent witnesses to an untold series of births and deaths, hopes and dreams. One of our US presidents had courted a young lady in the house when he was younger. When we went to Kinderhook, I was taken back two hundred years to a time when horse power was just that, and life, though much more difficult in many ways than today, was perhaps simpler, kinder and gentler as well. Our neat little house in Peekskill was brand spanking new and was of the new America— the jet age, the space age—suburbia. This was a throwback. Sitting on a few acres in a little town in the middle of the countryside, seemingly (at least to a little kid) without particular purpose, except to be a sensational vacationland for us! At that time, I don't remember seeing anything new anywhere near Kinderhook. American society at that time was on the backside of a massive shift from a farm based economy to an industrial based one, and it had been years since anyone had thought of heading out into the country to start something new. For the most part, the migration was to the metropolitan areas. When I was growing up and had the privilege of visiting this village, the last vestiges of a vanishing society had not yet gone away.

Usually, after the almost two-hour-long trek from Westchester, as soon as my dad parked the car I'd participate in the obligatory hellos at the main house and then make a beeline for our grandparents little cottage across the driveway. The front of Baba and Gama's cottage was picturesque and wreathed with a lovely garden, but the family always came and went through the back door which opened onto a nice little porch outfitted with a built in table and benches where they could enjoy a meal outdoors on a sunny day. Invariably I'd find Baba sitting in his chair, either reading the newspaper or watching TV—hopefully a New York Yankees game, which meant strict silence until commercials. Cornelius James Leary, the son of Irish immigrants, was a joyful man with a sincere love and respect for all of us. Although I knew him until he died in my ninth year, only once did I see Baba angry and that was when my cousin Conn and I were making fun of an elderly neighbor in his presence. One word, "Boys!" and a stern look was enough to bring us into line. Baba spent fifty years working for the Railway Express Agency and though he had a minimum of formal education (leaving school after the eighth grade) he rose high in its ranks. Eventually he was given the responsibility of building out the company's new air freight division, and while there, mentored John Emery who later founded Emery Air Freight. He also worked closely with World War I ace and head of Eastern Airlines, Eddie Rickenbacher as well as C.R. Smith the longtime President of American Airlines. Smith thought highly of him and made him an

"Admiral of the Flagship Fleet."

Dear Gama almost always seemed to be in the kitchen when we arrived, preparing either a delicious meal for us, or one of her famous desserts: cherry tarts, apple or cherry pie, baked apples or chocolate éclairs, all of which were delectable beyond description. Her macaroni and cheese—no doubt the best in the world—could also have made her famous if she had purveyed it to the masses. Born in Germany, her family moved to America when she was three years old. The saintly white haired woman I knew as my grandmother grew up in a day when almost all women stayed home raising their families and did not venture much into the marketplace, yet she and all of her contemporaries were no less valuable to mankind because of it—they were largely responsible for rearing what one modern journalist later called "the greatest generation." An intelligent and active woman, Marie Leary attained a degree through a correspondence course while executing the arduous duties of a mother. Later in life she reviewed books for a Pennsylvania university's literary publication while at the same time fulfilling the role as the ideal grandmother to the eight of us. The two children she and Baba raised turned out to be amazing and outstanding people who are loved by many. Gama lived another ten years after Baba died, and some of that was in my hometown which allowed me the opportunity to get to know her a little better. She was a precious woman, and as I was living some of the roughest years of my life at that time, my stops by her apartment to check on her while heading downtown were a quiet, peaceful pause in the middle of mounting chaos. Each time she would dream up something up for me to do and then reward me with a delicious snack of some kind.

One of the things that characterized our time in Kinderhook was a zany game of dress up we often played. There was a small closet between the front entrance foyer and the kitchen of the old house which was jammed with literally hundreds of articles of clothing. Conn would take charge and organize the high jinks and we'd crowd into the small closet and put on all kinds of mismatched garments, then come out and parade in front of the adults for laughs. One wintry day in the middle of a blizzard, Conn decided it was time the general population had a chance to see our handiwork. In the disguise of a jogger in the middle of a heavy snow storm, I was sent jogging to the town square to call on the local grocer. With shorts, striped knee-high socks, ski goggles, an old fashioned long tasseled ski hat with a scarf trailing behind, I jogged in to his store. Brushing snow off while jogging in place, I asked him which way Albany was. He pointed with a dumbfounded look. A year or two later we did a variation on the prank. With snow falling at a prodigious rate and dressed in a crazy outfit, I rode Conn's snowmobile into the village, parked in front of the grocer's door, and climbing off my mechanical steed sought directions to the town of Hudson ... again without a word he pointed. A few years later during the summer, with the agreement of our parents, Conn arranged for me to work on his friend's family dairy farm with him. When we stopped by the grocery store one day to get a snack, we discovered that our mid-winter pranks had not gone unremembered or unappreciated ... after the grocer gave us our change, without a word he reached under the counter, pulled out a quart bottle of soda and proceeded to balance it on his nose like a seal!

Another incident I'll never forget also occurred in this lovely, rustic village. As the only boy in my family, fighting my own battles (or running from them) was a familiar way of life. On Thanksgiving Day one year, I discovered how nice it was to have older male cousins. While playing at Kinderhook's only school that day with

Conn, I was delighted to see what it was like to have some material support for a change. Conn had wandered off when one of the older neighbor kids began giving me a hard time. This kid was almost twice my size, and things were getting tough. Just then, out of nowhere my cousin Vern rode up on his bike and converged with Conn who was coming to my rescue as well. In a flash they had subdued the bully, and thanks to a length of rope Vern happened to be carrying, tied him tight to a big tree! Vern jumped back on his bike and rode off, and as quickly as my predicament started it ended. Now that was what I had been missing! Later that day as our large extended family along with a friend or two were gathered around the long formal dining table in the bright, cheerful dining room glowing with the warmth of the holiday, the phone rang. As a doctor who practiced out of his home, Uncle Roy rarely answered the phone, but on an impulse he picked it up. It was the bully's father who complained angrily that my cousins had tied his "Butch" to a tree. Uncle Roy who evidently was not keen on remembering names, replied, "I don't see what's wrong with tying a dog to a tree!" We couldn't hear the man's response, but a puzzled look crossed Uncle Roy's face and he said goodbye. We laughed about that for years, but I'll never forget the one time I had others to stick up for me!

Aunt Cornelia was one of my best friends and one of the kindest people I've ever known. If Attila the Hun walked into the room, she would not have had an unkind word to say about him. Not that she by any means would have condoned his unkind actions, but because she never had a harsh word for anyone that I can remember. Many times I had comforting conversations with her over the telephone during my hardest years, and received many heartfelt and encouraging letters from her too. In the very worst days of my life, she and my older sister Pam were two of the few people on the planet (who knew me) who would even take a telephone call from me. I do not stand in judgment of all the others—it is only by God's grace and their kindness that anyone who knew me then talks with me, even today! Helping the most downtrodden, convicts especially, was her life's love. For years a volunteer librarian at the little Kinderhook Library across the street from their house, she went back to college and completed a Masters in Library Science at the age of sixty so that she could work within the walls of the New York State prison system. Uncle Roy was a generous and loving man also; during harvest time he opened his medical practice in the evening and treated the migrant workers who were laboring in the nearby orchards and fields for free. In his later years he came out of retirement to join Aunt Cornelia working at the prison. When she and Uncle Roy moved to Dallas, I was blessed to be able to visit them often. Everyone was a candidate for friendship with Aunt Cornelia … she truly did not see color, race, creed or class. After Uncle Roy passed away, several times upon finding guests with her, when introduced I'd discover that she'd met them on the bus or at the library or a store. A week before she died at eighty years of age, Aunt Cornelia was pursuing her greatest passion … ministering to prisoners. A great friend to all, including many others overlooked or looked down upon, when Aunt Cornelia went home to be with Jesus she left a bequest to the NAACP where she and Uncle Roy had been life members. Along with my Dad and Mom, my grandparents, my other dear relatives and a host of other terrific people, Aunt Cornelia and Uncle Roy were great models to me of how to " … love one another as I have loved you" as our Savior Jesus taught us to do.

Most of my mom's family lived in Poughkeepsie, New York

on the banks of Hudson River north of Peekskill. Driving there was a treat, especially when my Dad took Route 202 which hugs the cliffs overlooking the Hudson River. Known as the Rhine of America because of the spectacular path it carves through the state as it stretches from north to south, the river valley is one of the most beautiful sites I've ever seen and surely one of the most awesome in God's creation. Though we had no cousins in Poughkeepsie, seeing our Papa and 'Keepsie Gama, my mom's father and mother, was quite enough! They were very special, kind and gentle folks. Though they remained married, for most of my young life they were estranged and lived separately, so a trip to Poughkeepsie always meant at least two memorable visits. Papa, the son of Polish immigrants, led a very colorful life and had an army of friends. Joining the US Navy at age fifteen along with his best friend Crafty, he was decorated for pulling a guy out of a swamp in Cuba during World War I. After the war he served on horseback as a New York State Trooper and later as city policeman.

In his semi-retirement, the place we usually found him was at the parking lot he tended downtown. At the center of town, it afforded him a vantage point to keep his pulse on his lifelong hometown. After pulling into town we kids would run to meet him and invariably he'd give us each a hand full of coins. Back in those days it amounted to a fortune! I'll always remember his kind smile. Papa took me fishing several times, and I cherished being with him. Either he, his maiden sister Anne, or 'Keepsie Gama would take care of us when our parents were out of town traveling, and it was always a treat. One day when Papa was down in Peekskill watching us, my friend Eddie and I struck out exploring in a new direction. We discovered a new stream, fresh and crystal clear, with stepping stones sprinkled liberally across its bed. As we followed it deep into the woods, we slipped into the chilly water a few times soaking our shoes and pant legs. Eventually the stream led us to a clearing with a house in the middle of it. Disappointed it wasn't a meadow or a bear den or some other place to explore, we turned back and headed toward home. Along the way, we ventured twenty or thirty yards into a large storm drain. We must have tarried longer than we realized, because when I finally got home Papa was angry. I had never seen him that way before and was quite taken aback. He'd been out searching the neighborhood for me and had even contacted the police. He sent me straight to bed without dinner (an unknown punishment to me). As I lay there thinking about it all, Papa came in with a nice sandwich for me … now that was the Papa I knew!

'Keepsie Gama whose family came from Ireland, was of tough stock. Besides tending to the house and children, she worked many, many hours a day cleaning houses to help support the family during the depths of the Great Depression. Later in life, she had a successful and rewarding career working for the computer giant IBM at their old mainframe assembly plant in Poughkeepsie. Despite having had a pretty tough life, she always had a sweet infectious smile and often a kind word. A fabulous, large flower garden with bright fragrant blossoms filled much of her backyard and drew me like a magnet ... I'd never seen so many different and beautiful flowers! Behind the beautiful flower garden, a giant weeping willow tree and a nice big stretch of grass, was a pond that we skated on during the winter and swam in during the summer. The first of my many brushes with death occurred one otherwise perfect afternoon while our mom lay on the beach sunning, and my sister Pam and I paddled around the pond in our inflatable tubes. We were about twenty yards from the shore when I realized that my tube was leaking and almost out of air. At about three or four years old and yet to have had any swimming lessons, what moments before had been a cool, refreshing pond instantly became a terrifyingly murky grave, ready to swallow me alive. I cried out to my mother who couldn't hear me, and as terror tightened its grip on me, my dear sister Pam (safely in her tube which had not deflated) swam over and grabbed me, instructing me to hold onto her tube as she paddled into the shore, saving my life. She has remained my faithful friend and what my Dad calls a "big fan" of mine all of my life. I am a big fan of hers too!

The last time I saw my 'Keepsie Gama, somehow we both knew that we'd never see each other again ... it was a bittersweet moment. Just before our last goodbye that day, she told a story about our Papa which was both fascinating and indicative of his strong character. While on a routine thirty day patrol along the banks of the Hudson River with the State Troopers, he fell off of his horse and broke his back and was unable to ride again, so he took a position with a local police department. His time as a policeman coincided with the Prohibition years here in the United States when the manufacture, transportation, and sale of alcoholic beverages were banned. One day after a failed raid on an illegal liquor still, as the squad was changing back into their street clothes in the police locker room, one of his colleagues told him that he was suspected of tipping off the bootleggers to the raid. The other cops gathered by the door ready to jump him and beat a confession out of him. Calmly, my Papa cleaned and loaded his pistol, and snapping the magazine into place he turned the gun on them and said,

"You so-and-so's I'm walking out of here on the count of THREE!"

"Joe, Joe, take it easy!" one of them protested.

Papa responded, "One, two ..." and out he walked.

According to Gama, he then stole the town's only police car, picked her up and drove into the Catskill Mountains where he pushed the car off of a cliff. They lived there as fugitives until he was later exonerated.

Aside from a very few unpleasant incidents, life for me proceeded along pretty nicely during the early years of my life. At the age of seven my family moved closer to New York City where my Dad worked. It meant a shorter train ride for him and a new neighborhood for us. Unlike the new development in Peekskill we left, which had recently been carved out of farm fields, Pleasantville was an old, compact village with everything within walking distance. In fact, most of Westchester County was a series of neat little villages cobbled together, each with its own distinct flavor and often with not much more than a small area of undeveloped woods separating each one. There were a lot of kids to pal around with and I liked my new bunch. Our house was on Washington Avenue which ran parallel to the Saw Mill River at the base of a tall strong ridge of hills. One of the highest hills in the area was right behind our house, and occasionally we kids would race up the side of it and explore the high ground—you can just see the tops of the New York City skyscrapers from there. Without that vantage point though, we may as well have been 1,000 miles from the city. The Saw Mill River was populated with fish, muskrats, snapping turtles and crayfish which delighted us kids and afforded us endless hours of fun. It was really a just a stream, but someone named it "River"; either way we loved it. We spent many hours fishing, catching other critters, or just exploring along its banks. Catching then releasing crayfish (called crawfish, crawdads or mud bugs in the southern USA) was a frequent pastime …once I saw but did not catch a sky blue colored one!

Regular pickup games of baseball, football, basketball (and during the winter hockey) were staples for us, and there was also general horsing around looking for something to do and frequent hiking and bicycle forays to the surrounding area. We kept things interesting by declaring "war" on each other every now and then. One day it would be the Jones boys and me against the Giovanni and Svenson brothers, the next time the Giovanni and Jones brothers against me and the Svensons. We would each establish a headquarters, and the goal was to find and overrun the enemy's position. Weapons consisted of water balloons, mud balls, snowballs, sticks, rocks, slingshots, homemade bows and arrows and generally anything that was handy. Since I was the only one without a brother, every now and then the whole neighborhood would gang up on me—this gave birth to my fast acceleration and superior escape and evade capabilities which served me so well in football later on!

Our bicycle trips would often take us to the delicatessen in neighboring Chappaqua or to the corner store in Pleasantville for a snack. My favorite trip was to Roth's Delicatessen in Chappaqua. This was back in the days when Coca Cola came in a thick green bottle, and you could redeem those and other soda bottles for two to five cents each depending upon the size. My pals and I would head to the train tracks just south of the Chappaqua train station where there was a miniature hill, really just an outcropping of limestone. We'd collect bottles that the passengers on the train must have tossed out the windows as the trains approached the station. In the days before air conditioned everything and lawsuits galore, the windows on the passenger trains actually opened! With our booty of salvaged bottles, we'd ride to the deli and exchange them for enough cash to buy some snacks. My favorite was a Table Talk pie, a "personal size" pie about five-inches in diameter. They were terrific! Peach, blueberry, cherry, or apple, I couldn't go wrong. After buying my pie and a carton of cold milk and my friends had collected their treats, we'd pedal off to some nice spot under a shade tree and feast!

Although a stop for a snack was almost always part of our routine, I continued my habit of exploring nearby forested areas which began in Peekskill and brought my new friends along in tow. My new "best friend" was Mike Svenson. Mike, who had twelve brothers and sisters, was a very friendly kid with lots of orange freckles, blond hair, a quick smile and a ready laugh. Much like my friend Eddie from Peekskill, we got along famously and he was often willing to go exploring with me. One favorite spot was a dark stand of evergreens just off the main road in Chappaqua which hid a beautiful waterfall. Another was right across from Mike's house. On the downward slopes of the long low hill that ran along the other side of the valley formed by the Saw Mill River, was a large area which had probably been a farm pasture not many years earlier and had just enough brush and undergrowth that a kid could hide in it if he wanted to. Next to it was a beautiful wild area with a thick stand of pine trees on it which merged into woods of mostly broadleaf trees that stretched on for a number of acres. Once a part of the summer estate of the co-founder of the ill-fated Johns-Manville Corporation, it offered hours of fun for us kids as we tramped back and forth on various sorties. Due to the proximity to all of our houses, many of the "wars" we fought were waged in there.

During our first few years in Pleasantville, the happy life I'd led in Peekskill continued and expanded. Life was simple and carefree, and it too was a great place for a boy like me to grow up. In addition to the marvelous enclave of nature which surrounded our lovely village just a short drive from the huge metropolis of New York, there were kind, friendly neighbors and an old fashioned Americana look and feel to the place. The town had good recreation leagues for baseball, football and basketball and I took advantage of each. Our swim team was perennially the area champion. Since I couldn't swim very fast, hated to lose and rarely even got to compete, it was out of character for me to do so, yet I swam with the team for four or five years. The sun, the water and the exercise were so great, and the electricity and energy of winning one meet after another and being on a team of such talented athletes, was a privilege—plus it was good conditioning for the other sports. My sisters Pam and Beth were among the many stars of the team and up until the late 1990s a plaque at the pool still showed Beth as holding the record for 25 yard freestyle in one age bracket. An extraordinary accomplishment (and one that would be a sorely needed milestone for me to look back on during the terrible years to come) happened thanks to my rigorous years of swim practice. One year as summer came to a close, it occurred to me that I should swim 600 laps of the town pool on Labor Day. Although I was not much of a racer, the many hours training with the team must have put some meat on my bones. How I came up with the number 600 I don't know, but I decided to do it and started challenging my friends to bet against me—might as well make some money while doing it! One of the lifeguards was the only one to take me up on it, and with a five dollar wager and my honor at stake off I went! Come Labor Day I paddled methodically for many hours to win the bet. At a little over eight and a half miles it was no big deal considering the hundreds of hours of grueling practice we'd endured, but at only eleven or twelve years old and with no previous experience to measure against, it seemed quite a feat ... I drew a line in the sand for myself, and jumped it!

Even more successful than our swim team, our Pleasantville High School football team was another town institution with an even broader popular following. Though a small school, the Panthers were a dynasty in New York State with many championships stretching over the five-plus decades that Coaches Peter Kurachek and Richard Rote guided the team. Except for a few diehard local rivals, most of the schools in our class wouldn't even play us. With no alternative but to play bigger and bigger schools, the results were the same anyway. At home games, my family would join what seemed to be every other family in town for the Saturday afternoon festivities. The band struck up loud and strong about a half an hour before game time, and by kickoff our stands and sidelines would be bulging to capacity. In the visitor's grandstand sat one or two hundred lonely people …brave, loyal souls, since from their point of view the results were bound to be dismal.

Pleasantville in many ways resembled a slightly newer Norman Rockwell painting of middle class America. Memorial Day there in the late sixties and early seventies was like a picture book come to life that will likely remain etched forever in the memories of those privileged to have celebrated it in this lovely village. Bedford Road, the main street in town, is lined with large, ancient trees and runs between downtown and the Old Village, a cluster of shops east of and uphill from the main village, which used to be the center of town before the railroad came through in the mid 1800's. On the day set aside to honor the heroes who gave their lives for our blessed country, Pleasantville had a grand parade no doubt unsurpassed in any town anywhere in the country. Our volunteer fire department was proudly and vigilantly staffed by our fellow citizens who protected our lives and property, and almost all the surrounding towns and villages had them. Volunteer fire companies from all over the county along with their shiny engines led by their brass bands would march down Bedford Road. With a flag flying from every fire engine and every house and building which lined the street, it seemed as many as two or three dozen fire department bands, bright, brassy, shining, blaring and drumming, played all the stirring patriotic songs which are a part of our nation's rich heritage. Our excellent high school band and other local school bands rounded out the group and made the parade an unforgettable event. As vagrant breezes stirred the towering trees with their dark green leaves overarching and shading the street, an occasional glimpse of the beautiful deep blue New York sky or the sparkling bright sunshine of spring at its peak completed the dazzling and inimitable picture. The town swimming pool opened for the season that day, and a barbeque, picnic or some other pleasant distraction would round out the day as we enjoyed the unofficial beginning of summer in this most lovely spot. I for one, could have stayed for hours right there on Bedford Road if the bands would only have circled around and kept coming back. Although the dark clouds of unrest of the late sixties had begun tainting the love of many for our beautiful land, these were for the most part days before America bashing was in fashion. Days when your neighbor or your uncle or the guy who cut your hair had fought bravely at one of those faraway places for freedom, justice, goodness and truth ... back before we were regularly urged by unhappy people to be ashamed of our great country. No, we can't go back, but thankfully many of us have some sweet, pleasant memories of a far better time.

# CHAPTER 3

Before my exceptionally good life took a dramatic turn for the worse, I had one delightful summer in Kinderhook. The verdant dairy farm in Kinderhook that I was blessed to spend my thirteenth summer on was run by a small strip of a man who had left a lucrative career as an attorney in New York City to take over the family farm. Jim McCarthy was a man in motion: with farming in his blood, he worked from dawn until dusk and was always going or coming or doing. My cousin Conn and I worked hay that summer with his son Mark, his nephew Paul, and Jack, a college guy who was on summer break and lived in an attic bedroom of the big family house. There were many acres of hay to cut, rake, bale and store in barns, and our main job was bucking bales. We each had the privilege of handling about a thousand bales in the morning and a thousand in the afternoon, and above and beyond the athletic training I'd done, by the time that summer was over, the work had made me as tough as nails. My introduction to "doing hay" happened when Mark pulled the first wagon full of bales up to the barn where we were inside waiting. Since the hay was to be stored in the second story, Mark positioned an elevated conveyer belt to lift the bales to a door at the top. Conn stationed me under the top of the elevator, and Mark loaded the bales on at a lightening pace! My job was to grab each bale as it fell off the end of the elevator and throw it about twenty or thirty feet to the next guy. It was a large barn, and for what seemed like hours I pumped away like a piston: grabbing and throwing, grabbing and throwing as we unloaded one wagon after another. The end of the barn seemed to get farther and farther away. Mercifully, just when I thought I was going to collapse, the last bale rolled off the elevator. Doing hay was hard work, and that particular task seemed to be the roughest, but thankfully I quickly got used to the routine. Occasionally we had the pleasure of waiting a bit longer for the next wagon full of hay to come. Surrounded by the incredible summer of the Hudson River Valley, we were spectators as nature rejoiced to the fullest at the annual apex of God's creation. One day while we lay in the cool grass, tall stately oak, maple, elm and chestnut trees swayed lazily in the hot afternoon breeze, some of which may have been there since Hendrik Hudson made his first tentative voyage north. Brilliant white clouds floated across the rich, dark blue sky like billowing sails on a great ship from a bygone day, and the uneven symphony of birdsongs sweetly punctuated the balmy, aromatic air. I could have stayed there a long time!

Every day we kept up the pleasant rhythm of working and waiting (often not very long) until noon, when we'd hurry back to the main house for lunch. The family farm house was no modest place, but a great mansion. A vast lawn stretched out front, and behind the house a large swimming pool and cabana invited us to a quick dip before lunch to rinse off the scratchy hay which clung to us. After our swim we would head to the main house and sit at the kitchen table where Mrs. McCarthy had prepared large heaps of sandwiches and gallons of milk, placed strategically at both ends of the table so as not to accidentally create a tense situation as the ravenous farmhands reached for some sustenance. Wisely, the farmer provided a big lunch for the crew—fuel for the engine! Just about the time when the sandwiches ran out, she would offer up a couple of gallons of ice cream, or some homemade pie or cookies. In businesslike fashion, we'd dispense with lunch and head out to the front lawn for a half hour of softball before heading back to buck hay bales.

Almost everything was perfect except for Mark's cousin Paul. Paul was a southern cracker from Maryland, and for some reason he and I just did not get along. Conn and Mark finally got tired of us bickering and decided to put an end to it. On lunch hour one day they took Paul and I down into the basement of the cabana. Typical of my bright imaginative cousin Conn, he and Mark had cooked up a three-part competition, the winner of which would have bragging rights. Theoretically, when a victor emerged it would spell the end to our ongoing squabble. The first event was boxing, and as they strapped the gloves on us, no two combatants could have been more eager to join the battle. Paul plainly had some lessons whereas I hadn't, and in my furry to pound him into the pavement, as I swung furiously at him, he deftly blocked my punches and countered with well-placed jabs to my head. This did not go on long as Conn and Mark could see that Paul was going to punch my brains out if it continued, so they declared him the winner and we moved onto the next event. Now I was really mad since my pride was hurt too. But ah ha! The next event would be mine … the Indian Death Match! The contest began by tying the opponent's wrists together with a rope, then having us lock in a wrestling match to the end. It was more likely cooked up in my cousin's fertile mind than by any Native American tribe, but since I had about ten or fifteen pounds on Paul and had lots of practice wrestling, I had a sure advantage in this competition! Within a very short time Conn and Mark had grabbed a hold of me and were trying to pull me off of Paul. Given my wounded ego and the acrimony of our personality clash, I just *may* have killed the poor fellow hadn't they intervened. After those two climactic battles the cousins decided to cancel the third match and call it a draw, and we all went to lunch. It probably worked out better that way—since we had each dominated in one contest, our pride was intact and we now had a new respect for one another as well—after that we didn't argue much.

One day Jim McCarthy chose me to drive a tractor to rake one of the hayfields. Having never operated any machinery at all except for a lawnmower, I was both afraid and honored. After a rather short lesson on how to operate the Ford 2000 tractor, he directed me to a field on the far side of the farm. Successful in getting the machine to move, I managed to steer it safely to the pasture in question. Jim and his daughter Naomi were already there attending other chores, and after attaching the hay rake to the tractor she gave me short lesson on how to proceed. When I asked a question, she responded in a manner as if to say, "It's simple!" and though I was not at all sure of that, off I went. It actually went very well for the first hour, but as I was circling the field from the outside in, the circles became smaller and smaller as I went around, and a tractor pulling a rake can only make so small a circle. Being a novice driver, disaster struck! After a particularly tight turn I managed to land the hay rake on top of one of the large back wheels of the tractor. Naomi rushed over to ask how it happened, and after explaining how to do it the right way (and that those large back tires cost about $300 apiece, a fortune in the early 1970s) off I went again … only to run amuck a second time! This time when she raced over to investigate, she was a bit irate. Not taking a chance this time, Naomi climbed onto the tractor and finished raking the last part of the pasture herself.

By then the joy of driving a tractor had worn off and I began to head back to the barn. It was almost lunch time, and as I tooled down the dirt road which led back to the cluster of buildings which were the center of the farm, it didn't seem unreasonable to put the thing in high gear and open the throttle all the way. After witnessing my driving skills back in the pasture, I suppose my high rate of speed was salt on his wounds to Jim McCarthy, because as he pulled alongside me in a truck, he yelled, "SLOW DOWN." Throttling back, I admired the beautiful summer day at a lower speed until hunger began to gnaw at me, and anticipating the feast awaiting us, I again eased the gas up a bit. Approaching the area near the main house, the barn in which I'd been instructed to park the tractor was on my right. The rubber pad had fallen off of the tractor's clutch pedal, and since I hadn't throttled down yet, when my foot slipped off the clutch while down shifting from the highest to the lowest gear, the old tractor popped a wheelie and leapt forward like an unleashed stallion. Before I could react, it had torn off the corner of the wooden barn door and ground to a halt against the fieldstone foundation of the barn! Sweating bullets, I jumped from the tractor to survey the damage. Thankfully the only visible damage was to the barn door. Stepping out into the sunlight I looked this way and that ... there didn't seem to be any witnesses, so I slid the damaged door behind the good one being careful to leave it open just as far as before, then dragged the orphaned part of the door into the corner of the barn and covered it with hay before heading to meet the gang for lunch. After my mishaps raking the field earlier, this may have been enough to get me fired. Conveniently it was a few years before the evidence was discovered.

Besides the dairy operation, the farm also had many acres of apple orchards, the best apples on earth! McIntosh apples do not keep or travel very well, so I suppose that their reputation has not gone very far from the opulent orchards in which they grow. During summer the apples are not yet ready for harvest, but more than once on a brisk autumn day Conn and I rode our bikes to the farm and filled our coats with them and ate until we could eat no more. Fresh off the tree, they are a combination of sweet and tart that is incomparable! Working on the farm was a great regime for us growing young men and a fun way to learn about hard work. McCarthy's was a gorgeous piece of land in a beautiful countryside and it was there that I learned the luxury being far from any city. That vibrant summer holds many great memories for me which I continue to treasure today … it was a shining bright spot for me just prior to entering the darkest days of my life.

Just as our country was beginning to say goodbye to the days of relative, peace, innocence and wholesome good, my life would also soon take a radical turn for the worse. Early in life my worldview was based on the belief in the Almighty Creator, God. At about three years old I met Him in church one Sunday morning and felt His unmistakable presence and knew that He was real. Though I hadn't doubted His existence right from the beginning, my first notable encounter with Him was that day when my dad and I were standing singing a worship song, and a sense of awesome power and love came over me. Indeed I was surrounded by adults, a midget among giants, and the rare beauty of the polyphonic Gregorian chant we sang was steeped in reverence and piety, yet it was much, much more than that … at that moment I knew that Almighty God was real and that He too was joining us there that morning! Young children often tell their parents with a gleam in their eye, "I'm going to be a fireman someday!" or "an astronaut", or "a doctor." That morning as the Lord surrounded me with His presence, I knew beyond the shadow of a doubt that He was real and that one day I'd be working full time for the Him. Gleefully, but with a bit of shyness, I told my dad about my experience before we left the parking lot of the church that day. Little did I know that years later the memory of that moment would escape me and atheism would engulf me like a shroud.

The road to atheism was a gently sloping one, but there was no mistaking the direction of it ... down. Mom taught us how to read and write a long time before we entered school, and reading the New York Times became a pastime for me at a tender age. My attitude early in life was quite optimistic and idealistic, but as I learned more about the world around me and began to experience pain and disappointment on a regular basis, disillusionment began to set in. They taught us about our loving God on Sunday, but the disharmony and ugliness so manifest in the world from Monday through Saturday wore away at me. The religion I grew up in was confusing and illogical; much had been added to the simple good news that Jesus Christ died on the cross to pay for all of our sins, so that we can have eternal life. What had been added, to a large degree nullified that great truth by reason of contradiction. Since that religion was the only source of my knowledge of God (we were discouraged from reading the Bible) the one anchor for my soul began to appear no more than a flimsy, manmade crutch as so many voices of the day proclaimed God to be. The unrest and sadness in my own soul, my family, the neighborhood, the country, and the world cascaded upon me ... our beautiful flag was being burned in our streets, riots were rocking our cities and college campuses, and every institution was being challenged daily in the court of public opinion. Finally, when a dire personal crisis hit at about eleven years of age, my fate was sealed. Having long forgotten my experience in church that one morning, I came to the somber conclusion that although I very much liked the idea of a loving God, He was just not real. He was not dead, but had never existed. At seven o'clock on Sunday nights "Walt Disney's Wonderful World of Color" used to air on television in the New York Metropolitan area and offered adventure and a pleasant and distracting fantasy—I came to the dismal conclusion that the whole idea of God was just that: pleasant but a fantasy, like fairy tales told to children. Unlike the minor let-down of discovering Santa Claus was unreal, my false conclusion that God did not exist had deep reaching ramifications. If there was no God to explain all this mess and ultimately bring justice and peace, and to provide a reason for and a solution to all the pain and suffering, how could there be any purpose in life? If we are just going to die and push up daisies someday, what difference does it make what we do? It seemed as if all of our efforts at goodness and nobility in the face of ongoing evil and misery were like swimming feebly against the strong flow of a mighty river at flood stage.

Enter the days of beer, wine and whiskey. Satan is a master strategist and tactician, and after he had sucker punched the Lord out of my hands, he handed me a drink. Growing up in the shadow of New York City where kids tend to grow up too soon, and in the days when the drinking age there was eighteen, I was a prime candidate for trouble. Most of the folks in my home town were first, second and third generation Americans whose families had arrived from Europe not too long before. Alcohol had been a part of everyday life for our predecessors and soon became so for us too. Some of us grew up in homes where it was part of every meal. Neither our culture nor most of the religions in my part of America had anything negative to say against recreational drinking. Since many of my contemporaries had older brothers and sisters in high school who were drinking booze, it was only natural that we would eventually imitate the older kids we admired. Besides, it seemed fun, exciting and adventurous … and so grown up? By the time the first invitation to a drinking party came my way it had been about a year since I had fallen into the lonely abyss which is atheism, allowing just enough time for an ugly mixture of sorrow, confusion, frustration and fear to ferment. Add one ice cold beer and it was like taking away the little boy who had his finger in the dike. One wild young man was unleashed on the world. As my newfound painkiller secured more and more of a death grip upon me, it brought misery and trouble that was unsurpassed in its devastation. Eventually, held in its vice-like clutches, I was brought to unspeakable levels of humiliation, terror and depravity.

*Part 2*
# EATING WITH THE PIGS

# CHAPTER 4

The parochial school I attended when we first moved to town was a good place for a kid—it was safe, cozy place. The one problem was that there was only class per grade, and although I thoroughly appreciated my early start reading, it put me way ahead of my peers academically. The teacher would present a new lesson on Monday and some kids would get it then, others by mid-week and others by the end of the week. Since I consistently got it Monday and tend to be a pretty high energy person, I'd often become mischievous as the week progressed. Eventually the school's leadership suggested public school would be better for me since it would present me with more of a challenge. My transfer to Pleasantville Middle School for seventh grade closely followed my recent transition to atheism and the onset of puberty … a dangerous brew. I had been friends with and was acquainted with a lot of the kids in town, either by meeting them around the neighborhood or playing sports with them. Moving to the public school with them though meant that I was now the new kid who needed to be accepted. It went pretty well because I was a fairly good athlete, a fairly good student and played the class clown. But the fact was that I had an increasingly low opinion of myself and was seeking the approval of anyone and everyone. Getting a laugh made me feel good ... for a little while.

As I gained in reputation in my new school, one day I was approached by one of the elite of the class who asked if I wanted to join a secret club. Flattered, I readily consented. Revealing my not so broad appeal among my classmates, I later found out that a lot of the guys didn't want me in, but the two top guys said, "He's in or we're out." The club was really a gang, but unlike urban gangs we were not bent on violence, had no rivals, sought to control no turf and planned on intimidating no one. In fact, we were not supposed to tell anyone about the group. Our primary mission in life was to plan and finance drinking parties. Had I only known what I was letting myself in for, I would have run as fast as I could. Only a small percentage of those who drink, drink alcoholically, but I did right from the start. The fact is that if you never pour the stuff down your throat, you'll never have a problem. The first time I got drunk was something I'll never forget. A feeling of euphoria came over me as never before, and it felt as if I'd reached the Promised Land. For once I did not care what anyone thought about me, nor did any of the emotional burdens I carried matter. On top of that, since my style was to do everything in a very big way and my goal was to impress folks, when I drank, I drank with a passion. Determined to out drink everyone, I drank more, faster, and longer every time. The paths that alcohol took me down were both dangerous and horrifying, and I lived to tell about it only by the grace of God.

For a while, my reputation as a drinker and a wild man raised my stock as a big man on campus. It also gave me an identity. Before then I was a mischievous but "good" kid. Anything too far out was not for me. I stole a toy horse from a neighbor's sandbox when I was a little kid and later stole some candy, but felt very guilty each time and did not continue. Once booze entered my life, all bets were off. America was a very different place when I grew up than it is today, and one of the differences was that television back then was fairly moral and generally reinforced positive values. Police shows like "Dragnet", "The FBI" and "Adam-12" left me with the distinct impression that the good guys would win, and the bad lose. Although I sometimes tried matching my wits with the cops in my imagination while watching one of those shows, my considered impression was that it wouldn't be a good bet in real life. As I remember it "The FBI" ended with the bold statement that ninety-five percent of all cases they pursued ended in convictions. The odds weren't very attractive, and by God's grace I began developing a healthy fear of the consequences of breaking the law … but it took some hair-raising real-life experiences to cement that in my mind.

Our gang usually met every weekend somewhere in town, and we'd drink whatever happened to be available. We met in our secret clubhouse regularly to plan parties on a grander scale, and it was required that we fork up dues in order to finance the operation. At first, my newspaper route and the money I made mowing lawns and gardening easily met my dues, but the deeper I got into to the whole scene, the positive things I was doing (such as work) began falling by the wayside. The parties became more and more frequent, and I worked less and less. One edict that came down from our leadership was to steal (as instructed to by the author) and read "Steal this Book" by Abbie Hoffman. After giving a report to the gang to prove we had read it, two of us decided that we needed to test some of the theory and constructed a Molotov cocktail. After careful planning, we crept out in the middle of the night to see if it would work. We were smart enough to do so in an open, paved area on a windless night, and though the resulting fire was rather unspectacular, we had the satisfaction of knowing that it worked. Though the book was meant as an introduction to hippie and other radical ideas of the 1960s and was my first formal introduction to those ideologies, as far as I know none of the gang had any political axes to grind. Pyrotechnics were exciting though, and portions of the book were devoted to learning how to steal successfully which was useful to us at the time. Since the club rule was, bring the dues or you're out, I began to resort to stealing in order to meet my dues—it was understood that no one cared where the money came from and no questions were asked.

We'd schedule parties in the middle of the night so that our parents were less likely to catch on. We would choose a meeting place and time, usually about one in the morning, sneak out of our houses and the fun would begin. About a year later one of my classmates offered me marijuana. Like an open grave temptation loomed before me, and I jumped in without a second thought. Most don't get high the first time they smoke pot, and the guy who invited me, who as it turned out was a pusher, grew impatient with me. Once I did get high though he had a steady customer. So did several other dealers in town because my appetite for drugs was insatiable. Working less and less and needing more and more money to feed the demons, my friends and I began to come up with more creative ideas to raise funds.

The Village of Pleasantville, like most of the little towns in Westchester, had a downtown area the size of a postage stamp, and if they didn't go into New York City to shop, most folks did their shopping in White Plains. With about 50,000 residents, and due to its proximity to the city, White Plains had a branch of just about every major retail chain. As part of our fund raising program our gang began to plan shoplifting excursions there. Each foray was a contest to see who could steal the most. If I didn't win, I was usually first runner up. Since the goal was to generate income, my technique was to steal the most expensive and available items, so seldom was anything useful to me. Disposing of it wasn't my responsibility, but someone must have fenced it for cash to finance our parties. For me, it was the thrill and competition which motivated me … and the partying which it all financed of course. Two of us stood head and shoulders above the rest as the most adroit shop lifters, and it was decided that we should have a contest for the championship. On the fateful day, we entered our second store of the day, neck and neck. When my pal walked up to a marketing display right at the intersection of two main aisles of the store, grabbed the item on display and put in into his bag in full view of anyone within fifty feet, I couldn't believe it. Leaving the store immediately, I got on the next bus home—going to jail was not part of the game and that was it for me! Some of the other guys continued to do it and got caught not long after that. It was last time for me until years later when I was living on the street, and even then I didn't make it a habit. Once when I was really strung out, I attempted to steal a bottle of whiskey and failed, mercifully getting away by simply being yelled at. Besides that, I stole some food a few times when I was very hungry, but thankfully my early experience left no doubt in my mind that shoplifting and other types of crime were not careers with a future.

Burglary was another option the gang decided upon, and a scary one to me. Excitement was among the drugs to which I was becoming addicted to however, and being the wild man of the bunch it would have been unbecoming of me to flinch at the idea. Because we didn't take any cash from any of the break-ins, the idea quickly lost its glamour for me, and the last job we pulled wiped out my appetite for burglary forever. While casing the upstairs of a house as the others cased the downstairs, opening the closet in the master bedroom, directly in front of me at about eye level was a large caliber handgun locked and loaded! As I gingerly closed the door to the closet, and began to descend the stairs leading to the living room, I saw a black and white police car pulling up in front of the house! "Psssssst!" I called to the others, while frantically gesturing towards the window. Directing them to the back door, they left so fast that they almost let the screen door slam, but I caught it just in time. We raced through the woods and neighboring back yards and re-assembled at our hideout. Our take was meager and we were scared to death. I vowed at that time never to do it again, and never did, though once again some of my cohorts kept it up. Eventually they got caught and had it hanging over their heads for many years.

There were some high points mixed in during my steady decline into the pit. While still working regularly I had earned enough money to purchase a really nice French touring bicycle. It was far superior to my last bike and was lightweight and fast. Not wanting to wait to earn the entire $350 it cost, I asked my dad if he'd loan me the money and I'd pay him back out of my wages. Though dad had plenty of money, he was wise enough to offer to loan me half of the amount if I first came up with the other half … he wouldn't spoil his children! In the end I just saved the whole amount, but it was a good lesson and indicative of Dad's God given wisdom. Virtually every day, if I wasn't walking, I was riding my new bicycle up and down the hills of Pleasantville. With the combination of that exercise and my athletic training it occurred to me that I could probably bicycle pretty far, and I decided to ride to my Aunt Cornelia and Uncle Roy's house in Kinderhook—over a hundred miles. I obtained my parents' permission and enlisted my friend Dave to ride with me. Dave, one of my best friends, was a guy I sometimes couldn't decide whether to love or hate. He had a winsome personality and was a nice guy, but had a couple of incredibly irritating flaws—although I was a fairly talented athlete, Dave was just a little better in almost everything. Ping pong, basketball, tennis, you name it, he won ... *and* he was cocky about it. Although I never competed in wrestling, I was very good at it, and was especially determined to beat him. He had about thirty or forty pounds on me, which in wrestling is quite an advantage, and although I was in very good shape, he invariably tied me up like a pretzel. I did pin him one time ... but he wouldn't admit it! Our bicycle trip to Kinderhook turned out to be my chance to dominate.

In typical fashion, Dave purchased a bike almost identical to mine from a mutual friend only a week or so before our trip, and trained very little (assuming there was no need). We set out early on the appointed day and headed north on the shoulder of the brand new Interstate 684 long enough to make it to Rt.22. The weather was just right, and we covered a lot of ground by noon. Sometime after lunch we decided it would be nice to have a beer. We were both big for our ages, but before we entered the bar in the little country town along the way, I concocted a story to help us pass for eighteen. There had been a fire at Grand Central Terminal in New York City the day before, and as we bellied up to the bar, I commented that Dave and I were taking a few days of vacation after the tough job of extinguishing the fire. Whether or not any of the guys present bought the story I don't know, but I always figured if I was going to lie it might as well be fantastic. We got the beers. Fortunately we didn't have a lot of cash, so in a short time we were back on our bicycles crunching away the miles north. We hadn't counted on Rt.22 being a truck route so we had some pretty thrilling moments as the big semis swept past us within inches, but all in all the ride was progressing nicely. I'm not sure what material they make touring bike seats out of today, but ours were made out of a very hard smooth plastic or synthetic rubber designed to reduce friction. Not an issue for me since I had ridden hundreds of miles already on mine and had become accustomed to it, but although Dave was able to keep up with me, he complained increasingly of his sore posterior. Finally, after plunging down a very steep hill at breakneck speeds in the pitch dark (a thrill I've decided not to repeat) Dave called it quits and refused to pedal any further. Regardless of how I argued and cajoled he was not getting back on that machine. I'd finally outdone him! It was getting late and we were still about twenty miles from Kinderhook, and although I explained to him that we would probably have to walk all night to get there, he wouldn't relent. Thankfully, when we didn't arrive in a timely manner, my cousin Conn and his friends started searching for us on the western side of the Hudson River, and my Uncle Roy set out to search the north-south route on the eastern side. Shortly after our forced march began my uncle found us, and we rode the rest of the way to Kinderhook in the comfort of his Oldsmobile Toronado.

That summer just prior to when our class was to begin playing for our famed high school football team, I began physical training as never before. Weighing only 150 pounds I knew that as quarterback and one of two middle linebackers in a Notre Dame defense, I'd have to be pretty tough if my class was going to continue to uphold the town's championship tradition. Since we were a small school we all played both ways (offense and defense) and I punted as well. One day while running around our school track I began running with an older guy, talking as we ran. He was a police detective from Yonkers I learned, and we talked and ran for quite some time. When we stopped running he asked me if I knew how far we had just run.

"Nope" I answered.

"Ten miles!" he said.

"Wow!" I thought, and filed it away. A few weeks later, some friends and I went to the old Rome Theater in Pleasantville to watch a movie. While chewing the fat waiting for the movie to start, I recounted the story to my friends. One by one they expressed their disbelief, and before it was all over I had seventy five dollars-worth of bets riding on whether I could do it or not. One of the gamblers was wise and realized that anyone could run ten miles given enough time. Not knowing how long it took, I pulled the number "an hour and half" out of the air and the contest was on. A couple of Saturdays from then a small crowd gathered to watch as I chugged around the track ten miles … in an hour and twenty nine and a half minutes! When the boys got up a scratch football game after, when I began to join in with them someone suggested that I shouldn't, considering my recent feat. By insisting on playing to prove how tough I was, it made some of them uncomfortable and mad at me. It was and occasionally still is a characteristic of mine to do things my way, no matter what the effect on others (or on my reputation).

In spite of these and a few other bright spots, my steady decline continued as I drank more and more, and became increasingly dependent on the euphoric oblivion of marijuana. During my freshmen year at Pleasantville High School, because someone had thrown a gauntlet down, I'd decided (in uncharacteristic fashion) to fully apply myself to my studies, and managed to carry an A+ average. It felt good for a while, but one day after class when one of the better students (a nice person whom I admired) came to me and in awe asked, "How do you do it?"

I muttered something deflecting their praise and thought to myself, "I don't deserve this brain ... I wish they had it!" Adding to my already low self-esteem, my despicable extracurricular activities made me feel like such a worm and undeserving of anything good.

Students on the high honor roll were not required to go to study hall, so I usually took the time to go down the hill behind the school and smoke pot. Eventually all my free time was focused on one thing—getting drunk or stoned. Enslaved less than three years after meeting my courtly master, before I knew it drugs and booze reigned supreme ... and what a cruel master they turned out to be! As I descended into the pit of addiction, I grew more and more distant from my friends and family. Although most of my friends used and abused alongside me, my behavior so was radical that even they started distancing themselves from me. Once when I walked up to a couple of friends as they were discussing a party on the street corner across from school, there was an embarrassing silence. When I finally got them to fess up to what they had been talking about, they told me where and when the party was, but confessed that they were not sure that I was invited. "What is happening?" I thought as I walked away. Although I had always been somewhat controversial, twice I'd been elected to be Vice President of our class, was chosen to be co-captain of our football team, and seemed to enjoy the friendship of most of my classmates. Now I was becoming an outcast and even a laughingstock. Even among the hardcore freaks (drug users) I was becoming more and more unwelcome. Guys I thought were close friends were "busy" more often or would just happen not to be there most of the time when I called ... there was often "no more room in the car" for me. My reaction was to retreat further and further into the abyss of mind altering substances, and I became increasingly alienated, my mood growing darker and darker.

Right around this time, an interesting thing happened. Although many lively and interesting discussions on a broad range of subjects occurred between me and my brilliant family members, it was unusual for us to discuss our deeper personal thoughts or feelings or anything relating to our innermost selves. So I was taken aback one day when my mom stopped me in between our dining room and front door, looked me in the eye and said, "Neil, if you're ever in trouble, I mean serious trouble, just say these three words, 'God help me.' or 'Jesus help me.' It doesn't matter which, just say them."

The words and the scene became fixed in my mind in stark relief. Looking back, I know that she had spoken prophetically— little did either of us know at the time that my life would be in imminent peril many times for years to come.

A pitiful indication of how far I had sold out to my new master and the speed at which I was descending lower and lower into the pit, happened when our class student council decided that we needed to write a new class constitution. The president, a prominent member of our class and one time close friend was in favor of replacing our current governing model with a communist model. As vice-president that year I was strongly opposed to his ideas, and was ready to dig my heels in and campaign strenuously in favor of a more conservative model. Much to my shame, I concocted the idea of soliciting a bribe from him ... if he would get me high three times, I would give a speech endorsing his plan. In violation of my strong beliefs, I gave a rousing speech in favor of his Marxist constitution, and the measure carried easily. Not only had I humiliated myself for my new slave master, but I came to the terrible realization that I now had to buy friends. Now I was plummeting downhill—the next change would push me over the brink into a life I never would have dreamed of.

# CHAPTER 5

The summer of 1973 was a weird one. My Dad took a new job with a company based in the Midwest and he offered me the opportunity to work on a cattle ranch in East Texas that summer before we were to move. With the happy time on the dairy farm in Kinderhook fresh in my mind, I jumped at the chance. A banker friend of my Dad's had financed the purchase of the ranch and was able to arrange the job with the owner. Since my Dad is such a train buff and knew that I loved them as much as he did, he booked me on a train headed west out of Penn Station. Much of the trip I stood in the open half door between the two railcars watching the scenery roll by as the breeze brought the delicious scents of the countryside through the opening. The beauty of the brilliantly green valleys of central Pennsylvania were unforgettable. Scores of deer grazed alongside the tracks as we headed into the sunset on the first night of the journey, and it occurred to me that the eyes of our pioneer forefathers may have glimpsed a similar scene before reaching the Mississippi to join a wagon train headed west. Yet even those special moments were somewhat marred by the ounce of pot in my pocket, which I chained smoked as usual and finished before I reached Texas.

The first week or so of my time in Texas was rather

disorienting. Considering myself pretty worldly for a teenager since I had traveled the length of the east coast of America and been to Puerto Rico and Hawaii as well as a number of other somewhat exotic places, the events of the next week made me realize I had a way to go. Having read fairly extensively ever since I was a pup, my view of the world was well rounded beyond my years, yet Texas had a certain mystic about it outside of its borders (whether created by Hollywood or folklore) and in my subconscious I envisioned cowboys, tumbleweeds and oil wells abounding, and millionaires everywhere. My adventure began as I was met at the Fort Worth train station by my dad's friend who was wearing a tall, black, beaver skin cowboy hat. He drove his wife, daughter and me to the ranch which was several hours east, in a brand new Lincoln Continental. Arriving at Lone Star Ranch, we turned off the highway onto a long gravel road which after a third of mile or so led to the driveway of a large, rambling house where I was to room with the ranch manager's family for the summer. The house was nicely situated in the middle of a large stand of pine trees and bracketed by pastures where some of the 900 or so head of cattle grazed on the deep, rich East Texas grass. Appropriately the ranch house was quite spacious, and in the center of the living room was a large fireplace which seemed big enough to roast a side of beef in. There were two relatively new, midnight blue Lincoln Continental sedans parked in the carport, which I was told were there for folks "to look at the cows with."

"My!" I thought, "In Texas even a simple ranch manager and his family live like kings!"

I could understand my Dad's friend and his family when they talked, but when Jerry and Judy and their young boys Joshua and Jason spoke to me, I reacted like a recently arrived immigrant ...

smiling and nodding a lot but understanding little. This was in the days before the incredible media saturation with which we're familiar today had become commonplace, and regional accents across our country were much more pronounced than today—I barely understood what they were saying most of the time. Being generally disoriented due to the language barrier and remaining caught up in the lore of the Texas myth, I marveled at the opulence of the simple ranch family, and Texans in general. A week or so after I arrived, the ranch owners Joe and Peggy and their family came to spend the weekend. Amid the flurry of activity upon their arrival, little Joshua and Jason began to misbehave, and Judy turned to them and drawled, "If ya'll don't be good little boys ya'll won't be able to go to PARIS with us!" This was too much! Incredible! Not only did humble farm workers live in a mansion here in Texas, but they were going on a junket to France! I cornered Judy and incredulously asked,

"Judy, tell me you're not going to Paris!"

With a laugh, she said "Why shoor we are!"

Noticing my mouth hanging open, she said, "We're from thayre!"

Then realizing I was also astounded by this latest news, she said, "Paris is just a little moahr than an hour from hayre!"

Paris, Texas that is. Later I learned that Jerry and Judy were simply caretakers for the big house, and that the owners intended to settle at the ranch at some time in the future. I even learned to understand and speak East Texan before the summer was over!

It was a long, long summer. In spite of the incredible beauty of East Texas, for the first time since the age of twelve I was without my "medicine." After drowning in alcohol and drugs for about three years now in an effort to calm the seething caldron of my adolescent emotions, now I was a prisoner to them and had nowhere to hide! This was very different from my memorable experience on McCarthy's farm. I did not have the camaraderie of my Aunt Cornelia and Uncle Roy, my dear cousins Conn and Mary and the other farm workers. Without them, the old house and the familiar environment of New York, I felt very alone. At Kinderhook we worked as a team, while most of the time on the ranch I worked by myself. Whether fixing long stretches of fence, mowing hay or feeding the horses I was most often alone with my thoughts, and they were very poor company. Jerry would drop me off where the work was and come get me hours later. One Sunday morning while the family was away at church, hard up for a high I scoured the house looking for something intoxicating ... the only thing I found was a bottle of Angostura bitters used to flavor cocktails. It did have some alcohol in it, and I was ready to drink it but realized there wasn't enough to get a buzz. The rising then dashing of my hopes for relief made the rest of the day seem to drag out forever as I languished in misery.

In spite of all that, the summer was actually somewhat of a respite. Even though I was without God (or so I thought) which *really* made the world seem empty, He really never left me. Ever since I was a child, He has blessed me with the ability to draw rest, satisfaction and joy from a few areas of life. One of those is the incredible world which He created and which has always held a great fascination for me. More than once I've stood motionless for a half an hour or more gazing at the sky, a beautiful forest, the plains, the desert, the sea, the mountains or the stars. Throughout my years God has painted a vast number of wonder-filled canvases from which He allowed me to draw great peace and joy. The ranch, which was many miles from any large city, was a patchwork of gently rolling pastures, pine forests, and streams. On Sundays, our day off, I would saddle up Joe's big gelding which he allowed me to ride, and pick a direction, slowly guiding the powerful horse on a nice long walk while I drank in the sights, smells and sounds of the meadows and piney woods as they woke up. Occasionally I'd kick his ribs and slap him with the reins so he'd break into a full gallop, though for the most part I'd walk my mount slowly, since a large part of the joy was in the journey. After a half an hour or so I'd tether out the giant, gentle Palomino and sit under a tree and listen, look and revel in His fabulous world some more. True, I didn't know the Creator of all this beauty then, but that didn't keep Him from lavishing this special Balm of Gilead upon my tortured soul. Reading is another pleasant release He has blessed me with, and on my Sunday morning rides I always brought a good book along and would read for an hour or two before heading back to the barn. Mark Twain, Hemingway, Steinbeck, Kurt Vonnegut and others were my companions back then. Walking with them transported me away from the dark foreboding echoing within my head and created a certain kinship with these men who looked at the world from a different and sometimes more realistic or noble perspective. Years later, after experiencing the revolution known as being born again, I picked up some of their books again and realized how empty they must have been; but they were good company for me at the time.

My long days in the beautiful garden that is East Texas were filled with labors, but whenever things slowed down, I was haunted by restlessness and a longing which I could not put my finger on. The feelings were born from what has been described as a God shaped hole in my heart. If we do not invite God to fill our lives, whether out of ignorance or rebellion, we will automatically try to fill it with other things: riches, work, hobbies, sports, booze, drugs, sex, or any number of other sometimes worthless or downright destructive alternatives. None is good enough or big enough to take the place of the Almighty who made us for Himself and so longs to share His love and the goodness of His world with us. When we will fill ourselves with shabby substitutes and find that the emptiness is still there, we often then try more and more of whatever it is, until the substitute completely loses whatever joy and relief it brought and then becomes a cruel master. My fix was unavailable that summer, and I was adrift. One day at lunch, Judy asked me what was wrong. "Nothing" I said, but the truth was that there was a lot wrong … and I hadn't a clue what it was.

Being so far out in the country was a blessing though, because it kept temptation out of reach. Ranch work was good, hard, clean work … the last I would do with any regularity for many years. One of my daily tasks was to feed the horses the first thing every morning. Getting up at 5:30 A.M. is not in my nature, but it came with the territory, so get up I did. After walking from the ranch house to the barn which was near the entrance to the ranch, my job was to muck out the stalls and feed the horses and the lone bull in the barn a goodly portion of alfalfa hay, and then carry a fresh bale out to the horses in the corral. There were a half a dozen or so horses out in the twenty-five-acre corral and four or five in the barn, as well as the baby bull. The bull didn't have a stall and was free to roam the corral, but for some reason hung around the barn all the time (maybe to stay out of the hot Texas sun!). After handing each of the barn horses a handful of sweet stuff as a final treat (it was a mixture of grain, corn and molasses) I'd throw a bale of hay over my shoulder, grab a bucket of the sweet mixture and head for the far corner of the field where the other horses usually hung out. Why

they didn't come to the barn every morning for eats I don't know …
horses may be a bit like cats and prefer to display an air of
indifference and independence to their human masters. The baby
bull Luke followed me around the barn like a dog and also followed
me all the way out to the corner of the corral and back. (Perchance
it had to do with the fact that I'd slip him extra handfuls of the sweet
stuff every now and then?) One morning after many trips out to the
corner of the corral and back with Luke following faithfully, the
notion hit me,

"What would happen if I got on Luke's back?" I speculated,

"I bet he'd just keep plodding along right back to the barn!"

Luke was only about three feet tall at the shoulders and
probably weighed only 350 or 400 pounds at the time.

"He seems pretty gentle." I thought, "and he does let me scratch
him on the head all the time. What the heck, I'll give it a try!"

Being careful not to whack him with the empty grain bucket, I
petted him down while talking to him, then gently climbed on his
back. It worked! Sure enough he plodded slowly right back to the
barn. "A regular Doctor Doolittle I am." I thought, "Like Tarzan,
King of the Jungle!" Luke was my loyal friend, and actually helping
with the work!

A few weeks passed, and while I rode my trusty friend back to
the barn after feeding the corral horses one day, I mused to myself,
"It is a particularly beautiful morning." Meadow birds were singing
and the sun was shining, and a warm breeze danced around me. Just
then, Luke shrugged his shoulders then gave them a little shake …
the next thing I knew I was flying through the air like a bird! When
I picked myself up off the ground, I asked Luke why he had done
such a thing. Without responding he began plodding alone back to
the barn—he had officially resigned his position of servitude.

While tacking barbed wire fence back to the posts for long hours at a time, to stave off boredom, one day I began imitating the cows and calves which were standing not far away in the adjoining pasture. To my amusement, when I called with the deep throated sound of one of the mother cows, a calf jerked his head up from grazing to see what was required of him! Alternately, while practicing a particularly strident calf call, a mom cow whipped her head around in distress searching in my general vicinity for her furry charge.

At the end of the summer, my dad, mom and sister Beth came to pick me up for the journey to our new home in Indiana. As they drove up to the big ranch house, the owners Joe and Peggy (who had come again from Dallas with their children for the occasion) came out with me to meet them in the driveway. After sharing pleasantries with my folks, he cordially offered to let me take Beth riding. Since she was relatively inexperienced, Joe chose one of the oldest mares for her to ride. Ever since I was a young child I've had a strong affinity for animals, and during my atheist years I liked them better than most people. Although I am not a very skilled or trained horseman, my innate understanding of animals and my seeming ability to communicate with them easily has always enabled me to ride with confidence. Beth and I enjoyed a nice long ride through the lovely countryside and were circling back to head for the barn. As we passed a house several dogs came out barking angrily and spooked the old mare she was riding which bolted and ran away with her. Beth was terrified, and at first I was at a loss as to what to do. The old mare was frantic and ran a lot faster than seemed possible. Kicking my horse hard in the ribs and catching up, after unsuccessfully trying to slow her by holding her reins, I noticed that a fence line ran parallel to the road. In an instant I decided to run ahead of the mare and cut her off against fence—mercifully it worked. As we walked our horses back to the ranch house, after regaining her composure Beth thanked me for saving her life. The old mare would probably have tired before too long and Beth would likely have been unhurt even if I hadn't acted, but for a short time I was a hero. It would be many years before anyone would again think of using that adjective relative to Neil Leary. We left the ranch the next day and headed for South Bend, Indiana and our new home. Like the vortex which is created in water when you unplug a drain, my life would soon begin again a rapidly downward spiral.

# CHAPTER 6

Shortly after we moved in to our new house in South Bend it was time to go back to school. There I went from being a big or at least a medium fish in a small pond, to being a small fish in a very big pond. The new high school my sister Pam and I were enrolled in had over 2,000 students, as opposed to the 600 or so at Pleasantville High. I had felt like nobody before, and now I was. Feeling so out of place, my interest in school quickly disappeared altogether and I soon got back into drugs and alcohol even more fervently than before. Pursuing the next high became a full-time occupation, and instead of waiting for a break from school I began to just skip classes. Tentatively I went out for football, but since drugs and booze had already begun sapping the lifeblood out of me, my attempt was weak. Knowing no one on the team and seeing no signs of welcome or acceptance among the players or coaches, I quickly gave up. Without an unlimited source of wealth, staying high was a torturous exercise. The periods in between highs were times of restlessness and torment. Predictably, with the devil as my tour guide, I fell in with a terrible crowd and my behavior became more erratic and radical. After the school contacted my parents a few times about of my absenteeism, they sent me to a psychiatrist. Though they meant well, that only served to push me further towards the edge. Already I felt like an outcast—now I was weird, different—and sick. The guy's office was right on a main street of town and had a big lawn in front of it. Assuming that everyone in town knew that it was a shrink's office, self-consciously I'd approach the building from a route that would make it less likely that anyone would see me enter. He was a nice guy, but I don't remember anything that we talked about. It was my habit back then to relate as little as possible about myself to anyone for two reasons: my obsession with illegal drugs, and the likelihood that if anyone knew what I was doing or thinking they would reject me ... or lock me up.

One morning at school I heard that Buzz, a local drug dealer, had some purple barrel LSD. Having no money, I concocted a scheme to hustle some up. Telling all the freaks (druggies) that I was going to buy some LSD, I asked if they wanted some. Charging them a little more than the selling price would leave some money left over to buy some for myself. After having collected as much money as possible I set off for the dope. Buzz was an older hippie who lived in a small frame house on the wrong side of the tracks. We had railroad tracks in Pleasantville too, but there, even the other side of the tracks was a pretty nice place—not so here. Buzz owned a pistol which he kept in the drawer of an end table next to his chair. It was the first one I had ever seen that wasn't strapped to a cop, and it scared me. My friend who introduced me to Buzz said that he probably needed it because he was a known dealer and someone may come and try to rob him of his dope. Never the less, this was new territory for me and I didn't like it. Buzz was home that day thankfully, and after buying the LSD and smoking a joint with him, I swallowed some of the acid and headed back to school with it. Walking along the railroad tracks which was the quickest way back to school, a slow-moving freight came along.

"Ah ha!" I thought, "That train is going faster than I am ... if I jump on I'll get to school faster!" So on I jumped.

YEE HAH! What fun! Clinging to the ladder attached to the boxcar, the train gradually picked up speed going faster and faster. When I saw the school zipping by in the distance and realized that if I jumped off, I would probably break my neck, my train "trip" suddenly became a bummer. I soon adjusted though and decided to make the most of the ride. Climbing to the top of the boxcar, I sat cross-legged waving at all the cars at the intersections. When we reached the countryside there were less and less folks to wave at, and I began to wonder when my ride would end. Seeing an approaching rainstorm, I flattened out for a while to avoid as much as possible getting soaked. Eventually, seemingly many hours later the train stopped and I climbed down to seek help. Though the LSD had worn off for the most part, when I went to a store and called for help, I didn't anticipate being hauled to jail (actually Juvenile Hall, but yes, that is jail). A rough end to my trip indeed, and it got even rougher when the burly young man at the intake desk told me to empty my pockets and my hand touched the LSD. Yikes! I managed to get it past the guards and into my cell, and later taped it to the underside of the toilet. Consuming it several times a day for the next couple of days made my first trip to jail a little more bearable, but by the time my dad (who had been out of town) was able to come get me, the whole experience had me pretty shaken up. Oh, that I'd taken that as a lesson learned and tried to change my ways! Long ago I had lost the way though, and didn't even know where to look for it.

A few weeks later, after missing more classes at the new school they suggested that a change of scenery would be good for me. Dad drove me down to a military academy near Indianapolis which seemed like a barren harsh place, and I told him I'd prefer not to go there. Dad's kind, gentle spirit kept him from forcing the issue. Eventually, the public school in South Bend expelled me and Dad found a private school in another state that would take me. Loneliness was to be my plight there too as there was no one to share my dorm room with, and I made few friends. Deeper and deeper satan sucked me into the hole he was digging for me, with plans to bury me in it. Although I had little or no interest in school, I was told that the "townies" didn't like us "preppies" at all and were liable to beat us up. Since there was little to do except go to school, I managed to get a few more credits toward graduating from high school, but certainly didn't do so in an exemplary fashion. Since the main goal—living for the next high —was now firmly established, and those times were far too infrequent to bring sustained relief, my misery grew ever deeper. A high point, if you could call it that, was when they brought in the Beatles movie *Yellow Submarine* ... which I went to alone.

One night before my mom was to come and visit me for Family Day, while generously helping out at a parent's fundraising rummage sale being held in the school cafeteria (my intentions were good) at the end of the event I noticed a man stash the night's proceeds under a counter in the kitchen. Quick action procured me my prize and I was off into the night. Needless to say, the time with Mom was not what it should have been. Although I had plenty of dope and booze for a little while, joy did not permeate my soul. A few weeks later I got sloppy and took a few of the dorm rats out to a steak and lobster dinner so that I didn't have to eat alone. To repay me, they turned me into the school and I was caught with some of the evidence. The administration was merciful and allowed my dad to pay the money back, and even gave me credit for the semester before putting me on a plane back to Indiana.

It turned out that my mom was miserable in South Bend too, and since Dad's job allowed him the flexibility to work from New York City as well, we moved back to Pleasantville. "It could be that this will bring some normalcy back into my life." I thought. But at that point I was already a runaway freight rain.

My hair had gotten pretty long by then after not having a haircut since thirteen. The status quo was clearly not a formula for happiness, so I became an easy target for the revolutionary ideas which turned the world upside down at the time. Being a pot smoker, a child of the sixties and having read "Steal This Book" I considered myself a hippie ... a conservative Republican hippie! Being young, impatient and preoccupied I had not taken the time to fully know or understand the arguments for or against the Vietnam War, but I could not stand to see my beloved country and flag dragged through the mud every day in the national media. Nor could I believe that the great men and woman who had stood so bravely, sacrificially and righteously for the world against Hitler and the Axis powers would now be leading an evil deception of our country, needlessly allowing the butchering of our soldiers to fulfill some selfish, greedy and arcane scheme. I could see the truth in some of the other anti-establishment hippie doctrines though. The idea of open thinking not constrained by convention or tradition was logical to me, for it seemed that the alternative was narrow minded and intellectually short sighted. The ideas of completely unfettered liberty which included the freedom to partake in massive quantities of drugs, booze and free sex, and that we were able to blaze new paths for civilization because we were brave enough to fly in the face of the established ways, were also appealing. Regardless of living the good life in my father's house and the many material blessings of the "Establishment", because of my separation from God I was miserable and empty inside. Swallowing the propaganda which was being spoon fed our generation that the "rat race", the mindless pursuit of wealth and the material world was a dead end,

I followed the Pied Piper in to hippiedom. Why spend time chasing money when it would never bring fulfillment? Eat, drink and be merry, for tomorrow we shall die! Since this life is largely consumed with attempting to meet our physical needs (and as an atheist there was no afterlife to pursue) this left me with very little to live for. I was a ship without a rudder, a loose cannon. Having learned to skip school in Indiana, attending school for me now was the exception rather than the rule. More than ever, my full time job was looking for the next high.

My second stint at Pleasantville High School, where once I'd been somewhat of a big man on campus didn't last long. Not even bothering to go out for football or even pretending to care about my studies, life was all a big joke now (or at least that was my front).

One day I walked in late to Math class and Mr. Sonberg greeted me brusquely:

"Mr. Leary, where have you been?"

"Oh here and there!" I replied, which drew a healthy round of chuckles from my classmates.

"And *what* have you been doing?" he asked.

"Oh, this and that!"

An uproarious burst of laughter followed and it was another trip to the Vice Principal's office for me. I so loved making people laugh, but I had increasingly less and less to laugh about myself. Where once I had been a star pupil, athlete and class leader, now I was way out on the margins of society, and I knew it. Still ostracized by my old friends who I used to drink and use drugs with, and now under scrutiny at school, it was decided that a change was needed and at the suggestion of my parents I started counseling with Dr. Cohen, a psychiatrist and a dear man who really listened, cared and wanted to help me. Though I didn't mind going to see him, I shared few of my thoughts, and certainly nothing radical for fear they'd lock me up and throw away the key. Eventually Pleasantville High School had enough of me and kicked me out, and I was enrolled at an elite private school nearby.

My stay at Canterbury School in New Milford, Connecticut (where John F. Kennedy attended) wasn't long enough to afford me the time to delve into its history. Once again, I was not in a normal dorm situation and was assigned to a room in the basement of a faculty or staff house which I was to share with another boy. He must have taken an immediate dislike to me, because I do not remember having more than one short conversation with him or seeing him much. Having arrived before the school year and alone most the time, things didn't start well. Trying to fit in, one day after the end of football practice and angry at the cool indifference with which my teammates greeted me, after punting the ball as hard as I could and running it down a few times (partly to burn off my frustration and partly to show those monkeys who they were snubbing) I then went to the locker room, stripped off all the equipment and left it in a heap on the floor and walked away. Going straight to my room and gathering my few belongings (along with a crisp hundred dollar bill which belonged to my unpleasant roommate) I mounted my bicycle and rode home. On the way I stopped to call one of my friends in order to arrange to buy some marijuana with my newfound wealth. He didn't have a line on any pot, but was very excited about some LSD he had just gotten wind of. I made it to his house late and was disappointed to learn that I'd have to leave the money so he could purchase the stuff later. He was a very good salesman though and talked me into it even though he hadn't sampled it yet, and he delivered it to me later. When my parents who were out of town on business learned that I was "loose" again, they shipped me off to my uncle's house until their return. Before my uncle left the house for work the next morning, he gave me the job of mowing the lawn. Prior to heading outside, I went into the bathroom and put a hit of the "Four Way Sunshine" LSD under my tongue. Ignoring instructions to take only one quarter of it, I took the whole hit. After firing up the riding lawnmower I began mowing while waiting for the stuff to take effect. Nothing! After thirty minutes or so I took another hit of the stuff. By now I had consumed eight times the "Recommended Daily Adult Requirement."

In the middle of my umpteenth pass around the yard the hellish concoction started to work. The stuff I'd had in Indiana was nothing like this! Abandoning the riding lawnmower in the front yard and wandering around to the back, it felt like great volumes of energy were surging in and out of me as I breathed. The incredible amounts of power seemed to be generated from within me, and along with it came the impression that I'd always had it and just never used it before. The leaves on the trees were waving at me like hands (not blowing with the wind … for there was no wind that day) and in fact seemed to be moving in small groups in opposite directions with a surreal motion, something like a gigantic school of fish turning and alternately turning back upon itself. This fascinated me for a quite a while (or so it seemed). It may have been a combination of the feeling of incredible power, my own pride and ego, and the raging anger that had built up in me over the years which inspired me to address Almighty God then (the One who I momentarily forgot that I didn't believe in). Pointing to the heavens and yelling at Him, after not getting a response soon enough, in arrogant, blood curdling anger I demanded that He come down and speak with me. He did not, so I took my rampage into the house.

It was nothing that an average teenager couldn't have done, but I reveled in my strength, punching out the screens on my uncle's screened in back porch. After exulting in that victory for a few moments, I entered the main part of the house. It was then that I decided that the President of the United States needed to answer a few pertinent questions. Picking up the phone (without dialing) I boomed,

"I want to speak to the President! Immediately!"

After a few moments without a reply, I screamed "I said IMMEDIATELY!"

Getting no results, I ripped the phone off the wall. Moving to the living room as a sense of fear and unease crept over me, I decided to listen some rock and roll, which I often sought solace in. No matter what I did though, I couldn't get any sound out of my uncle's stereo which had worked fine before. Giving up on that, I decided to take a stroll. Walking out the front door and to the end of the driveway, turning I headed to the main road, the whole time rejoicing in my newfound power and magnificence (completely out of touch with reality). Continuing to seethe with "power" as I breathed in and out, nearing the intersection with the main road, a little old lady carrying a handled paper shopping bag began crossing the road in front me.

"Excuse me ma'am," I boomed. "Do you know what time it is?"

After getting no response I demanded in an even louder voice,

" I said EXCUSE me ma'am do you know what TIME it is?"

She cast a quick glance over her shoulder at me and silently continued on her way.

Then I screamed, "LITTLE OLD LADY, TELL ME WHAT TIME IT IS OR I'LL BREAK BOTH OF YOUR LEGS!"

My rage was in vain, so I crossed the road and headed down the hill. The last thing I remember I was standing in front of a store at the bottom of the hill … then nothing.

What was probably a day later, I awoke lying flat on my back totally immobilized. Having no immediate memory of what had transpired prior to coming to, I looked around alarmed. Straight above me was a high bare ceiling. Straight behind was a very tall, wide and translucent window. Able to move only my eyes, apparently there was nothing in the room but me. Not hearing a sound, I yelled, "Help, Help, Help!" After what seemed like ages, a man wearing an all-white suit (without a tie) with jet black hair and goatee appeared.

Terror raced through my mind, "I've died and gone to hell, and this is the Devil!"

In a sweetly sarcastic voice the man said, "Oh, so *you're* back with us!"

"Back with you WHERE!", I croaked.

It turns out that they had thrown a net over me and hauled me off to a psychiatric hospital, put me in a straightjacket and then under an insulin sheet. Realizing I was now coherent, they undid all of the restraints and allowed me to walk around the ward freely. Since I was no longer acting irrationally, a few days later after warning me to alter my behavior they released me to the custody of my father. That was a bone chilling experience, but I managed to get away with it with almost no consequences. Remarkably, I continued to take LSD at every opportunity for many years after that.

Since I'd run out of public schools my dad decided to try me in another private school, this time a place for kids with "special needs." That there was a liquor store directly adjacent to the campus didn't bode well for the future, and it took me less than a week to blow that set up. One night after getting warmed up on Budweiser beer, I craftily walked next door to the liquor store (which like the school, sat on the main road through town) smashed the front window, reached in and took a half gallon of whiskey. Walking fifty yards back to the stoop in front of my dorm and going to great lengths to act inconspicuously, I sat down and began drinking. It didn't take Sherlock Holmes to figure out who did it. My Dad was morose when he came to get me at the police station. After squaring things with the store owner and the school, he gave me two choices: hit the streets, or go to a psychiatric hospital where they might be able to help me. Though not keen on going to the loony bin, when I thought of the big bad world out there, I opted for the indoors. Though not yet considering myself a lunatic, frankly I didn't see much future for me the way things were going. The mental hospital was somewhere ... and I was going nowhere fast.

# CHAPTER 7

Shady Rest Psychiatric Hospital was situated on the tree covered top of a hill near the banks of the Hudson River in New York, not far from Sing Sing the infamous New York State Prison often referred to in old American movies as "up the river." It was a beautiful place for sad, mixed up folks. Feeling like I'd hit the end of the line and already struggling greatly with feelings of inadequacy, I dreaded what my friends would think about this if they knew. At this stage I'd already been relegated to the fringes of society by my contemporaries who considered me a drunk, a doper, a loser ... now I was a certified nut! Considering that the other patients there were crazy, isolating myself from them seemed a logical move. Guilt by association was a concern—if I felt at home with them, I may be one of them! I was also a little afraid of them. Although normally very much a people person, the blackness of my mood also drove me to isolation. Most of my time during the first few weeks of my stay were spent sitting in the shade of a huge, ancient, beautiful shade tree which graced the front lawn of the old mansion that served as offices for the hospital administration and some of the doctors. For hours I poured over volumes on psychology and psychiatry borrowed from Dr. Morales, the founder and president of the hospital. At that time, I had considerable confidence in science and the ability of mankind to triumph over the adversities and challenges of life by his own devices, and found it logical that I might find answers to my dilemma in the books. I also wanted to know what incantations and potions these guys might use to shrink my head. Years later I realized that the "giants of intellect" who concocted the sciences of psychiatry and psychology by which men think they can solve other men's problems, were merely broken pygmies like me. I was reading the wrong books. For a time though, it distracted me from my misery. It was quite tranquil sitting under the boughs of that great tree reading as the soft summer breeze rustled the foliage, the gentle sound soothing my weary soul. The front lawn of the old manse dropped off quickly, revealing a magnificent view of the Hudson River and Valley stretching south towards New York harbor. I'd read a while, then pause and gaze out over the miles, soaking in the beauty. Occasionally I dropped by Dr. Morales office and would I'd ask for an impromptu audience. He was not my therapist, but the fact that he was the top guy there and carried himself with a cheerful self-assured confidence inspired me to check in with him from time to time. This was supposed to be one of the top ten psychiatric hospitals in the country, and he was the head … maybe this guy would be able to steer me in the right direction. We had a few informal talks, and one day when we were chatting he quipped, "Neil, marijuana makes you crazy." It made no sense to me though—from my standpoint, booze and drugs were the only things that made my life bearable!

After languishing in despair for a while and seeing no solutions close at hand, I walked into Dr. Morales office and volunteered for Electro Convulsive Therapy—shock treatments. Always a radical guy, I reasoned that big challenges called for bold action. Longing for nothing less than a brand new start in life, I was willing to do anything to achieve that ... perhaps if they hit the restart button? In reality, it was going to take a power much greater than a series of regimented electrons to do the job. With the advent of many new drugs to treat mental illness, I don't think shock treatments are very common today, but this was a number of years ago before the physicians began to rely more heavily upon pharmaceutical solutions. The treatments began by administering a general anesthetic then placing electrodes on the temples on either side of the patient's head, then blasting electrical current from one electrode to the other—right through the brain. The recommended course for me was regressive therapy which was usually prescribed to bring a person out of psychosis or very deep depression. Conceivably I didn't qualify on either grounds, but I didn't doubt the prescription—these men were brilliant and at the top of their field. With regressive shock treatments, the person is subjected to a series of treatments until they become almost completely out of touch with reality. Though people in this state can understand and function to some degree, they generally go into stupor like state. Once the desired effect is produced, the treatments are stopped, and after a short period of time the person returns to "normal", hopefully better off than when they started. I can only speculate as to the overall benefits this therapy had for most people, but one of my favorite lines in any book in the world says, "... nothing, absolutely nothing happens in God's world by mistake." If nothing else, shock treatments gave me a fresh starting point. One of the side effects of the treatments is memory loss. I'm not sure if there is a uniform pattern to it, but I could not recollect most of the few months leading up to my stay at Shady Rest. Though later many of those memories returned, the break with reality served as punctuation mark in my life and may have helped to stabilize me somewhat.

April Anne McQueen was an angel sent from heaven. A vision of loveliness (and part tomboy too) she was everything a young man could dream of when imagining a young lady to fall in love with—bright, beautiful, cheerful, exciting, mischievous, thoughtful and romantic—I was enraptured. All the patients who were allowed to roam free on the campus at Shady Rest ate their meals in the dining hall in the old mansion, and April Anne always sat with her friend Jenny. At first, I was careful not to talk to any of the other loonies. One day though, I couldn't resist grabbing a seat next to her at lunch. We hit it off right away and before long were talking every time we had an opportunity. Our friendship quickly blossomed, and soon she became my first girlfriend and my very close friend. Sharing with each other for hours on end about ourselves and our lives, we fell deeply in love. Throughout my life I have been blessed with many great friends, and even to this day I'd count April Anne among the very best. As a teenage guy with a checkered past and an even messier thought life, the likelihood of me sharing my innermost self with anyone was infinitesimal—until she came along. Holding nothing from her, she reciprocated. How exciting, freeing and refreshing it was to share *everything* with her knowing that she would continue to love me and be my friend no matter what! What an honor it was to know that she trusted me to share all of her life with me as well. My tremendous love for her grew deeper every day and ushered me into a whole new dimension of life. Although April Anne had been through some pretty rough experiences in the preceding years, she came from a loving family and had a good head on her shoulders, and I listened carefully to everything that she said. My life had been a train wreck of my own making, but her story was quite different. She suffered severely from a disease called Lupus. Latin for wolf, it is a devastating disease and she had very serious case of it, spending most of her life in the hospital until she was thirteen. The nurses got so used to her being there that they began to talk about things when around her that a child should never hear. By the time she reached puberty and went into a long remission, she had grown up way too quickly. Her mom, who was a Registered Nurse, was understandably very protective of her and kept her on a very short leash allowing her little freedom once she was finally released from the confines of the hospital. Finally able to and wanting to do the things other kids could, April Anne felt smothered. After struggling a while, she ran away from home. The first guy that picked her up as she hitchhiked away from home claimed to be a photographer for a well know soft core pornography magazine, and offered to put her in the magazine's centerfold. April refused, telling the guy that her dad would probably shoot her if she did! In lieu of that the guy took her virginity and started her quickly down a steep slope of sin into a kind of hell on earth. She ended up living with a heroin addict and becoming addicted herself. In the end the dope fiend held her captive and would rape her at knifepoint and forcibly inject her with dope. Her decline and fall happened quickly, and by the time I met her at the age of fifteen, this was all in her past. As I came to know her, she seemed to be on solid ground and pretty well adjusted to life. Once she was separated from the drugs and the thugs, her life came together in a fairly short time.

By playing my cards close to the chest (as always), behaving in a subdued and rational manner, and telling Dr. Cohen and the hospital staff what they wanted to hear, I was released from the hospital at about the same time April Anne was and our budding friendship continued to flourish over the telephone. We spent hours talking whenever possible ... she was one of a very few sources of joy in my life. Since I could no longer attend the public high school in Pleasantville, I was enrolled in yet another exclusive private school far away from friends and family, this time on Long Island. Given my extreme circumstances and mind warping experiences of the past five years, and without a roommate once again, loneliness and isolation were again my constant companions there. The children of some luminaries of the world attended there, and among those was one of my few friends, a very nice girl who (tongue in cheek) I called "Mean Mary Jean." Her family owned an oil company among other things, and just before Thanksgiving I asked her if she was going home for the holiday.

"No, she replied, "my dad said we can't afford it."

Without thinking of how my answer would affect her, I said, "Mary Jean, your dad could charter a 747 to come and get you and not miss the money!"

Yet to regain any significant desire to achieve scholastically, or to be a part of what others were doing, I was soon back to skipping class and wandering off campus (which was forbidden) looking for drugs, booze. The spirit and the flesh were quite weak at this point, and although part of me wanted to succeed, my grasp on the normal had long ago slipped away. In a small effort to reintegrate I went out for the school's football team, but was humiliated and frustrated however, when I, the former star quarterback, middle linebacker and punter was relegated to the offensive line. Trying to take it in stride and figuring that I'd excel as a lineman and they'd see my true worth and restore me to the correct position, I gave it a shot. During my first drill the coach had me line up in front of a 300 pound guy from the city. At about 160 pounds I slammed into him as hard as I could, yet just bounced off repeatedly as he lumbered ahead. So much for proving my worth! My ego took another battering while I sat in calculus class and realized that I did not have clue what they were talking about—I who had been an A+ student in advanced placement math courses was reduced to an idiot! Although I took into consideration that it had been almost two years since I had applied myself at school (or even attended regularly) these two failures one after another hit home hard and I began to fear that I'd dug a hole that would be impossible to climb out of. Fear and depression drove me harder toward the unhealthy pursuit of my self-prescribed painkillers. When April Anne called from Penn Station in New York saying that she had run away again and wanted to come to me, I gleefully directed her to the right train and met her at the station when she arrived. In the midst of this crisis we bonded even more closely. When I missed chapel the next morning and the Dean came looking for me, April Anne popped up from the top bunk in my dorm room, and my short stay at that school was ended. I put her on the next train back to New York City and uneasily awaited the arrival of my dad to take me … where?

Within a short time, April Anne and I were reunited at Shady Rest and we grew closer and closer. On December 29, 1975 I asked her to be my wife and she accepted and embroidered the date on my jeans. Since I did not take my last drink or drug for another thirteen years, I thank God that we never married. We did rejoice in a wonderfully rich relationship for a number of months though. She loved me as much as I loved her, as witnessed by the dozens of love poems we wrote back and forth over the time, and the memorable hours we held and caressed each other while talking about everything under the sun. She was in my thoughts all the time, and when I was with her my world was very good. With no God to worship, no doubt I came close to worshiping her. When we were walking up the hill from the hospital's swimming pool one day and she complained of the steepness, I picked her up and carried her in my arms like a treasure. We talked about virtually everything that occurred to us, and if the subject was a problem she would occasionally counsel me to "trust God, have faith in God."

I'd say, "Oh sure Babe," but to myself I'd rehearse Karl Marx's statement that "Religion ... is the opium of the people." She had her God and I had my dope and booze. Yet something in me was stirred by this. She had bared her soul to me in every area and had held nothing back, not even the things that would shed a very bad light on her. Why would she lie to me about God? Though nothing changed for me at the time, her faith (and the unshakable faith of my dear mother) had a bigger impact on me than I realized.

In the midst of terrific darkness April Anne McQueen was a gift from God and shone like bright sunshine. She was an oasis in my life. It was a brief interlude of thrilling excitement, adventure, beauty and love sandwiched between the dark days before and the darker days after. She loved me! An all-time loser and freak of the century! One day when I was in elementary school I looked into the mirror and thought, "My head is way too big for my body!" That and many other hurtful ideas constantly baited and goaded me for many years, leading to a very poor self-image regarding my insides and my outsides. My relationship with April Anne was such that, when she told me that I had a great body and my looks were way above average I believed her! Because she let me know that she found value in me in many ways, for a little while I felt like a worthwhile person to SOMEBODY (if not myself). My days were filled with her. The times we could be together were like heaven, the times apart filled with writing to her and dreaming about her. The demons that continued to pursue me tirelessly would not let me go though. The despair of "knowing" that life was in the end empty, meaningless and without an ultimate reason haunted me. The thought that apart from my new love, the world was filled with gut wrenching pain, sorrow, horrific suffering and emptiness, to be climaxed in death—black nothingness—wouldn't go away. It was hard for me to want to stay in the game when the prize at the goal line was … nothing. As such a sorrow filled, unstable and confused being, how could I expect to be any good to April Anne or anyone else. The nurturing and building of a relationship between a man and a woman is a very intensive and difficult process and takes dedicated commitment and a solid foundation within. Since my self-image and understanding of who I was, my person and indeed my very world itself was an amorphous ever-changing blob, there was very little I had to offer April Anne besides my own deep need for love and my desire to be kind to her and shower my love upon her. Sadly, the well of love I had to draw from was almost empty.

Over time, my dear April got better. Time in a safe, quiet place with the opportunity to talk and think (and the love of her precious heavenly Father) were healing to her. My own therapy was stuck in the mud. Whatever value there is in psychotherapy was lost on me. In keeping with my learned survival techniques, I tried to be who I thought they wanted me to be and hoped that sooner or later things would get better. The goal was to get out and to go back to the real world, but in retrospect I was afraid of that possibility and wasn't ready for it. My stay at the hospital was tragically unsuccessful, and the only thing I really wanted to do (besides be with April Anne) was get high, and by then I was beginning to see that there wasn't much of a future in that. So what did the future hold for me? I tried not to think about it and lived in the moment.

One beautiful spring day her parents came to take her out for her sixteenth birthday. Although her doctor had repeatedly warned her away from me, in deference to her wishes I was invited along for lunch with the family. Though always a stunning beauty, April was a blue jeans kind of girl. On that day however, when she walked into the waiting room of her dormitory where her parents and I waited, in a satiny, flowery dress, looking more radiant and beautiful than ever, it took my breath away. I'll always remember her like that. Her mom and dad were good people and were polite and friendly to me, and we had a nice lunch. (As a father today, I cannot imagine how I would react to a boyfriend/fiancé that my daughter met in a mental hospital!) The lunch was to be one of our last pleasant memories.

Not long from then, April Anne was deemed well enough to return home. Unable to imagine being without her, immediately I decided to leave the hospital against medical advice and move to be near her. After more stern warnings from her doctor it was decided that I should not see her for a month, during which time I was to prove myself an upstanding citizen. Hah! I'm sure no one was taking bets on me. My Dad, frustrated with my unwise decision to leave the hospital, was just about to move to Texas and had just enough time to install me in a nice motel in a town near April's. The only way to easily do that was to leave an open tab on his credit card so I could eat my meals there. The bad news was that it also meant an open tab at the motel bar too. Although I found two jobs right away, the open bar tab spelled my doom in short order. After losing both jobs, I called April Anne to arrange a forbidden meeting. By this time she too had grown quite tired of my behavior, and when I met her that night on the edge of her parent's property high on booze and marijuana, it was not a cheerful reunion. After a few brief, tense exchanges her dad appeared on the porch with a shotgun. She turned to him and assured him in a friendly tone that it was just me. Perking up, assuming that her attitude towards me had softened, that wasn't the case. When I asked if we could go inside and talk, she reluctantly agreed. Once inside, her whole family (father, mother, and two sisters) joined us in the living room—they were on one side of the room, I on the other. As the lopsided discussion commenced, I was in a losing position. They asked a few questions I could or would not answer, and made undeniable points about my bad behavior. When they finished, I made a lame attempt at pretending to be the injured party.

"I've been down here less than a month and have two jobs already. I know that I should be doing better, but I guess I'm kind of slow." (Neglecting to inform them of course that I'd lost both jobs). With that I turned on my heels and left, "quitting" before I got fired.

April's family lived on about ten acres of land, and I walked toward the road devastated, and dropped to the ground in front of some large hedges that ran along the front of the property. This precious young woman who had been the one ray of hope in my ever darkening world, had just gone away … it seemed likely, forever. As I contemplated this, it felt as if I had just stepped off a cliff overhanging a deep, dark, bottomless gorge. What now? After a few minutes of stunned silence, the thought crossed my mind to start praying again … to seek God.

I thought, "Why would I want to do that? I don't believe in God. I mean I *really* don't believe in God!"

Then, "But you have no *proof* that there is no God!"

True! So how could I know for sure? Echoing what I'd learned from my great teachers at Pleasantville High School, next I reasoned, "Scientific method says that if I have an hypothesis I need to prove it by experimentation." It seemed reasonable to conduct an "experiment" of praying, seeking an answer to the question, "Is there a God?" In an experiment it's imperative to include all possible answers to the question—eliminating any answer without cause ruins the experiment and the results will be invalid. Seriously doubting that it would yield any results or evidence of God's existence, it occurred to me though, that I had nothing to lose. More and more people were abandoning me (for good reason) and I was alone often already … it seemed that would be the case in the future too.

"It will give me someone to talk anyway!" I thought. "Even if He is only imaginary, like Jimmy Stewart's Pooka in the movie Harvey. The way that I'm going I'm bound to die young, so what do I have to lose? If by some remote chance God *does* exist He would be the *only* hope for me."

Then I prayed for the first time in about eight years. "God if you're real, please show me. You know how much I need you. And Lord, if I cannot make April Anne happy, please make it so that I never see her again."

I supposed that my words were rising about ten feet above my head, then falling lifeless to the ground … and yet maybe …

You'd think losing April Ann was enough of a crisis for one day, but the night was young. A former co-worker had given me a ride to April's house that night and had been waiting faithfully the whole time just on the other side of the big hedges. Rejoining him, we headed back for town. Weary from the heart wrenching experience of the breakup, I decided the journey of only a few miles back to town was too much for me and suggested that we get a room for the night in the little hamlet where April's family lived. "Downtown" was a few buildings at a crossroads, one of which had been an old country inn and was now serving as a residential hotel. Forgetting that it was now late at night, I went inside in search of the proprietor. After knocking on numerous doors with no results, I wandered out into the street fuming in drunken frustration. As I crossed the street to my friend's VW bug, a car approached. Once again with lightning speed, my sharp mind formulated a plan. With a grandiose gesture, I stepped out in front of the car which was slowing for the stop sign at the intersection, and held up my hand like a traffic cop. Moving around to the driver side I made the illogical announcement that I was a policeman from that town and needed directions to the nearest motel! I got them alright. The man was an off-duty police officer from that very town, and within a minute my friend and I were surrounded by a number of angry officers. After some conversation they let him go and escorted me off for a goodnight's sleep … under the watchful eye of the local jailer. I say jailer, but this town was so small it didn't have a jail. Sleep completely eluded me, for when they placed me in a courtroom to wait out the night, realizing the gravity of what I'd done, all I could do was repeat over and over, "Oh my God, oh my God!" The arrest had sobered me enough to realize that I was now in very big trouble. Although largely ignorant of the law, even drunk I could guess that messing with the police must be a very serious crime. I was scared to death! Thanks to a good lawyer (and the fact that I subsequently spent almost two more years in psychiatric hospitals), eventually they dropped the charges.

# CHAPTER 8

My dad, once again patient and helpful, bought me a bus ticket to Texas where he had just moved weeks before. The fact that it wasn't an airplane ticket was an indication of his growing dissatisfaction with spending money on me and generally having to deal with me—the bus would take much longer to get me there. He loved me, and always has, but was approaching a breaking point. Arriving in Texas like a meteor, more trouble was on the way. The guy in the seat next to me on the last leg of the bus trip was a young teenager whose mom worked at a local club (read bar). The next day I set out to find the place. Penniless as usual, I reasoned that after striking up a friendship with her son, she would be good for a couple of free drinks. Not wanting to get a late start I arrived at the place by mid-afternoon. She wasn't there yet and I was left to fend for myself. Noticing the place was almost empty, I gravitated to the pool tables in the back and spotted a short guy wearing a cowboy hat and drinking a beer. Without even the fifty cents to challenge him to a game of pool, a brilliant thought struck me.

"If I *had* five dollars, I'd bet you five dollars that I can drink a pitcher of beer faster than you can!" I challenged.

The gauntlet thrown and the bait swallowed, he was off to the bar for a couple of pitchers. Pitcher one I beat him by a decent margin. He offered to pay for the pool table while we drank, and within a fairly short time I dispatched of pitchers two, three, and four with similar alacrity, beating him at pool as well. The cowboy stormed out in disgust. With some grog under my belt and holding my head high in victory, I walked out the front door looking for more adventure. How I came up with so many zany ideas and stories back in those days is hard to tell, but I seemed to be able to think pretty fast on my feet. Walking out into the late evening sunshine and spying another bar directly across the street, I headed in. Although it was early the place was already hopping. Stationing myself at a table, by the time the scantily clad server came to take my order I had formulated a scheme for more free booze.

"I own a club in New York City called Adams Rib and I'm down here scouting for new talent!" I puffed to the young woman.

One by one the pretty young servers came by to make my acquaintance, and as I spun the tale again and again each one willingly brought an offering of a double Tequila Sunrise in an attempt to ingratiate herself to me. Considering the four pitchers of beer I'd already consumed, by the time I spilled out into the parking lot at closing time, I was flying like a bird. Walking over to the road to hitchhike home, one by one the cars emptied out of the parking lot and it occurred to me that since it was after two in the morning it might be difficult getting home. Also, this was my first day in the city, and I didn't know where I was going!

It's fuzzy how it happened, but before long I was driving an old car, had gained confidence in my ability to find the way home, and headed north on the highway. With only a vague idea of where to go, as I went zipping along looking for the "right" exit, I began what became a trademark practice for me …. the drunker I got, the faster I drove. Turning around two or three times I looped back under the freeway again and again trying to find the elusive exit, each time pressing down harder on the accelerator as frustration mounted. Riding the white line with the pedal to the floor and the speedometer buried past 120 miles per hour, I spied the "correct" exit! Quick thinking told me to jerk the steering wheel to the right to make the exit. Drunk thinking failed to consider the tremendous speed at which the car was traveling, and panic set in. Standing with both feet on the brake pedal and plowing parallel furrows in the dirt on the grassy area between the highway and the exit ramp which I'd overshot, I took down a few metal sign markers and hastily assessed the situation. Sober, I may have thought to correct my slide back onto the off ramp, but instead, looking up and noticing that dead ahead was a small forest with a lake or pond behind it, and immediately to my right was a ten foot high dirt embankment—in a split second I reasoned that if I made it alive through trees I'd probably drown in the water. The dirt had to be softer than the trees, so I decided to end the ride quickly. A glance at the dashboard indicated my speed was still ninety-five miles per hour. Remembering my mom's advice from four years earlier, I yelled out, "Help me God!" Jerking the wheel hard to my right brought the car to an almost ninety degree angle to the embankment. Still standing with both feet on the brake pedal, arms braced against the steering wheel, within an instant WHAM! My forehead smacked into the steering wheel, then my head snapped back and slammed into the roof the car. Incredibly, though the car went from ninety-five to zero in a split second, my only injuries were a couple of bumps on the head! The prayer of an atheist was answered and a miracle had occurred. Considering the tremendous rate of speed (and that I was not wearing a seat belt), I should have been skewered on the steering column like a shish kabob, thrown a hundred yards into an immovable object, or crushed to death in a jumbled pile of steel.

Like my childhood friend, Woofie the cat, having spent another of my nine lives, the next day I set out to find a job and within a few days landed one at a fast food restaurant. We were working to open a new store in North Dallas and the hours were as long as I was naïve … the manager convinced several of us to work for *free* "until the store opened." My experience as a solid citizen however didn't last long. One day as I hitchhiked east on Forest Lane after getting off early, an open top Jeep pulled over with some kids in it. They were headed to the country to party and asked if I wanted to go. "Heck yeah!" I said, and jumped in the back. As we headed north on Preston Road, it wasn't long before we were rolling through lovely green pastures filled with contented grazing cattle.

"What a beautiful day!" I thought, as the air blasted through the car. They shared their beer with me, and by the time we made it to our destination, an old rock quarry near McKinney, I was in a festive mood. The old quarry had filled in with water and had become a gathering spot where young people swam and partied. On this lovely summer day the place was crowded, and though unprepared, I managed to mooch a few more beers and before too long was drunk again. Fixated on playing with a Frisbee I'd found and unable to find anyone to play with me, I began throwing it and chasing it and throwing it again. It must have looked a bit odd, and even more so to the sheriff's deputy who drove up to monitor the situation. The crowd immediately stopped everything they were doing and kind of bunched together, watching to see what the lawman would do. Being from near the big, liberal city of New York, I didn't have much fear of the police and I felt free just to continue my solitaire game of Frisbee. Uh oh! I caught the attention of the sheriff who called me over to his car. Shortly after that, I was on my way to the county jail ... end of party.

Although I'd had some brushes with the law before, I'd yet to see anything like the old Collin County Prison in McKinney, Texas. Today, some human rights organization would probably make sure that the place was shut down. It looked like something out of the Wild West and in fact dated back that far. The cell block they put me in was on the top floor. Rectangular in shape, in the middle was the old cell block which was constructed of what looked like hand forged slats of steel which were interwoven the same way a basket is made. Outside of the cage around the perimeter and against the exterior walls of the building where at one time guards probably patrolled, were metal frame cots where most of the prisoners slept. All the beds on the outside were full, so the cage was the only place left for me to sleep. There were no lights in the cage, and the steel slats allowed very little light in—it was a particularly dark, dirty and dingy place.

There were windows on three sides of the perimeter wall, wide open to the outside world—bars only, no glass, no screens. It was summertime in Texas, and it was over a hundred degrees each day during my time there—the place was like an inferno—if it hadn't been on the second floor and caught a breeze now and then we probably would have cooked! On my second night there, I woke up to see a cockroach with a head an inch wide sitting on my chest staring at me. Immediately I became airborne. Panting, with sweat pouring out of me profusely, sleep didn't come back quickly that night. Needless to say, this was a rude awakening for a fine young fellow like me, whose only crime (this time) was having a bit too much fun. My Dad was about through with me by then, and was by no means going to bail me out of jail again, but after a few days he did bring a pack of cigarettes to me. The only one I'd had up until that point was a Bugler, a nasty roll your own brand common in jail at the time. Being in jail, any jail at any time isn't fun, but withdrawing from nicotine only makes it worse! Since the charges against me were minor the suffering didn't last too long, and when the judge finally got around to seeing me, I was released.

Back in Dallas, although increasingly reluctant to have me around, Dad and his wife decided to chance allowing me to stay at their house again. My nineteenth birthday was fast approaching, and with it came another hair-raising escapade and an interesting introduction to the Deep South for a Yankee from New York. Although I had worked as a cowboy on the ranch in East Texas, I'd never worn western clothes. While at his house visiting one day, one of my new friends gave me a straw cowboy hat as a birthday gift. I had recently purchased a pair of Dingo boots which were not really cowboy boots, but similar enough that I decided to be a cowboy to celebrate my birthday. Decked out in my boots, hat, denim shirt, mirror shades and my light blue leisure suit (a gift from April Anne), I walked in to Lily Langtree's, a country western bar which used to grace upper Greenville Avenue. Swaggering in, I must have been a sight to the locals as I hunkered up to the bar. The place was half full as, beer in hand, I made my way to an open seat beside a pretty blond who was seated at a table alone, and kind enough to let me join her. A guitar player starting banging out some tunes and the place was hopping before long. After finishing off the first pitcher and buying a second, I poured another glass and left the young lady at the table, stationing myself right in front of the guitarist.

Clapping, singing and yelling, I returned to the table only to fill my glass every ten minutes or so. Each time I'd chat with the lady briefly but never stayed for long, as romance was never on my mind until I drank massive quantities of booze (and then it was usually too late!). It was a regular hootenanny for a couple of hours as singing, hollering, stomping and yelps of approval rang out from the crowd for the guitarist who was belting out all the old country favorites.

Talking is one of the things that comes most easily to me, and when I drank my words multiplied exponentially. It seems that my motor mouth had become an irritant to some of the patrons, and my New York accent probably didn't help things either in this part of the US where many had not forgotten the defeat of their ancestors in the Civil War. When I sat down at the table to replenish my beer again (thankfully the blond had left by then) someone hit me on the underside of my jaw with so much force that it lifted me up out of the chair. There must have been an angel aiding me, because as I flew up and over the heavy oak bar chair, while airborne I reached down and grabbed the arms of the chair and in one motion lifted it over my head and to the right, landing on the balls of my feet facing my aggressor. As I held the chair as a weapon, the guy, who I later learned was six-foot, seven-inches tall and weighed 290 pounds, made a move to come at me, and I said, "I'll kill you, you so and so!" Instantly a crowd gathered around which included the bartender who said to me,

"Get out of here!"

"Me get out of here! It was that so-and-so who hit *me!*" I protested.

"I said get out of here! If you don't leave, I'll call the police!"

Baffled, I grabbed my hat and my mirror shades and went out the back door. Standing there for a minute, I lit up a cigarette, mulling over why the guy hit me. After straightening my hat on my head, I walked slowly around the front of the building towards Greenville Avenue. When I was about thirty feet southwest of the front door, a bunch of people burst out the door … the big guy was trying to come after me and a group of his friends were trying to stop him. As they struggled to restrain him, he fell to his knees on the porch, threw his arms back knocking them all aside, then got up and started coming after me. My dad often said that discretion is the better the better part of valor, so I walked away from him and turned halfway around to address him, "I don't know who you are, I don't know what you want, but leave me alone!"

He continued to come towards me, and turning I repeated, "I don't know who you are, I don't know what you want, but LEAVE ME ALONE!"

Still he kept coming and made a lunge at me. I grabbed his head, gave him a hip throw, and as his big body hit the sidewalk, I hammered his head with punches. Whether it was the punches, the booze in him or the impact with the sidewalk it's uncertain, but realizing that he was out cold I stopped punching him, stood up and straightened my hat and glasses. Standing over his limp body I lit another cigarette, turning the whole thing over in my mind. The crowd disappeared back inside, but moments later a lone man appeared and approached me.

"You'd better get out of here right now." he said.

"Friend", I said with a self-assured air, "I'm standing here smoking a cigarette and he's lying on the ground unconscious. I think I'm okay."

"Yeah, well, his friends inside all have rifles in their pickup trucks, so you'd better get out of here now!"

"Thank you friend." I said, maintaining my cool tone of voice.

Turning, I walked casually away … and then ran like lightning as soon as I was around the corner.

After putting up with my part time working and full time partying for a while, the last straw for my dad came when he was awakened by my friends who I had invited to come by the house at two in the morning, after they got off of work. After sending me to tell them to leave, when I had tarried too long talking with them, dad came out on the front porch madder than I have ever seen him and demanded that I come in the house. After waiting for a few moments my friends suggested I'd better go. As they drove off, I approached the house cautiously. My dad was furious …grabbing the beer out of my hand and slamming it on the sidewalk he growled "Get in this house!" and for the first time in my life I was frightened by him.

Hesitating I said, "I'm not going to fight with my own dad!"

He responded by repeating his command, "Get in this house." in a tone it seemed better to obey, so in I went. Once inside he followed me to my room where I broke down in tears. Clueless as to what drove me on in my desperate quest to escape reality, I asked him to please send me back to the hospital. A few days later I was on my way back to Shady Rest.

Now I was in a really deep hole. Before I had April Anne, now had only myself and my misery. It was harder and harder for me to imagine how I could survive and exist happily in this fallen world. Shortly after my return to the hospital, I once again volunteered for shock treatments. This time was quite different from the first though. Initially things went as before … I was led downstairs to the treatment room and administered the drugs, and later taken back upstairs to the dormitory. One day something went very wrong though. Whether the anesthetic was not administered correctly or it was another reason, I was not completely under when they threw the switch. Like an explosion the electric current coursed through my skull in a terrifying rhythm, then I felt and saw myself falling rapidly into a deep black hole. Sensing that the breath of life had gone out of me, silently I screamed into the abyss into which I seemed to be falling head over heels, "I'm too young to die!"

Thankfully I did not, and when I regained consciousness petrified at the thought of undergoing another treatment, I related my experience to the aides and pleaded with them to allow me to speak with the doctor. My second brush with death within a few months was even more terrifying than the first, because I knew that another treatment was scheduled for the next day. The tricky thing was that in the course of regressive shock therapy the patient slips into a fog losing touch with reality ... would they believe me and allow me to talk to the doctor or would they assume that I was already loony and dismiss the whole thing, only to wrestle me onto the table for the next treatment? Thank God they let me see him, and although Dr. Volt (as we lovingly called him) said it was impossible for a patient to experience what I did, he relented and discontinued the treatments. It may be that the Lord had allowed that anomaly to happen so that again, I could "taste death" in preparation to learning about eternal life.

# CHAPTER 9

The rest of my stay at Shady Rest was fairly uneventful, except for when a friend and I ran away in a vain attempt to find drugs. Casing a local seminary looking for cash was miserably unsuccessful, and after my friend decided to give up and go back, I attempted to befriend some local kids partying in a nearby park, hoping to share some of their booze. It turns out that my fellow escapee had ratted on me to the staff at the hospital, and I was "captured" just before being jumped by some local toughs. Although my misery continued to deepen, it didn't appear that staying there would solve anything, so I convinced the doctor that I was stable and was released again. Quickly falling back into hardcore drug and alcohol abuse (accompanied by my typically radical behavior), I looked for an out. Greyhound Bus Lines was running a special: anywhere in the country for fifty dollars. Once again penniless, this time on the streets of New York City, my dad was kind enough to ask a friend of his to give me some cash. The man's office was in the old Gulf + Western building at Columbus Circle (since converted to luxury high rise condos by Donald Trump). In a short while the gentleman graciously gave me the money and I went to straight to the Port Authority bus terminal and bought a ticket to San Francisco. Just before getting on the bus I exchanged the eight dollars left in my pocket for eight silver dollars which I envisioned (and succeeded in) slapping down on bars for a drink as I traveled to the "Old West." Obviously I'd seen too many old movies. With only the eight coins and the clothes on my back I headed for California.

Having never been to the far west, adventure was in the air. The tales of the Old West and the exciting exploits I'd read about as my American pioneer predecessors had fulfilled our "Manifest Destiny" and settled the western portion of this great continent have always intrigued me. The eastern part of our land had been "civilized" for a number of centuries, but the west as I envisioned it was still relatively fresh and raw from its wild days. That, and of course California, one of the cradles of the hippie movement, lay at the end of my journey as well. California also made sense because it was as far as you can go from New York in the lower forty-eight— my thrifty side wanted to get the most of fifty dollars' worth of travel. Besides, my cousin Mary was living on the coast at the time, so I'd have a place to crash when I got there.

As the bus rumbled west, I thought about what lay ahead. Hollywood beach movies with Frankie Avalon, Annette Funicello, Elvis Presley and company had painted a fun image of the Golden State for me, and I looked forward to spending a lot of time near the sand and surf. As the bus pulled out of New York City an air of high adventure and promise reigned. Like castles built in the sky though, reality would be more of the same, simply in a different locale, and the adventure was generally not the kind to write home about.

"More whiskey barkeep!" I barked, slapping a silver dollar on the bar at the first long stop the bus made as we headed west.

Even though one dollar would buy a shot of bar whiskey or a beer in those days, my money didn't last to the western border of

Ohio, and I didn't "waste" any of it on food either. It was winter, and during our stop in Chicago I wished for more than just my denim jacket to protect me from the cold. Though I had shoveled snow at twenty-one degrees below zero in Pleasantville and walked around the block in Kinderhook one cold dark winter night when it was thirty-six degrees below, I cannot remember ever being so cold as when I dodged from one storefront to another trying to get back to the Greyhound station in downtown Chicago that day. Unbelievably, it was only thirty-two degrees, but with the bitter wind coming off Lake Michigan (and I suppose the lack of fuel in my engine) I was chilled to the bone in a very short time. Wistfully I remembered that my Dad had planned on being in Chicago at approximately this time, but realized that even if he was, in the days before cell phones it would have been difficult to find him … and if I did there was no guarantee it would be a warm welcome.

Heading west again, just out of Chicago I became acquainted with a guy who had just boarded the bus and taken the seat next to mine. Richard Wolf, who was headed home to Denver, looked like the Indian on the old American nickel, but with blond hair. Half Native American and half Scandinavian and with long hair which hung down to his shoulders, it was easy to imagine him perched atop a paint horse adorned with eagle feathers and holding a spear.

He was a nice guy and a good conversationalist, and as the bus sped west, I learned that he had some marijuana to share as well. I will not glorify drug use or drunkenness, but at the time, drugs and booze were the only solace that I had … without Christ (or so I thought) it seems that the intense ongoing pain in my life may have crushed me otherwise.

More and more hardened by sin, by the time we arrived in Denver I'd unashamedly cooked up another scheme to continue the party. It was unrealistic to expect Richard to keep supplying me with dope for free, and I had no qualms about asking my Dad if he could again arrange for some more cash there in Denver on the pretense that I needed to eat. Sure enough, my dear father also had a friend there, and Richard and I made our way to a downtown high rise to meet the guy. (NOTE: this is before the addict/alcoholic label had been pinned on me and before the concept that enabling that behavior was deadly had become more widely known.) We probably looked an odd sight, two bedraggled hippies fresh off a cross country bus ride, sitting in the lobby of a stuffy financial establishment. Eventually the man invited us into his office and handed me the cash. With prize in hand, we proceeded to the dope supply where I promptly spent the entire $25 on LSD. Before parting ways with me, Richard who had to run an errand, was kind enough to give me a healthy amount of pot from his stash to keep me going until he returned.

My stomach began to growl and I decided to sell some of the pot so I could eat. Walking down the somewhat crowded sidewalk in downtown Denver, I soon found a likely customer. Just as he pulled out his money and I pulled out the pot, a policeman stepped up. He told the other guy to get lost, took my baggie of marijuana and poured it down the drain and told me to follow him. Follow him! Every cell in my body wanted to run, yet something (probably the Lord) held me in check. As we weaved through the crowd, scared to death I followed him into a liquor store. He told me to stand right on the spot I was and not move. This was quite a few years ago and the penalties for possessing drugs were still draconian in some places. As I stood there I squirmed inwardly wondering what would happen. Just then my hand touched the LSD in my pocket and panic shot through me. The store was crowded and the cop had picked up the phone to make a call. He turned his back for a moment and in a flash I grabbed the baggie containing 25 hits of purple barrel acid, jammed it into my mouth and (assuming the baggie wouldn't digest) swallowed it. To my great relief the cop didn't see it. A minute later he came back, and after giving me a stern warning and promising to arrest me if I wasn't on the next bus out of town, to my amazement he let me go. Scooting out of the liquor store as quickly as I could and intending to head back to Richard's house in hopes he'd returned by now, I made my way down the street. The baggie insulating my bloodstream from the LSD I'd swallowed was no match for the hydrochloric acid in my stomach, and an overdose of LSD quickly began to take effect, sending me on a walking tour of Denver of indeterminate length. Combine the effects of the drug with the fact that I'd never been to the area before, and although Richard lived in downtown Denver in the near vicinity of a bright purple building, I searched for his place vainly for long time. Finally giving up out of sheer exhaustion, it occurred to me that I was in a nice upper middle class residential neighborhood miles from the downtown Denver. Realizing it was hopeless to expect my fried, hallucinating brain to get me anywhere, I stepped out into the street and flagged down a passing motorist,

"Sir", I spoke candidly, "I'm tripping my brains out on LSD and I'm trying to get back to my friend's house. Can you help me?"

Instead of speeding off and calling the police, the guy told me to get in. When I told him where I was trying to go, he patiently told me that I had transposed the address and that the place where I needed to go was many miles away ... and he drove me there.

Nothing but God's mercy! So high that I could have been run over by this guy or any number of other speeding drivers not on the lookout for a dope crazed hippie, the morgue, or at least the county jail could have been my destination. Instead, I was being chauffeured downtown and dropped off in front of my friend Richard's pad—to my disappointment though he wasn't there. Burned out and hungry but still wired up on the acid, I wandered around downtown Denver for a quite some time. Teaming up with a wild looking street guy, we roamed about for a while, him clutching a big piece of tree branch about five feet long, and me a piece of inch thick steel rebar about the same length. I guess we figured we were navigating the urban jungle! It's a wonder that the cops didn't pick us up. Without any planning on my part, our route eventually brought us to the Greyhound bus station. My ticket, though balled up and somewhat illegible was still in my pocket. Bidding my buddy goodbye and throwing my club into the gutter, I went inside. Providentially, a bus was just about to head west for San Francisco. Relieved, I settled into a comfortable chair in the front row of the bus and headed west again. An hour or so later, as we crested the continental divide, the brilliant beams of the setting sun burst through the windshield of the bus hitting me in the eyes, and I melted into the chair collapsing into a dreamless sleep, after many hours of sleepless insanity.

When I came to it was nighttime and we were approaching Steamboat Springs. To me it was the stuff of dreams. I'd seen my skiing heroes race down the slopes there on a number of telecasts, so as the bus stopped briefly at the little store which served as the bus station, I climbed off the bus hoping to get a taste of the glory. How I expected to get to the top of the mountain or ski down it without a nickel to my name I don't know, but youth is never fazed by much, so away I went. Though January first, that day it had been seventy degrees in Denver, and at Steamboat Springs it wasn't much cooler. There had been a drought for quite some time, and according to one of the beautiful people at a chic local watering hole, the only place where there was snow was the top of the mountain … another burst bubble. Because of my recent adventure, my confidence and energy levels were not up to the hard work of schmoozing the local populace in hopes of extracting a few free drinks, so I walked back across the street to the Greyhound station and camped out waiting for the next westward bound bus.

Gratefully one came shortly so I didn't have to sleep outdoors that night, and after climbing on the bus again I was able to get some more badly needed rest as the bus droned westward. Angst brought on by reality and lack of food began to take the shine off my adventure to the "Old West." At Salt Lake City I became sidetracked again, pursuing an abortive attempt at a party in Ogden. After another futile night's effort trying to find some companionship, joy or happiness through a bottle, I stumbled on to what appeared to be an Interstate (and was) and stuck my thumb out, forgetting about my bus ticket for the time being. Eventually I made it to Pendleton, Oregon arriving just after sunset. The town had an Old West look to it, and when I discovered that they hosted a big rodeo there each year I perked up. Yet it also had a small town feel to it—everybody knows everyone and a stranger sticks out like a sore thumb. When I gravitated to a local bar which actually looked just like an old saloon out of the Wild West (with swinging half doors and all) I immediately caught the attention of the half dozen people in the room. Realizing that trying to bum a drink would probably not work so well here, I turned and walked out disappointed. The western atmosphere brought the cowboy and adventurer out in me though, and upon hearing that there was an Indian Reservation right next to town, my sleep starved, booze and drug addled brain struck on a "bright idea":

I would go to the reservation, find the Chief and ask to borrow a horse and a rifle in order to ride over the coastal mountains to the sea! Surely the honorable red man would feel a kinship to this pioneering paleface and extend a hand! It was pitch dark by the time I reached the Indian land, and knocking on one door after another trying to find the chief's house, no one would even answer the door. Later on, a local told me that behaving like that I could have been shot!

Somehow I made my way back to the Interstate and reached Portland late that night. A week or so out of New York by now I was cold, exhausted and really hungry. As I stood in the rain beside the highway without my denim jacket which was a casualty of the trip, the lighted billboard beside the road announced the temperature grimly, "Thirty-three degrees" and informed me that it was a little after three o'clock. Something had to give. To my relief, I remembered that I had a bus ticket to San Francisco. When I reached the bus station my hopes were dashed when I could not find it. Hoping against hope, I climbed aboard the southbound bus thinking that possibly the driver wouldn't notice me. Settling into the seat next to a very nice young lady who turned out to be a student at a college south of Portland, my night took a turn for the better. After sharing my story with her, including the fact that I lost my bus ticket, she kindly offered to buy me a ticket to her stop if the driver discovered my dilemma (which he did). She even offered to let me stay with her for a few nights! She had no roommate, so when we arrived she took me to her room and gave me some food, and within an hour I was asleep in the spare bed for the first time in many days. The situation wasn't ideal though; she was a poor student and had a meal ticket to eat at the cafeteria, but no money to feed me. Quite grateful for the sleep and her company, I hung out for a couple of days on campus before bidding my new friend goodbye and headed south.

Hitchhiking through the rolling hills of southern Oregon and noticing some wildflowers growing beside the road, a 1960s song came to mind that said, "If you're going to San Francisco, be sure to wear some flowers in your hair." Really getting into the hippie thing, I picked some and put them behind my ear. My first stop in California turned out to be Berkeley, called Berserkley by some. The University of California at Berkeley had been a hotbed for the cultural revolution of the 60s and early 70s, and those years were not so far in the past as to have left the area unaffected. Flower Power, Love Ins and the Vietnam War may have passed by now, but the freaks were out in full force here! Telegraph Street, one of the main roads near the university, dead-ended into the campus, and the sidewalks were lined with a curious admixture of people, young, middle aged and old, and all seemed to have Bohemian leanings. One day while walking away from the campus, it occurred to me that suddenly the streets were deserted. As a police cruiser idled slowly past on my left, glancing to my right, about fifteen or twenty people were flattened against the walls in an alley hoping to avoid the cop! Blown away by that, I stopped a local to ask about it and he informed me that Berkeley was the run-away capital of the country … they were probably kids trying to avoid a trip back home.

On the UC Berkeley campus one afternoon I caught wind of a rally that was to be held that day for Angela Davis, a well-known radical from the 60s. Harry Edwards and several other luminaries of the period were to be in attendance as well and I was curious to hear from some of the celebrities of the movement. Preoccupied with chasing the next joint of marijuana or bottle of booze, I arrived after the rally was over, though many people were still milling around. Looking for what might be gathering of key radicals so I could join their conversation, I noticed a guy who I am convinced was Bob Dylan. Approaching him I said, "Hey Bob, I saw you in concert during your Rolling Thunder Revue tour (although I hadn't) ... it was really good." He did not respond but looked at me disdainfully, and I walked away. Curious to know whether it was actually him or not, later when he started talking with a couple of tall black gals, I approached the group on the pretense of needing directions and asked where the Communist Party headquarters was. The biggest deception a liar ever pulls off is fooling himself into thinking that people actually believe what he is saying. Bob (or whoever he was) and the folks with him saw through me, and he invited me to leave.

Berkeley soon lost its luster for me and I headed over the bridge for San Francisco, my sights set on Haight Ashbury. Though I really didn't know much about the genesis of the hippie movement at the time, I knew Haight Ashbury was ground zero. Expectantly I mused that dope would be flowing in the streets there, along with free love and all the other trappings of the movement. As I walked down Haight Street headed toward Golden Gate Park, I looked in every doorway, nook and cranny hoping to see people smoking pot or any other signs that the 60s were still alive here. There were some hippie looking folks walking around and a lot of interesting shops and things, but none of what I anticipated. Stopping once to make sure that I was really on Haight Street, and pausing again at the intersection with Ashbury, I wondered what had happened. Was I five years too late?

My brain was a bit addled from the long trip and six years of hard partying, but eventually I came back to earth and began thinking about where my next meal would come from. Just about then I looked up, and coming toward me on the sidewalk was an old buddy of mine I'd grown up with in Pleasantville carrying some groceries! 3,000 miles away from home, Patrick and I greeted each other. Following him around the corner to an old storefront where he and three other guys, all friends, brothers of friends, or acquaintances from Pleasantville were living. Expecting a fun (and food filled) reunion, like a mirage on the desert though, the long anticipated good fortune evaporated before my eyes. When we stepped through the door we interrupted a loud argument and I was immediately invited to leave. Help disappeared from view as I glanced over my shoulder astonished at how quickly relief came … and went! The trip to Mecca was a big bust and before long I was on the highway headed south.

Travelling on the inland highways since reaching the west coast, though quite close in San Francisco, I had yet to be enraptured by the beautiful Pacific Ocean. My ultimate destination was the little fishing town where my cousin Mary lived, and approaching it from the landward side I was greeted by a magnificent rock over forty stories tall which stood out of the Pacific Ocean a short distance from the shore. A lava dome, the remnant of a volcano, dominated the vista and a broad causeway of boulders and dirt stretched from the shore out to the rock. Together with the sand dunes and bars that had built up south of the rock, a harbor was formed for the many fishing and pleasure boats which called the village home. The tantalizing smell of the salt air, the sound of the crashing waves, and the endless blue green horizon before me enthralled me for many minutes, and all seemed to spell the end of my journey. Very tired by now, I was ready to crash. Except for the short stay with my new friend in Oregon, I had hardly slept at all since leaving New York. During all my years on the streets I rarely slept in the alleys or the "bushes." Not only was it difficult falling asleep on the ground, but I didn't feel at all safe sleeping out in the open in a populated area. Even when in the countryside, lack of proper camping gear or just my hard-headed determination to press on to my destination almost always kept me driving myself through the night, rarely sleeping while I traveled. If not for the many Christian rescue missions and the Salvation Army which provided food and an occasional good night's rest, I probably wouldn't have lived long enough to tell this story! After a significant effort searching I found Mary's apartment, but no one was there and I was becoming dejected, when thankfully she arrived home from work. Mary was sharing a tiny two bedroom place with two other young ladies and I had the couch to sleep on. All three of the gals were working and were quite generous, so I was able to eat and get rested in a short time; it helped that I was only nineteen years old. The cramped quarters wasn't the perfect setup though and the situation quickly became uncomfortable for her roommates. After a few days I wore out my welcome completely when I stole Mary's absent boyfriend's pot plant off the back porch, smoked it and denied it … and didn't even get high!

Though disappointed in myself and ashamed, the time to get rested there gave me new vigor, and I headed into town to begin to look for work, food and a place to live. The town is one of the loveliest I've ever seen. Nestled between the coastal hills and mountains and the beautiful Pacific Ocean, and hundreds of miles from the nearest metropolitan area, it is a real gem. With a great love for the sea, I headed straight for the harbor to look for work.

"A job on a fishing boat would provide a place to live as well!" I reasoned.

Most of the boats were unmanned, and the few guys I was able to talk with said that they didn't need anybody. Making my way down the dock, I came upon another small fishing boat and hailed the man working on deck.

"Hello! Do you need to hire anybody?

He looked me over and said, "Why do you ask?"

The Polynesian man's dark skin reflected the many days he must have spent on the open sea, and as his deep dark eyes appraised me critically, he seemed like a guy who'd seen a lot of life but couldn't quite place where I fit in. Not sure where he was coming from either, I asked again if they needed anybody or if he knew if any of the other boats were needing a crew member. He answered no on both counts, but then told me that there was a place in town where I could stay for a few days and get something to eat, for free. Suspicious, I grilled him a bit then decided to give it a look. Following his directions off I went.

Heading inland and reaching the edge of town, I continued east on the road that now paralleled California Highway 1 which connects many of the coastal towns for the length of the state. Pasture land and farm fields flanked the highway and an occasional house clung to the edge of the road. About a mile outside of town a small dirt road ran south to the base of the string of mountains which, along with the foothills to the north, cradled Highway 1 as it headed inland to join up with US 101. Noticing a cluster of buildings a hundred or so yards closer to the mountain on the little dirt road, I realized it was the place he mentioned and turned in. The people at Salem Christian Commune welcomed me warmly and said that the reason that they were helping me was because of Jesus's love for us all. The rustic camp at the base of the steep green mountain was a welcome respite, but after staying for a few days resting up and regaining more strength, my restless wanderings began again.

# CHAPTER 10

Drifting around the country for a while, I heard that my cousin Conn had recently moved from New York to Houston and I decided to visit him. Finding his apartment easily, I was quite disappointed to discover that he and his new wife had, like good hippies, already opened their home to three or four guys that had either come with them from New York or who Conn had met there. There was no room in the inn. Seeing that I was bummed out, Conn invited me to his favorite bar which was conveniently located about fifty yards from his front door. "Well," I thought to myself, "at least I'll get drunk out of this!" Even that didn't work out because no one had very much money. Now in a foul mood, as we sat around a table with two of his friends, my mighty mouth got the better of me. Jokingly harassing one of Conn's friends to the point of distraction, he finally got up and came after me. Something told me that this guy was not to be messed with, so I headed for the door. He followed close behind, and just after we stepped out the front door, I tried yelling at him to get him to back down, but to no avail. There were a bunch of wooden folding chairs set up out front, and he picked one up and swung it at me sideways so that the full weight of the chair smacked me. Since it hit my hard head it had no effect. When I just stood there and cursed him, he became even more enraged, and in the moonlight I saw the flash of a blade as he pulled out his knife to kill me! For a change, common sense grabbed hold of me and I ran away while cursing at him and telling him that I'd be back. Later word came back that he was a fugitive and was on the lamb for murder ... God had spared my life again.

Heading for downtown Houston, I was about to gain some new experience surviving on the streets. Settling in at the Greyhound Bus Station which in those days was a magnet for street people, drifters and other undesirables, it became my temporary refuge. Because the city was growing at a tremendous rate and there was a consistently large and shifting crowd in the bus station at all hours of the day and night, I was able to catch some sleep a few minutes at a time in the waiting area without drawing the attention of the security guards. Day labor was readily available, so enough work to buy food was to be had, but this level of existence was not sitting well with me, and I decided to do something drastic ... join the Marine Corps. In spite of the obvious drawbacks, it would surely mean three meals a day and a place to sleep!

This was years before most of our computer systems had become as tightly integrated as they are today, so they did not discover my problematic past and quickly growing criminal record. With very little fuss all the preliminary steps were finished except for passing a physical examination, and I would be ready to enter the service. It was Friday afternoon and they told me to go home (oh sure!) and return on Monday to take the physical and swear in. Relief was in sight—if you would call the Marine Corps relief. Granted, my room and board situation would improve and I was comforted by the idea that the regimentation of military life would probably be good for me. Rather than hang out at the bus station all weekend I determined to hitchhike to Dallas, throw myself a farewell party and return Sunday night in time to make my appointment Monday morning. The rides on Interstate 45 North were not coming easily though, and by 1:30 A.M. I was barely out of Houston. Walking north along the highway, down the embankment to the east I saw what looked like a hopping bar. The parking lot was packed and people were milling around outside as music and laughter drifted towards me. "I'll just party here for while!" I thought, descending the slope. Hoping for some chemical relief and taking in to account the time of night (just before closing time) I decided against shooting pool to raise money or spending my last money on one drink, and instead to invest the $1.25 that was in my pocket in a joint of marijuana. Asking around though, I had no luck. They shut the place down, and as the crowd filtered out of the bar towards the parked cars and motorcycles, I asked around some more but still had no success. Wearily I climbed back up the embankment and stuck my thumb out again. My antennae and street smarts were not very well tuned that night, because when a car pulled over a few minutes later I climbed in, failing to notice that while the front seat next to the driver was empty, there were three guys in the back seat. After driving a short distance, they pulled off the Interstate and drove up to a house. Two of the guys in the back seat got out and picked up the third guy who was stone cold drunk and carried him to the house. Laying him on the front porch, they got back into the car.

We made our way back to the Interstate and shortly after the driver pulled the car into one of the northbound lanes, in a flash the guy behind me put a knife to my throat! As shock rolled through me, I heard his demonic voice say, "Look in the mirror you so and so!"

I looked and saw a Bowie knife at my throat and an automatic pistol to the back of my head! My blood ran cold as I thought, "I'm only nineteen years old! I'm too young to die!"

The guy with the hardware growled,

"Give me your money you so-and-so!"

"I only have a dollar and a quarter!" I protested.

"You lying so-and-so!" he said, "You were trying to buy pot at the bar!"

"I was trying to buy one joint!" I said, "All I have is one dollar and twenty five cents!"

"Check his pockets!" the guy with the weapons said to the other guy.

He rifled my pockets and confirmed that I was telling the truth which made him mutter in disgust. Then he took off my belt and used it to tie my hands behind my back. Just about then, I noticed a latex tube on the dashboard. Junkies! Chills ran through my body as I stared ahead, trying not to move ... trying to pray. Thoughts raced through my mind. Since I had been consistently practicing lying for seven years now either to escape consequences I deserved or to obtain drugs or booze, I resorted to it again.

"Have you ever heard of Carlo Gambino? I ventured.

"No." one of them answered.

"Have you ever seen the movie *The Godfather*?" I asked.

"Yeah. What about it?"

"Carlo Gambino is the real life mafia guy that they patterned the movie after. He is the head of all the Mafia in this country. All that stuff pretty much happened the way it showed in the movie."

"So what!" he said.

"My grandfather is Carlo Gambino, and if you mess with me, you're dead!"

Not only was I a liar, but I was a stupid one. With my big mouth and loose tongue I had just signed my own death warrant. One of the rules of the street is that dead men tell no tales. If what I had just told them was true, if they were to let me live their own lives would be in dire jeopardy. The only way to insure their own safety would be to kill me. There was a long silence and I again revived the prayers that I'd begun again a year before. Minutes later the driver turned off of the Interstate and headed east on a narrow farm road. After not much more than a mile, he turned right onto a dirt road which was recently cut through the thick pine forest. The red south Texas dirt was mounded up in a neat row about six inches high on both sides of the road where a scraper had recently left it. Ahead to the right not too far from the main road was one house, and beyond that; blackness. Fear crushed in upon me. "They're taking me down here to kill me!" The car rumbled a mile or so to the end of the road which stopped abruptly facing a wall of pine trees.

"Get out of the car!" one of them growled.

Terror gripped me as I wondered when and if I could make a move to escape. They all got out of the car, and one of the guys motioned to me with the Bowie knife (about a foot long with a three-inch-wide blade) and said, "Follow me!" as he walked into the woods.

"Where is the gun!" I thought. "One of the other guys behind me must have it. I can't make a move unless I know where it is!"

As I followed him into the tall brush, great fear rose up within me. "Sit down." he said. Of course I did, and then oddly enough he began a conversation with me, just as two people who meet traveling might do: where was I from, where was I going and that sort of thing. At first I responded truthfully—if I'd continued he may have just left me there unharmed. Without knowing there was Someone else who I could rely upon to help me though, instead I turned to my own faulty wits and began again to tell him about my grandfather who would not take kindly to anyone harming me. Without a word, in one motion the guy stood and punched me as he did.

"Hey! What did you hit me for!" I blurted out.

He didn't answer and just kept walking.

Blood began gushing down my chest and I realized that he had not just punched me but had stabbed me. The car then started up and my assailants drove away.

During my short time as a Boy Scout I'd learned to put pressure on serious wounds, and I pulled my hands loose, pulled my shirt off and balled it up, pressing it against my chest. The wide, long blade of the knife had pierced my chest just below the inside tip of my right collar bone. Knowing I was hit badly, as the blood ran steadily down my chest and stomach, immediately I began walking back up the road to find help. Desperate, I began praying to the God that I did not think was there. First an "Our Father" then a "Hail Mary" … what else could I do? An interesting thing happened. When I prayed the "Our Father" a calmness came over me and my heart rate seemed to slow. When I prayed the "Hail Mary" fear would grip me, my heart would begin to race and I'd begin to go into shock. I said my last "Hail Mary" that night and have never said one since. As the profuse bleeding continued, I kept repeating the "Our Father" as I walked. Things seemed okay for a while, but eventually shock began to overcome me. Cold fear gripped me, "I may die right here on this road before I can reach help!"

Just then I looked up, and way off in the distance the lights of the house I'd seen as we had turned off the main road sparkled in the night. My sprits renewed, "I can make it to the house." Minutes later after reaching the goal and stepping a few yards into the driveway, I looked hard at the house. As is often the case with houses way out in the country, it was very well lit; at each corner of the house there were two flood lights, each one blazing light into the otherwise moonless black night of the deep piney woods. Taking comfort in this and in the fact that there were three or four cars parked in the driveway indicating that there were surely people inside, I decided to lay down a minute in the driveway to compose myself before knocking on the door. The *very second* that the back of my head hit the driveway I heard a car engine, and within fifteen feet of me the early 1960s model station wagon rumbled past. They were going back to finish me off! Frozen to the ground until the sound of the engine faded away, I cursed myself for talking after he stabbed me (otherwise they would have counted me as dead already).

Once certain they were gone, I leapt to my feet, went to the door and banged on it, looking over my shoulder every few seconds. Within a minute or so (thank God!) a woman peeked through the curtains covering the window in the door, gasped and went away. I'm not sure what I'd said to her but then realized that I must have been quite a sight, bare-chested and soaked in blood. Although it seemed like forever as I kept glancing toward the road, straining to hear the sound of an approaching car, within a short time a man and his three young adult sons piled out of the house and told me to get into one of the cars, and off we went. Feeling somewhat relieved, they must have been shaken when I mentioned the guys in the old station wagon down the road. All four of them sat staring straight ahead and not another word was spoken until we pulled up next to a cop car which was parked under the Interstate. The driver got out, exchanged a few words with the cop, and shortly after that I was installed in the back seat of the squad car as my rescuers drove away. Breathing a sigh of relief as I waited for the ambulance to arrive, I thought, "What if I hadn't jumped up and started walking for help right after he stabbed me? They would have encountered me on the road and killed me! And how could they have not noticed me lying on the driveway so close to the road illuminated by all those lights, in contrast to the inky black night that made everything else nearly invisible?"

As hard as I pressed on the wound, the blood continued to run down my arms, off my elbows, into my lap, down my legs and into my boots. Before too long it occurred to me that I may well bleed to death in the back of the cop car.

"Officer!" I said.

"I'm not an officer boy, I'm a Depaty." he spat back with a thick country drawl.

"Deputy, when will the ambulance get here?"

"This is a small town." he said, "The ambulance driver is a business man. He needs to get up and shave and shower before he goes to work."

I didn't reply, but sat as still as possible and chewed on that. It seemed as if a half an hour passed by and I continued to bleed. The cop had gotten out of the car and was standing a few yards away when I called out,

"Deputy!"

"What is it boy?"

"Do you think that ambulance driver will get here before I bleed to death?"

"Shut up boy!" he said, and walked away.

My mouth was getting dry and again it felt that I was slipping in to shock. The fear of death seized me and I began to pray more fervently again, pleading with the unknown God and hoping against hope that I was not talking to an abyss. Within a few minutes a gentle peace came upon me and low and behold the bleeding stopped! The approximately three-inch-wide knife entered the uppermost part of my chest horizontally, about six inches below and inside the right side of my jawbone. Imagine the major blood vessels which must pass from my head to my heart through that area! That type of bleeding does not simply stop because pressure is applied! I sat in amazement at the remarkable turn of events. Within about fifteen minutes, the ambulance finally arrived and took me to Houston North Hospital. Once on a table in the Emergency Room the matter of fact Doctor Cho inserted a probe four and a half inches into the wound in my chest as he explored the damage. He was a rather taciturn chap, and once he was sure of the extent of the damage, without a word he went about his work sewing me up. The miraculous ending to what should have been my last night on earth was another stepping stone in my journey from atheism to belief in God. With each new sign the Lord was dispelling my doubts by displaying His love and His great power to me. The evidence was becoming insurmountable.

Needless to say, I did not join the Marine Corps on Monday morning. Making my way back to downtown Houston, and knowing no other way to survive, tucking away the sling they gave me for my right arm and buttoning up my shirt to hide the bandages, I hired out of the day labor place again. The first job they sent me to was unloading a boxcar full of disposable diapers with two other guys. That was easy enough, but from there they sent me to unload a boxcar full of fifty-pound sacks of flour by myself. I must have been nuts! But having started the job I was determined to finish it, and bearing most of the weight on my left arm, I attempted to unload the boxcar. Although I worked at it for hours I made little headway, and when the supervisor came back and commented on my lack of progress, I opened my shirt showing him the bandages and told him what happened. Feeling sorry for me he allowed me to work until quitting time. In a typically insane moment demonstrating my slavery to mind altering substances, instead of going for some food after getting paid that night, I asked one of the guys who hired out with me if he could help me buy some marijuana. When we reached his neighborhood on the bus, after handing him the money I watched as he disappeared around the corner. After waiting too long, I tried to find him but my search was fruitless—he was gone. Knocking on doors and madder then heck, I was met only with blank stares and shakes of the head. Thank God it was still daylight, because it dawned on me that I was the only one of my race in sight, and that I was in the middle of a city housing project and a very dangerous part of town. Deciding that looking further was unwise, sheepishly I made my way back to downtown Houston.

Thanks to the gracious generosity of my dad, before long I was safely in a hospital bed recovering. Dad then called The Menninger Clinic which was then based in Topeka, Kansas asking if they could help me. The people at the clinic (supposedly the best psychiatric hospital in the world at the time) responded that they had a two and a half year waiting list, but that there was a hospital in Dallas that was just as good as they were. Returning from Houston, after a brief interview I was admitted to New Beginnings Psychiatric Hospital for another dose of therapy. Unknown to me, the Good Lord continued to lift me up and give me the motivation to keep living under terribly depressing circumstances. He blessed me with a highly resilient and optimistic nature, without which it's likely that I would not have survived my years as an atheist, nor would I have wanted to.

# CHAPTER II

A funny story my Dad told of two young boys illustrates the extremes some of us go to: one boy was an incurable optimist, the other an incurable pessimist. It seems that they both displayed rather obtuse degrees of their particular leanings, so much so that their parents were driven to distraction. Christmas was fast approaching, and they devised a plan to cure the lads once and for all. On Christmas morning with their plan fully laid out, the two parents hid behind the living room couch to see how it would play out. The pessimist came down the stairs first, and as he approached the Christmas tree, he noticed a brand new red bicycle with a big bow and his name on it. His face lit up with glee and he jumped on the bike and started ringing the bell and honking the horn, laughing with delight. Dad and Mom looked at each other smiling, and yet as they savored their victory suddenly the boy became crestfallen. He climbed off the bike and sat down with a deflated frown on his face.

Mom came from behind the couch and asked, "What could possibly be wrong? You just got a beautiful new bicycle for Christmas!"

The boy said, "I know Mom, but aw, I'll take it out the door and ride down the sidewalk, and I'll fall. I'll be hurt, and the bike will be all scratched up. It will be terrible!"

The parents, both exasperated, grabbed the boy and pulled him behind the couch as Dad, comforting Mom said, "Well dear, let's see how it goes with his brother"

Soon the optimist bounded down the stairs and raced up to the tree, a broad grin crossing his face as he chuckled and began to rip the wrapping paper from the giant box which had his name on it. As he opened it, a look of horror struck him and he froze. Dad and Mom glanced at each other with a wink—the box was full of horse manure! But in the next moment, the air was electrified as the boy laughing and cackling, began to dig through the box, throwing manure everywhere. This was too much for his dad who jumped from behind the couch and grabbed him by the shoulders, "Son, son! How can you be happy! Don't you see that all you got for Christmas is a big box full of horse manure?"

Smiling from ear to ear the boy said, "Gee Dad, with all this horse manure, there's got to be a pony in there somewhere!"

Positive outlook notwithstanding, it seemed that I'd been on the receiving end of all the worst in life, and time after time my positive spirit was being stretched to its limits. Realistically I did not have much hope that the folks at the New Beginnings Psychiatric Hospital could help me, nor any confidence in their methods, but with little or no alternatives at hand, I forged ahead. During this time I continued to send up exploratory prayers on a regular basis searching for "the unknown God" as I struggled through. A Christian church service was conducted every Sunday which I attended a number of times hoping to find some sign or feeling that God was real, yet I remained adrift and unconvinced. Only a handful of people attended, and it occurred to me that our collective lack of motivation to follow God was why we were all so messed up. Two of my very regular petitions to the Unknown were "God if you're real, please show me!" and "Why me Lord? WHY ME? What have I ever done to deserve a life like THIS! I'm not Hitler or Stalin or Genghis Khan! I'm not the greatest guy in the world but look at the hand you dealt me!"

One day I concocted a fleece to put before Him ..."God, if you're real, please cause me to wake up at seven minutes until seven tomorrow morning." At precisely 6:53 A.M. I was awake ... and it happened many, many times! It took more and more effort to explain these "signs" away, though I continued attempting to do so. There was a character in the original Star Trek television show from the 1960s here in the United States by the name of Mr. Spock. He was portrayed as being from another planet called Vulcan, and possessed extraordinary mental and intellectual capacities. Having been blessed with a solid grounding in science while at Pleasantville High School and admiring Spock's habit of analyzing everything with an empirical and carefully calculated methodology, it seemed that this was a good way to tackle life. My approach to unanswered questions and unknowns was molded by this as I analyzed this phenomenon of repeatedly waking at seven until seven. It seemed that the electromagnetic radiation generated by the electro-chemical reactions in my brain (a reflection of my own thought processes) were somehow in sync with the electromagnetic field surrounding the earth, and therefore as time marched on, my own "inner clock" kept in step. Though it sounded like a viable argument and I had constructed it myself, I didn't quite buy it.

Participating in numerous group therapy sessions and many private sessions with both my psychiatrist and my psychologist, many different kinds of Freudian, Jungian, Skinnerian and other therapies were practiced on me. A number of psychotropic potions were also tried to affect a cure. However, to my dismay (but not my surprise) all proved unsuccessful at helping me. My psychologist, a nice man with many letters behind his name and several books on his shelf which he had authored, eventually said that we should discontinue our sessions since we could not seem to make any progress. Now THAT was encouraging! A line from the nursery rhyme Humpty Dumpty came to mind, "All the kings' horses and all the kings' men couldn't put Humpty together again." If the best minds the world had to offer couldn't help me ... who could? I was running out of options.

A few times I ran away from New Beginnings, only to return with my tail between my legs. Sometimes I went to my dad's house, but others I wandered far afield, hitchhiking hither and yon. Early on I didn't know the highways in Texas very well yet, and one time I wrongly assumed that US75-Central Expressway, a busy highway in Dallas, went on to its eventual terminus in a similar fashion—not so. Taking a northerly tack out of the city, the road gets narrower and narrower until it is no more than a country road. On one of my excursions north I ended up at a little country coffee shop right on the "highway" in a creek bottom surrounded by a forest, and it seemed like the road was about to disappear altogether so I went inside. Having some idea by now how to handle myself at the big truck stops on the interstate highways, I was at a loss as to what to do way out in the country The few local folks there immediately knew that I was not one of them—my Yankee accent and lack of money made them even more wary of me. On top of that I was more than likely half drunk or stoned as well. Just about the time I thought I'd better leave, an old man parked in front of the place and came in. He seemed to expect to see me, and asking if he could join me, struck up a conversation. My countenance brightened as he appeared to be someone who could help me in some way. The old guy was in the company of a very young, pretty lady and at first I didn't realize the incongruity of their relationship, then realized that she was his mistress. Sensing that his probing questions were likely born of morbid curiosity rather than kindly concern, I became uneasy. Glancing out the window at his car, I noticed that his license plate read, "KKKK."

Does that mean what I think it does?" I asked.

"Yes." he said.

"Are you the head of the group around here?"

"Yes" he said with a sly smile as the young lady squirmed in her seat and moved closer to him flashing an awkward grin.

I thought it wise to drop that subject, and our conversation reverted to what it was before, though it really was a strange and meandering talk. A little while later he asked if I was hungry.

"Sure" I replied.

"Why don't you go over to the counter and order some food? "

I shrugged, "I haven't got any money!"

"So." He said.

We went around the circle with this for a minute or two, yet considering that a few times generous folks had volunteered to buy me food when I was out on the road, part of me was thinking that this was his way of inviting me to a free meal. Something just wasn't right though, yet I couldn't put my finger on it. Finally he convinced me I ought to do it, so I sat down at the counter, ordered the meal and began eating it. A short time after that (sooner than usual) the waitress came and handed me the bill. I looked at him and he just smiled a big old smile and got up and walked out. I explained to the waitress that the man had invited me to eat, but my words fell to the ground. Since it was dark now and it was the middle of nowhere, and I had no intention of defrauding them of a meal in the first place,

I just sat there not sure of what to do next. My dilemma was ended when a Sheriff drove up a few minutes later and offered to give me a ride into town. He seemed to sympathize with my plight and even mentioned the possibility of me staying at the local Salvation Army, *but* they had closed their doors by that time of night. As we pulled up to the curb in front of the old stone County Courthouse (and jail) he suggested that I go inside and get a good night's sleep.

Politely deferring his offer, I said, "Oh that's okay, I can just start walking back to Dallas."

"No, you should go up there, it would be better.", he said. "We don't like people wandering around the streets in the middle of the night around here."

I protested, "Really, I don't mind … I like to walk!"

"No, you just go in there."

He was polite but persistent, and though he made no threatening moves or gestures, and in fact hardly even turned around to look at me, I knew that the discussion was over. He was a pretty confident guy too, because he was content to sit in his squad car and watch me as I walked up and checked myself into the jail for the night. The next day they let me go, and I decided to backtrack and return to the big city and the hospital.

Whether or not the therapies provided at New Beginnings had any positive effect on me was up in the air. It might be that simply being without booze and drugs in my bloodstream, my thinking and behavior was not that far out of line. Thankfully I was able to finish high school while there, and my therapy team eventually decided that I was well enough to venture out to attend a local community college as a stepping stone to returning to society. This worked well for a while as learning is something that I've always excelled at. Just around the corner from the college on the way to the bus stop however was "The Library", an inaccurately named establishment that, rather than helping people find out more about their world was focused on separating them from reality by serving that old toxin booze. Rolling downhill again, one day I hooked up with a few other friends (soon to be released fellow patients who had a pass to town) and after partying a while, scored some pot and brought it back to the hospital. Five minutes after checking in that day, they searched me, found the pot, and my "town privileges" were revoked. That meant I could no longer continue at school, and since at the age of twenty years old my Dad's medical insurance would only cover me if I was a student, it also spelled the end of my career as a long term mental patient.

That fateful day was also the last stop on the gravy train for me ... my parents had finally had enough. When I broke the news to Dad he said, "Neil, don't call me, write. In fact, only write if it's good news. If you set foot on my property I'll call the police ... and stay away from my friends." He shook his head in a silent warning that said more than words. Phoning my mom collect shortly after that, the conversation was quite short. "Please, just leave me alone." were her last weary words to me for quite some time.

"For the enemy hath persecuted my soul; he hath smitten my life down to the ground; he hath made me to dwell in darkness, as those that have been long dead. Therefore is my spirit overwhelmed within me; my heart within me is desolate" (Psalm 143: 3-4).

Walking away from the hospital carrying my garment bag and suitcase, and not knowing where I would live or where my next meal would come from, I remembered that one of my friends who was recently released from the hospital had an apartment just down the road. When I knocked on his door, he was kind enough to let me in. Though two other former patients who left the hospital against medical advice were already sleeping on his floor, he invited me to stay for a while. After about a week of misery and some of the most immoral, debased behavior I had yet committed, I'd about had it. It was around two-thirty in the morning on a Saturday in early October 1978. The lights were all on, the TV off, yet we were all awake—it's hard to say why because we had no food, money, booze or drugs left, not even a cigarette. That was a typical end to a "party" for me—the only things left were exhaustion and moral and emotional bankruptcy. As was always the case when drinking and using, my monotonously obnoxious behavior had driven everyone away from me, and the other two guys were lobbying our benefactor to invite me to leave. Just about to lie down and go to sleep, the thought struck me that I should pack all my stuff, walk down to Interstate 30 and hitchhike to California. An unusual peace and a sense of certainty came over me and I got up and started to pack. When they noticed me packing, all of a sudden the guys changed their tune and were concerned about my welfare. They tried to convince me not to leave and seemed to genuinely care, and yet I knew that this was what I was supposed to do and that everything would be alright.

With bags in hand, I walked down to I-30 and headed west. Even though I was starting in the middle of the night near the downtown area of a large city, which is usually a difficult place to get a ride, I reached the west side of Fort Worth by morning rush hour. Beginning the long trip totally exhausted after my week long binge, I was elated when a pretty young nurse just getting off shift at a local hospital stopped to pick me up. If you have ever hitchhiked, you'd know how exceptional that was ... women

NEVER pick up hitchhikers! She was only going a short way though, simply to home after work. When she looked at me with a sweet smile and asked if I wanted to come home with her for a cup of coffee my jaw must have dropped! It seemed like a dream and too good to be true. In spite of the golden opportunity it appeared to be, I thanked her for the offer and stayed on the road. Still an atheist with few moral absolutes and no apparent reason to turn her down, I was fascinated by what had happened and even more so at my response to her invitation. There is a scripture in the New Testament of the Bible which describes a time in Jesus' life when "He steadfastly set His face to go to Jerusalem" (Luke 9:51a) and would not alter the course of his journey. I too was in some way deeply bound to make this trip and knew that I must not turn aside for any reason. Never before had I been invited home by a beautiful woman, but something (or as I know today, some One) caused me to decline. Pressing on, I slowly made my way further west. Before leaving Dallas, I knew my destination would be the Salem Christian Commune where I'd stayed the year before during my first trip west. Though scant memories remained of my time there, I remembered that it was a peaceful place. The hours wore on and day turned in to night, then day again. In spite of becoming more and more exhausted I pressed on knowing that if I went into town seeking food, water or shelter, I'd likely come across a jug of booze or a joint of marijuana and may never get back on the highway: nothing was going to keep me from my goal. At one point I woke up from a deep, dream filled sleep sitting on my luggage, head in hands on an onramp to I-10 West ... though probably only asleep for a few minutes, it seemed like hours as my worn out brain appreciated the short reboot.

Lost Boy Found

# CHAPTER 12

Before long night had fallen again and the last ride of the night left me just outside of the small town of Wilcox in the desert west of Tucson, Arizona. It was very late (around two o'clock in the morning) and the spot where he dropped me was right near a small truck stop several hundred yards off of the Interstate. Normally a truck stop was an ideal place to catch a ride, but because of the long driveway leading up to the place and because it was late at night and there was very little traffic, they would see me coming from a long way off. The Sheriff would have me in the local boot before long—hitchhikers are unwelcome at truck stops. "RATS!" I thought. As I stood beside the road in the pitch dark with my thumb out, a car or truck would fly by at seventy or eighty miles an hour every five minutes or so ... most of them probably didn't even see me until they were right on top of me. It's notoriously difficult to get a ride hitchhiking at night and I was so tired. Though only twenty years old I felt like a 120-year-old man. Since my dad was well off, I'd been many places for a young man—beautiful hotels at lovely vacation spots up and down the East Coast of America, Hawaii, Puerto Rico—and we'd always lived in very nice houses in the nice part of nice towns too. Between my dad's relative wealth and the catalyst of substance abuse, I'd been places and done things by the age of twenty that many people will never experience in a lifetime, and had sinned almost every sin imaginable as well … I felt old and worn out and was tired of living. Standing there cemented to the ground with the weight of the world on my shoulders, all the years of frustration and anger began to well up in me. As my exhaustion reached its depths, the truth of the adage, "There are no atheists in foxholes." proved itself again. Looking into the night sky I said,

"God please get me a ride!"

And ten or fifteen minutes later, "God *please* get me a ride!"

My anger came to a boil and I turned it towards those who were not picking me up, fantasizing about planting a machine gun in the middle of the Interstate and stopping those who were carelessly whizzing by in their nice, shiny new cars and motor homes and leaving me to languish hungry and exhausted on the side of the road. My emotions swung back and forth from rage to despair as I seriously considered jumping in front of the next semi-truck that came by and ending my unendurable misery. Finally, I turned my eyes heavenward and screamed at the top of my lungs,

"God, you so and so! I've been praying to you all of my life and what have you ever done for ME!"

Then I took a few steps away from the road, took a deep breath and thought for a moment. Remembering some old cartoons where a lightning bolt would flash out of heaven and incinerate an offender, I thought,

"What if He's really up there? I'd better not talk to Him like that."

Then out loud, looking up in to the starry desert sky I said, "I'm sorry Lord, but I just can't take *another* step!"

Just then, like a brilliant sunbeam in the middle of a frigid, dark wasteland, the most beautiful warm feeling of love hit me on the top of my head, and feeling like warm oil, washed through me to the bottom of my feet! All at once I was no longer angry or despondent or lonely or tired, but bursting with joy and peace and light! The presence of the God of the universe, the One I had been seeking for the last two years filled me and surrounded me! How Merciful, how Wonderful! All at once, without hearing any words or seeing a burning bush, I knew in my heart of hearts that God was real and that He was the same God that I knew as a little child. He reminded me of our first meeting in church when I was a toddler. Amazing love! He also showed me (I cannot tell you how, but I knew that I knew and I still know today) that every word in the Bible is true from "In" to "Amen." Later I learned that those are the first and last words of the Holy Bible. That revelation was of the utmost importance to me since I did not trust a living soul. Because of my own enormous fallibility and the overt shortcomings of all those around me, people were not trustworthy guides. God knew that my cynicism towards men dictated that I have some "true north" to fix the compass of my life on. Jesus showed me that I could trust his Word to be a consummately reliable roadmap upon which I could pattern my life and begin to build a foundation for a future. In the next glorious moment, He answered with soundless words the question I had asked so many times, "Why me?"

Do you remember the old Native American saying: *Never judge a man until you have walked a mile in His moccasins*? Well, it's also true that because you have suffered (yes, and even sinned) in so many different ways, in others words walked a mile in the shoes of so many others, that you will be able to minister to them as you never could have if you hadn't walked this difficult road.

That moment, right there on the desert floor, it seemed as if I grew from lower than an ant's belly to ten feet tall.

To think that the Lord had chosen me to suffer for His Name sake that I might be able to better minister to His hurting and broken "little ones." What a tremendous honor!

Filling me with unspeakable joy, His love washed over me and answered a thousand questions, healed a thousand wounds. He spoke another Word before the moment passed.

"Someday" He said, "everything will be alright."

"What does He mean by that?" I asked myself.

As the years passed, I understood that in His mercy He had revealed that last blessing because He knew I'd remain in bondage to drugs and alcohol for another ten years … He didn't want me to become discouraged and give up.

What a kind, merciful God. I now had a new life. A reason to live! Within moments I went from a hollow wasted being, despairing of life, to a man on fire. As I stood under the spectacular star filled canopy of the still, quiet desert night, I finally understood. Beyond a shadow of a doubt I now had a basis to live and knew the reason that He had created me …to spend my life bringing the life changing Good News of His love to any and all who will listen.

# CHAPTER 13

My journey west continued along my planned route, but everything was now brand new and teeming with life! Within a short time a trucker in an old rig did the unusual and pulled over to the side of the Interstate to pick me up. He grinded through the gears in order to gain highway speed again and we became acquainted. Realizing how exhausted I was he allowed me to climb into the sleeper and crash. Waking up briefly probably hours later, it was still dark when we rumbled into Barstow, California. Even that dusty desert burg clothed in muted predawn colors and shadows was nice to see through my "brand new" eyes. Before the day had ended, I had reached the beautiful coastal plain where Salem Christian Commune was located. Making my way up the dirt road which led to the small gathering of buildings, I felt the warm, special feeling one gets when coming home after being gone for a long time. Not the home of my childhood, but it was as if I was arriving at a long lost homeplace ... somewhere that I could not quite grasp in memory, like a blissful place in a dream that vanishes when you wake leaving you with a warm feeling. It assuredly wasn't just the lovely agrarian setting of the place that engendered this, but in fact I *was* back home ... in the arms of God!

The main campus of the commune lay close to the base of one of a line of steep coastal mountains which are actually lava domes or volcanic plugs and run almost perpendicular to the coastline. The mountain was very steep, and came to a sharp point at the top. Except for some trees at the base, the mountain was blanketed with only a carpet of low brush which grows rich and green in the rainy season. The dirt road which led to the commune also led straight to a creek which ran along the base of the mountain. Heading south towards the mountain, as I turned right into driveway the pleasant sound of children playing reached my ears, and in a few moments I was welcomed back, not as a visitor but as part of the family ... I felt like a million dollars!

Salem was like a church where people lived together according to how the early church in Jerusalem lived as described in the second chapter of the Book of the Acts in the Bible, "Now all who believed were together, and had all things in common, and sold their possessions and goods, and divided them among all, as anyone had need" (verses 44-45). One of the missions of Salem was to reach out to the outcasts of society as Jesus did. Anything but a hippie commune, Salem was a "regimented" community, somewhat like being in the military, though considerably less rigid and formal, and without any focus on martial warfare. Our lives were shaped by discipline and a code of rules taken from principals and teachings in the Bible. Some of the rules didn't adhere exactly to it, for instance not only was drunkenness forbidden but even drinking or possession of alcohol as well. That was wise though, because Salem was much like a rescue mission in nature since the main campus was situated just off California Highway 1 which hugs the coast and runs the length of California, and a lot of hippies and drifters came through. Many wrestled with alcohol and drugs, and—thank God— some stayed long enough to begin a new and better life. New arrivals were given a three-day grace period during which they were allowed just to eat, sleep and rest and were not required to work; after that they could either start working or just move on. Whether a visitor or not, all were required to abide by the rules. Nothing that violated Biblical principles, which were delineated in practical terms by rules such as no foul language, no alcohol or drugs, no sex outside of marriage, no gambling or violence was allowed.

All of us worked for the Lord and were responsible for our duties during work hours six days a week. Some worked in the kitchen regularly, others with special skills were assigned to critical jobs such as auto mechanics, carpentry or electrical work necessary for the construction and upkeep of the property and vehicles. Many of us were assigned to semi-skilled or unskilled outside jobs, often as a group. Besides running a small fleet of fishing boats based in the beautiful harbor a mile or so west, we contracted to do migrant farm work during harvest time, and other jobs in the off season. When no outside work was available, we general workers would be assigned to various projects involving the maintenance or improvement of the property, either at the main campus or on the other property which was inland in the northern part of the county. Our main purpose was to glorify God and make disciples for him, to be a special people separated to God who were willing to devote our lives full time to His work. Everyone was required to attend worship service which was held six nights a week for about two hours—free time was from Saturday after work until worship service began Sunday evening. Although I was truly born again, all this was new to me, and sitting still for hours at a time during worship was very difficult. If someone needed to use the restroom during the service, they asked permission by raising both hands and the pastor or elder leading that night would grant permission. If you didn't like that or any other rule you could leave at any time. No big deal.

What happened during the worship services was a challenge to me as well. The religion into which I was born followed a liturgical format—before the service began and when one of the scripted activities weren't taking place, you could hear a pin drop in the place. In comparison to those solemn, almost crypt-like conditions, these folks were old fashioned Pentecostals and the services were pretty wild. The service began as people prayed out loud, often speaking in tongues, sometimes crying or moaning, sometimes shouting out to God! During this time it felt to me as if the place was on fire, and I wasn't sure that the folks with their seemingly incoherent babbling and extreme emotionalism were not crazy … it was all I could do to keep from running out the door! After that we would sing for a half hour or forty five minutes and then the pastor or one of the elders would preach for an equally long period. Invariably once if not twice during the service I'd raise both hands to escape to the restroom. Not that I didn't want to worship God, but everything was so different from what I knew growing up and the services were almost three times as long as well. No doubt the enemy was working hard to chase me away too—he would have loved to get me out of those meetings which were food for my soul, and just what a new Christian needed. Eventually though it all began to feel right and I saw the evening services as the capstone of my day. Each night I went to bed feeling more at peace than I'd ever felt in my life

It was harvest season when I arrived at Salem, and in short order the Lord had me doing something that I loved, was good for me, and was excellent therapy: heavy physical labor. Hard labor has always been a joy to me, whether it's digging a ditch, loading trucks or boxcars or swinging a sledgehammer, and when I do it, I feel as if I'm using the body the Lord gave me for what it was intended. Although I had been in great shape at the beginning, the over three years as an inpatient at the psychiatric hospitals were not good for my body at all. During my lengthy stays, in addition to getting soft and chain smoking cigarettes, I had put on quite lot of weight. My high metabolism and frequent physical activity usually counteracted my naturally healthy appetite and always kept me trim in the past, but due to the fact that I was restricted to the building during much of the time in the hospital and had a tendency to park myself in front of the television for hours and vegetate, I walked out of the last place weighing 236 pounds. Though average in height, I have wide shoulders and a large frame and did not really notice the extra weight I'd put on until a few months before getting out. While standing in front of a full length mirror one day it occurred to me that I looked like a watermelon with arms and legs! In the hospital setting, where romance or job hunting or anything that could have inspired me to pay acute attention to my appearance were absent, I didn't make an attempt do anything about it. Shortly after my arrival at Salem while walking across the property though, some of the children called me Fatso and Tubby! It was just the kick start that I needed to get moving. Apathy was a frequent state of mind for me as an atheist, but with my whole life ahead of me, my *new* life, I decided to whip myself into shape and lose the extra weight. Being a radical guy, the plan I devised was to work extremely hard physically and to eat one generous plate of food a day ... if I hadn't also taken a high potency multi-vitamin with minerals after my meal each night, that regime probably would have killed me!

Our first job that fall was an avocado harvest, and I attacked the job with gusto. We picked the fruit from the trees at first using our hands on the low hanging avocados, then using a long pole with pruning shears on the end operated by a rope to harvest the fruit higher up. Placing the avocadoes into burlap sacks, we'd then carry the heavy sacks to a wagon where they would be weighed for payment. Each time I filled up my bag, I would volunteer to carry three other bags of my fellow laborers to the wagon, rejoicing in the ability of my healthy body to do more and knowing it would burn off more calories and make me stronger as well. The heavy physical labor and fresh air were a tonic to my sin weary body and soul, and as I worked, worshiped and rested, I blossomed and grew in God's love.

Central California is so beautiful, and there are few better places than a farm to observe the beauty of God's creation! Rising early each morning to do a long hard day's work, returning to a good square meal and a worship service, and then settling in for eleven hours of sleep each night was a prescription for health. My sleep was a deep and restful sleep such as I had not known for years. The part of His earth where God sent me to live the first few months of my new life was a beautiful place to come alive again! Approximately halfway between the two urban centers of Los Angeles and San Francisco, the area is far enough away from each to be relatively untouched by the effects of urban culture. Farmland, ranchland and other relatively undeveloped land stretches for miles beside the highways beginning at the edge of most of the towns in the area. The natural magnificence of God's handwork is visible everywhere, from the coastal mountains and valleys to the great Pacific Ocean which relentlessly throws herself at the shore oblivious to the activities of man and all members of the animal and plant kingdoms. Working out in the sun under the bright blue canopy of the California sky was a blessing beyond description, especially after my dark, devastating years of rampant sin. At every opportunity I'd pause for a moment to drink it all in and thank my newfound Savior for these bountiful gifts.

Our second job that summer was a walnut harvest in the foothills of the coastal mountains. The nuts were harvested by attaching a cable to the back of a tractor, slinging the trunk of a tree and powerfully shaking it so that the ripened walnuts dropped to the ground. A team of migrant laborers would swarm the trees, collect the nuts into burlap sacks, sew them up, and quickly move to the next tree leaving the sacks where they lay. The crew I was assigned to was tasked with picking up the sacks and throwing them onto a wagon which was slowly being pulled behind a tractor. As the tractor crawled between the rows of trees, two of us would scurry under the trees toss the sacks onto the wagon and move onto to the next tree, swinging our arms and bodies like machines in order to keep up with the pace set by the tractor. We paused only when the wagon was full, and I sometimes wondered how it could possibly hold any more as my body, still somewhat unused to strenuous work groaned a bit under the load. But oh the bliss as we climbed on to wagon and perched on top of the mound of filled sacks for the ride back to the barn ...the cool, aromatic breeze blew in our faces as we gloried in the majesty of the verdant coastal orchard. Bathed in sunlight, the dark green patchwork of the walnut trees set against the crystal clear, blue sky was a vacation for my sin weary eyes and a tonic to my soul.

After a quick few minutes unloading the wagon, we would enjoy another ride back to the row where we left off, and begin again. Although some of the orchard was on flat ground, much of it was on hillsides, some very steep. When we began work on the steeper slopes, our driver switched from a tractor to a Burma Jeep, a special four-wheel drive truck designed during World War II to help the Allied Forces conquer the swampy jungles of Southeast Asia. When the driver threw the gears into low range it would creep along at about one mile an hour, inching up the hills. Eventually the hills became so steep that even that impressive machine could not make it and we had to switch to a bulldozer which had tracks on it like a tank. With the tracks kicking up a cloud of dust, we scrambled alongside tossing the filled sacks onto the trailer, sometimes choking on the dust. As both we and the tractor slipped and slid up the sides of the nearly vertical foothills we had to be careful not to fall under the tracks and be crushed! The intense work made the trip back to the barn all that much sweeter. With blood coursing quickly through our veins and perspiration dripping from our brows, we could look down upon the sacks we were sitting on and see the literal fruits of our labor. Feeling ever so alive under the bright, sparkling, diamond-like sun, how could one miss the monumental evidence of the existence of our Creator, Father God? Considering all of the breathtaking features of His creation, I often think, "How can anyone not see the Hand of God in all of this?" Since I denied the existence of God for years though, and in fact seemingly could not believe, I can never forget my own blindness as I reach out to the lost world around me.

It is not because of my own keen insight that I came to know Him. The Bible says, " ... the natural man does not receive the things of the Spirit of God, for they are foolishness to him; nor can he know them, because they are spiritually discerned" (I Corinthians 2:14). In His mercy the Lord Himself opens our eyes to the mysteries of the universe, things He said were kept secret from the foundation of the world, so that we may come to Him for salvation and healing. As I worked in God's beautiful sunlit orchards in those early days, I basked in the newfound glory of His marvelous love and the testimony of His presence in nature all around me.

What fantastic days those were when I first walked with the Lord! The exciting and enriching nightly worship services, the musical sound of children playing, the smells and sounds of chickens, roosters and other farm animals punctuating the day, and our weekly forays into town, to the beach or a nearby coastal park were the rhythm of my life for a time. It was so refreshing after the years of suffering! I'll never forget the incredible mixture of the salty sea air mingled with the pungent aroma of the eucalyptus trees which towered over all but the mountains near the Pacific shore … the intoxicating sights and smells of the seashore drew me back many times. Once at the beach I would often walk for miles, talking to the Lord as the breakers crashed ashore. Our trips into town on Saturday evening usually meant a stop at the Thrifty Drug Store, where fifty cents would buy a double scoop ice cream cone! Another quiet and gentle new pastime was reading my Bible. When not reading, often I'd listen to it intently and hungrily on a portable tape recorder, soaking in the words of this "owner's manual" for my new life. Listening came easily and I heard the entire Bible through shortly after being born again, gaining a solid foundation for my new life …what astounding, great, Good News is contained in the Holy Book! In the religion in which I grew up, there are a few select verses of scripture read each Sunday, and each year the cycle is repeated on the corresponding Sunday as the liturgy dictates. After attending church regularly for about fourteen years, I was exposed to a very small portion of the Bible. Now, turning to it at every opportunity, I rejoiced as His Word washed over me like a cool spring rain and brought light and insight I never imagined existed. God gives us the Bible "That He might sanctify and cleanse it (the church) with the washing of water by the word, That He might present it to himself a glorious church, not having spot, or wrinkle, or any such thing; but that it should be holy and without blemish" (Ephesians 5:26,27). The Lord had saved me from a living hell on earth, and now He was beginning to make a new man out of me ... day by day changing me into the image of His Holy Son Jesus!

One of the levers the enemy used to push me towards atheism as a boy was that when participating in the weekly sacrament of confession, he would bludgeon me with the fact that my sins were the same every week ... no improvement was being made, and in fact, new ones were cropping regularly. Try as I might, victory over my failures was elusive. As my sins became more and more hideous, so much so that that I dared not speak of them to my confessor, the weight of them crushed me down. How was I possibly to get to heaven? Surely I'd be damned to hell! With a brand new perspective now, reading and listening to the Bible and also hearing the good preaching and teaching of our pastors and elders I realized it was true .... there *was* no way I could change! If I could have simply willed to do good and thereby save myself, there would have been no necessity for Christ to have died on the cross for my sins! Praise God that Jesus did indeed die on the cross once for all and that He still does the hard work of redeeming us from the ongoing pitfalls of our lives on a daily basis. For all who will come to Him, He continually supplies the motive, method and power to purge us of our sinful nature! The Bible spells this truth out many times in many ways, but some of my favorite illustrations of this are, "For by grace you have been saved through faith, and that not of yourselves; it is the gift of God, not of works, lest anyone should boast" (Ephesians 2:8-9). And, "Not by works of righteousness which we have done, but according to his mercy he saved us, by the washing of regeneration, and renewing of the Holy Spirit" (Titus 3:5). And, "Being confident of this very thing, that He who has begun a good work in you will complete it until the day of Jesus Christ" (Philippians 1:6). Who began the work of salvation in my life? JESUS! Who will complete the work of salvation? JESUS! Thank God that I do not see my name (or anyone else's) in that scripture! He began the work and He will finish it. My salvation is a free gift! My good works are not tallied up and cashed in to receive a ticket to heaven, nor are they balanced against my evil deeds to determine if I deserve a ticket. We are SAVED BY GRACE and GRACE ALONE! What a fabulous revelation! Like a death row inmate who had received a full and complete and pardon, I now knew joy, happiness and freedom that only a condemned man who has had his sentence reversed could know. Having received this priceless truth, I've forged ahead from that day until this, ever reading and being washed by His Word, ever seeking His face in prayer, ever striving to make myself malleable clay in the hands of this Master Potter as He makes me more and more like Himself every day ... and always relying upon His mercy and grace in order to reach my goal.

# CHAPTER 14

During this blissful time, I felt like a little boy who found a giant patch of berries growing wild in the forest and could not wait to tell his friends! On our day off I purposed to go and share the Great Good News of Jesus Christ with the other people. My goal was to work with teenagers, since it was at this age when I took a radical turn for the worst. At the time there was a pool hall and game room in town geared toward kids and I went there one night looking for an opening to share Jesus. Ordering a Dr. Pepper at the soda counter, I noticed on the stool to my left was the girlfriend of a local tough named Bobby who I had been trying to build a relationship with. Gloria began flirting with me, and when I realized what she was up to and began to ignore her hoping she'd get the idea and back off, she got up and left. About twenty minutes later another kid came and said,

"Gloria told Bobby that you called her a slut and Bobby is madder than hell!"

Bobby was stocky kid and an accomplished liar and had me half convinced that he had been a boxer in the Navy and had never lost a fight, so I immediately went on guard waiting for him to come through the door. Passing the time at the pool table, I kept a watchful eye on the door and one on the game, the whole time praying silently that the Lord would turn this bad situation into good for His glory. A long time passed yet I didn't let my guard down knowing that a confrontation was inevitable. After what must have been an hour I knocked over the can of soda I had been nursing and quickly picked up a rag from the bar to clean the mess up. As I bent over to wipe the floor, Bobby walked in the door on my blind side and grabbed my wrist, and pulling me toward him he smacked me in the nose with his other fist and walked out. Bleeding profusely and more concerned about making another mess than pursuing Bobby, I grabbed the rag to mop up as much blood as I could. The proprietor of the store was rattled enough to call the police, and before long my Pastor was driving me to the hospital.

The Emergency Room was a familiar place to me by now, and I sat up on the gurney looking at the X-ray of my broken nose—the bridge was shattered into a couple dozen or more pieces—would it ever be the same? After pushing my nose back into place as best as he could, the doctor paced a splint over my nose rounded to conform to the contour of what a nose should look like, and taped it on in an X pattern with white medical tape. As I rode back to Salem with the Pastor, my "white badge of courage" prominent on my face, he admonished me to avoid problems in town and restricted me to the property for a while. Drawing the attention of the police was not in Salem's best interest (we already attracted the wrong kind of attention since Salem tended to attract the dregs of society).

When we arrived back at the commune the curious all wanted to hear the story, and after that I settled in to bed, grateful to have suffered for Christ. It occurred to me as I lay in bed, that referring to the miracles and healings He performed while walking on this earth Jesus taught, "Most assuredly, I say to you, he who believes in Me, the works that I do he will do also; and greater works than these he will do, because I go to My Father" (John 14:12). From my recent exposure to the Bible I'd learned that Jesus, the apostles and other disciples prayed for many people and they were miraculously healed. The leadership at Salem believed that the same power of God which He showed through these men is still being demonstrated today. Contrary to what some modern Christian denominations teach, I had yet to see any scriptures in the Bible that indicate that God does not still miraculously heal people today. Armed with that conviction, it seemed right to put some feet to my faith and practice what I believed. Overjoyed in my newfound faith and at the prospect of God doing a mighty work in me (who was hardly deserving of anything good) I asked Him to heal my nose, and then lay in bed and quietly sang songs of praise prior to going to sleep. Ever since childhood I've always gone to sleep laying on my stomach, and after finishing the last song, rolling over to close my eyes for the night I realized that would require putting my face into the pillow with the weight of my head pressing on my mangled nose. This gave me pause and I came to a turning point—was I going to believe and take Almighty God at his Word or not? Yes I would! Realizing I needed to step out in faith without turning back, I decided to take the bandage off and simply believe in lieu of any evidence. A little tentative, thinking that hot water would loosen the tape and make it easier to peel it off, I showered while singing hymns, joyful in a newfound freedom and power because of the free gift of faith from my Heavenly Father. After throwing the splint away and returning to bed, I lay down and committed my shattered nose to the Lord and went to sleep.

The next day dawned cool, crisp and cloudless, and my nose seemed a little sore and may have been a bit swollen, but I didn't let that deter my faith and went on with life as usual. Two days later I was led to witness to the doctor about my healing. Hitchhiking into town I managed to see him without an appointment, and once in the examination room, he asked me what happened to the bandage and splint. Explaining to him that Jesus my Lord had healed me, I demonstrated the fact (for both his sake and mine) by grabbing the end of my nose bending it from side to side. The guy almost jumped out of his skin and said that he'd have to put another bandage on right away. "That won't be necessary, I've been healed!" I exclaimed. He was as adamant as I was and had me sign a paper saying that I had refused treatment and released him from liability. Within a few days any trace of soreness disappeared completely and my nose seemed as good as new. Many times since then I've seen the Lord heal me, my wife, my children and others of various maladies without the intervention of medicine or man (apart from prayer). God has proven Himself to me time and again to be worthy of all of our praise! In the years following, my Jesus has taught me about miraculous healing and other things, and some of what He's shown me does not conform to many of the standard teachings I've heard, though I am by no means the recipient of special revelation on that or any other subject. If I discover that anything I ever think, do or say is contradicted by the Bible, the subject is settled for me and I no longer need to debate the validity of it. From that point on my goal has been to strive with all my might (relying heavily on the life and heart changing power of God) to adhere to the high standard—God's written Word is my final authority on all things.

One thing that had been bothering me about my newfound faith was this speaking in tongues thing. I hadn't yet heard the theological arguments for or against that particular "gift of the Holy Spirit" as described in the Book of Acts in the Bible, but I had serious reservations about the whole thing. It seemed without purpose and more than a bit wacky to me. When one of the elders approached me about the subject one night and asked me my thoughts about it, I admitted my reticence and then confessed: "but I've been wrong about almost everything most of my life, and if God wants me to speak in tongues, I am okay with it."

The Saturday after having my nose broken by Bobby, I felt the Holy Spirit compelling me to go and tell him that I had forgiven him. Though that would violate the Pastor's edict not to leave the commune, I was certain the Lord was directing me and knew that the Pastor would want me to obey the Spirit. The enemy (satan and his demons) tried to hold me back by putting fear on me, reminding me of Bobby's "experience" as a boxer in the Navy. Praying fervently while walking into town and growing more and more tense as I approached the places where he and the other kids usually hung out, after searching for him for an hour or so, I decided to go and wait for him where he lived. When we first met, he showed me a house where he said that he used to live with his parents. Supposedly his parents had moved out of town and the house was for sale. Though he wasn't supposed to, he'd kept a key and either stayed there at night or in a neighbor's garage across the street.

As I sat waiting on the curb in front of his house, the devil continued to try and scare me off, so I whistled and sang hymns and praise songs to the Lord and drew strength from Him, as those beautiful songs drew me closer to Him. At times the fear seemed almost tangible as satan and his minions fought viciously to keep me from my heavenly mission of helping Bobby toward salvation. The longer I sang though, the more the fear faded and was replaced with peace and joy. The Bible says that the Lord draws near to us when we draw near to him (James 4:8) and that He inhabits the praises of His people (Psalm 22:3) and as I sat there glorying in the presence of my Lord, I was overflowing with a joy. Suddenly the words that I was singing became words that I had never spoken before! Beautiful sounding words which I could not exactly understand were flowing from within my heart and out of my lips as I ascended to a spiritual mountaintop. Most of the words I sensed were praising God, but my main focus was not so much understanding the words, but wonder at the nearness of God and the certainty that He had come to visit me in such a special way. I spoke and sang in "tongues" (Acts 2:4) for what seemed like fifteen or twenty minutes, and in the end, fear of Bobby or the devil or anyone else had long vanished. Feeling like a new man, I decided to check the neighbor across the street, thinking that Bobby may have come home before I'd gotten there or had slipped past me when I wasn't looking. Hearing a television on inside, even though it was late I knocked on the door. The woman who answered had a very strange look on her face and her eyes were riveted to mine. Relating to her what Bobby had said about his sleeping arrangements I asked if he were there.

"No, no he's not", she said with a worried, quizzical expression on her face. "Where have you been for the last half an hour?" she asked.

"I've been sitting across the street for quite some time waiting for Bobby to come back."

"What have you been doing?"

"Singing" I said.

"No that wasn't it." she shook her head.

"I was whistling earlier." I said.

"No it wasn't whistling either … it was … a strange sound, an eerie sound … something I've never heard before."

Her voice trailed off, but her eyes never left mine, imploring …

searching. I shrugged, thanked her and walked back across the street. Thinking about the odd interchange, I realized that the Lord had caused her to hear my speaking in tongues as "strange" sounds, and that was meant as a sign to me validating the experience. My tendency is to be very pragmatic, careful and even skeptical, and not to invest myself in something unless there is corroborating evidence to substantiate it. Given my reluctance to buy into the more unusual manifestations of the gifts of the Holy Spirit as described in the New Testament, my experiences with LSD, and the fact that psychiatry had classified me as a "certified" nut, I also needed a sign to assure me that my experience was not an hallucination or some other form of psychosis. Considering my tumultuous past, this outward confirmation of my experience was part of the bedrock of faith that Christ built for me in the early days of my walk with Him, and has continued to build upon throughout the years … a foundation which would be much needed in the long and difficult years which followed.

Down from the that mountaintop, shortly after I had an encounter of another kind with the spiritual world. Salem Christian Commune was within a few miles of what was at that time the largest prison in the world, and we got word one night that a prisoner had escaped. They asked for volunteers to guard the commune overnight and I stuck up my hand. Hanging around the front porch of the main house until the last of the folks drifted off to sleep, I then stationed myself in the circle in front of the house next to the campfire to begin my watch. No matter what time of the year it was a fire was usually burning in the circle at Salem, since nights on the Central Coast of California often come with a chill. The fire was good company that night, yet as the night drew on a certain fear fell upon me suddenly, seemingly out of nowhere, as I contemplated making a round to patrol the property. Yes, there was an escaped convict possibly somewhere nearby, but this was something else … something elusive yet tangible.

Although a baby spiritually, I knew that it must be satan or one of the other fallen angels (or demons as they are referred to in the Bible). Although the "enemy of our souls" does not get a lot of space in God's Word, nor should he, scholars believe that he was the most glorious created being at one time and led a rebellion against God, drawing one third of the angels with him. The Lord put a stop to his mutiny and banished him and his hoards to the earth until the time of their final judgment and eternal punishment. Though earthbound, the demons still retain the supernatural powers that God gave them and dwarf the power of men in comparison, yet as with all things in the universe they are subject to and in fact puny in power compared to God (and they were created by Him). When we His children call on our Heavenly Father for help, there is no dispute as to who will prevail. The fear I felt was justified and very real, but even more real was the One who had opened my blind eyes and raised me from the dead!

Armed with this knowledge, at once I decided to walk the entire perimeter of the grounds and command the demons to leave in Jesus Name. The Holy Spirit reminded me that I was a joint heir with Christ and God's son by adoption and that we who have received Him are called kings and priests. God's Word states that , " … greater is He that is in you [the Holy Spirit], than he that is in the world [satan]" (1 John 4:4). With very little exposure to theology (which in my experience often waters down the powerful truths of the gospel), some youthful enthusiasm, and a fire burning within me lit by God's Spirit, I walked the commune grounds. Alternately singing hymns and praise songs, then proclaiming God's dominion over the place, I commanded satan and his hoards off the premises in a muted voice so as not to wake up my sleeping friends. The joy I felt as the Power of God flowed through me was inexpressible! The exhilaration of the moment was such that the spring in my step almost became a hop! Though without any empirical evidence, I knew that demons were scurrying for cover as I commanded them out in the name of Jesus.

Having begun at the front, approaching the very back of the commune I looked up at the peaks of the mountains which ran just behind the southern border of the property. This string of peaks, really one long ridge, run for about a half a mile or more beginning just next to Pacific Ocean and stretch east another eighth of a mile perhaps, where there is a break before another in the string of peaks begin and run further inland. The mountain is very steep and comes to a sharp point at the top—so steep that even though it is covered with brush, it looks as if it would be difficult to climb to the top without some climbing gear. Now, as I looked up at the mountainous ridge black against an almost black starlit sky, shaken, I saw what appeared to be more than a hundred of pairs of eyes lined up along the entire ridge! They shined like spots of white light, somewhat like LED lights except that this was many years before LED had come into common usage. They seemed to be eyes because they were paired two by two with uneven spaces between each pair. A chill ran down my spine as it occurred to me that these were demons peering down at me! As a new Christian, within a few weeks I had gone from atheism and complete disbelief in spiritual things, to talking to spirits … and SEEING them! Fear tried to overtake me, as it seemed that I may have bitten off more than I could chew with my exorcism walk. After pausing for a minute to take this in, in faith, I resumed my mission, praying and singing while walking (a bit more quickly) back towards the circle. Moving on to the porch of the main house across from the circle, I sat down and looked again. The "eyes" had disappeared from the top of the mountain ridge.

"What else could it have been? It's extremely unlikely someone crawled to the top of that ridge and strung lights up there!" I thought. Besides, there was something very other-worldly about what I saw ... and felt.

Just then, an oppressive fear seemed to descend upon and surround me, so intense that all I could do is pray the "Our Father" over and over again as I had that night a year before when God prevented me from bleeding to death.

Although it had been a cloudless starlit night, a thick coastal fog began to slide in from the west. It looked malevolent, and praying harder, my concern grew as to whether I had unknowingly opened a dangerous Pandora's Box. Sensing that the fog rolling in portended evil, as I prayed silently but intently, astonishingly it reversed its direction and started heading back out to sea! Just about then three women joined me on the porch, one at a time as if they'd all been awakened by someone. It was a very strange experience and almost seemed as if it were all a dream. Although I knew all of the women and was friendly with two of them, none of them spoke directly to me, or looked at me or the others when they spoke. They gathered on the porch as if summoned, and were manifestly aware of the battle that was going on. We all seemed to be perched there on the front porch of the main house watching the fog as if we were watching a great sporting contest—then I realized that it was! On one side I had been interceding with the Lord and on behalf of the members of the commune and the kingdom of God to cast demons off the property. The surprising realization struck me that the women seemed to be intervening on behalf of the enemy!

My mind raced as I considered this and continued to pray. Astoundingly for about twenty minutes the fog would roll out towards sea, and then roll in again. Each time it would reverse directions and come towards land the women would cheer up, and each time it turned back to sea they'd mutter disapproving comments about the tide of events, and seemingly about me. Speaking about me in the third person they made comments like, "Why did he have to go and do that?" and "There he goes again." Recalling what I'd heard about satanists, shuddering I thought "What if they have male counterparts who might appear at any moment and attack me" Baffling was the fact that although one of the women was a relative newcomer to Salem, the other two were not—and one of them was an elder in the church. Later a friend told me that he saw that elder smoking pot, which stood to confirm my experience that unforgettable night. The contest seemed to grow in intensity until finally the fog went all the way west disappearing beyond the horizon towards the sea, indicating that the "battle" was over. The three women, as if on cue, all stood up and walked away, commenting as they left that I hadn't seen the last of this.

# CHAPTER 15

The first months knowing the Lord were both joyful and quite eventful, yet my life was not transformed immediately as has been the case with some. The continued stealthy and vicious attacks of the enemy wore away at me, and my broken and tormented heart was still in need of much healing. It turned out to be almost ten years before my life began to return to a semblance of normality. As weeks passed into months satan began to exploit the weaknesses related to my emotional baggage and the wrong thought habits which I had developed growing up. It's not that the Lord cannot and does not set some people free from habitual sin immediately (as He has done for many) but it seems that there is a fairly large group of us that, for reasons we likely don't understand at the time, He sets free and heals over a period of time. After the pressure from the enemy's continued attacks wore me down, he craftily had one of his human agents invite me to indulge in alcohol and drugs, and I capitulated. Before too long my sin found me out and I was thrown out of Salem for the first time.

That invitation to "hit the road" began a long series of wanderings up and down the coast of California and back and forth across the United States. In "recovery" circles (folks who are trying to or have gotten free from alcohol and drug addictions, or those treating them) they call such wanderings "geographic cures", vain attempts to change our lives by physically relocating. The story was told of one old boy who said that he must be allergic to alcohol because whenever he drank, he broke out in spots ... New York, Washington, Los Angeles and so on! Many get the mistaken idea that if they just move somewhere (the farther away the better) things will be different. The catch is that when we get there, we are still there! The place isn't the issue. As the old time comic character Pogo once said, "We have met the enemy and he is us!" Though vain for the most part, relocating did have practical aspects to it. At the beginning of each road trip I was usually penniless, almost always homeless, and had worn out my welcome with the locals. It seemed a good idea to move and find people who had yet to grow tired of me. Whether or not it actually served the purpose, it did seem to help me leave behind memories of my incredible sin which was now very repulsive to me, and the feelings of failure and guilt which accompanied that. To some extent a change in scenery served to wipe the slate clean and allow me a fresh start.

One of the most creative (or at least the most alluring) plans for a geographic cure was one I hatched up while in Monterey, California. The beautiful harbor is home to a marina which is shared by commercial fishing boats, charter fishing boats, party and pleasure craft and a yacht club. Always a bit of a dreamer because of the many great books I'd read and old movies I'd watched (or simply because of my God given nature), while walking by the yacht club one day I hatched a scheme to crew on with one of the lovely sailboats headed on a South Seas adventure. The idea was to leave my current legal troubles behind and in the process, build a restful new life wandering among the islands of the South Pacific. In reality, most denizens of those verdant tropical paradises probably spend their days toiling away at one vocation or another oblivious to their remarkable surroundings, but at the moment I envisioned endless days sailing under the tropical sun, interspersed with equally strenuous days of lying on the beach under swaying palm trees. However reality may have played out, my first sortie into the yacht club in an attempt to insinuate myself into their community was unsuccessful. It was a private club, and when I walked in to the place my usually glib tongue couldn't produce a smart remark to break the ice with the three people in attendance that day, so I turned and walked back out.

The next time the idea crossed my mind, my intention was to take a more straightforward approach—my legal troubles were much more pressing this time, and I planned to search the docks until I was successful. It was the middle of the night and quite a while until sunrise though, so tired, hungry and homeless, I decided to ardently pursue a drink first. Ever resourceful and often successful, I didn't count it too difficult a task even though it was illegal to sell alcohol between the hours of two and seven in the morning in California. Success wasn't in the cards that night though, maybe because the sole tactic I employed was trying to convince the 7-Eleven clerk to unlock the beer cooler before hours. Without a nickel to my name, if I could just have gotten him to *open* it I would have tackled the money hurdle next. For a few hours I alternately hung out on the edge of the parking lot, then entered the store to attempt to persuade him to bend the rules for me—he wasn't budging and I was pretty frustrated. Add exhaustion to that, and when Captain Jack appeared out of the Monterey fog, it seemed that my fortunes might be changing. Except for the clerk, I hadn't seen anyone else for hours, and he was a sight for sore eyes.

Captain Jack's sun burnt skin, sun bleached hair and beard, and his captain's hat attested to the fact that he was a local with strong ties to the sea. He was easy to talk to and in just a few minutes we became friends. Obviously a divine appointment, Jack had also once contemplated shipping out to the South Seas to "begin a new life." Upbeat and persuasive, in a short time he convinced me that my plan was a poor one and unlikely to succeed. Abandoning the idea, I went with him to visit a private alcohol treatment center in Pacific Grove for a morning Twelve-Step meeting. A former champion surfer, it turns out that he too was an alcoholic and was living with his mother. At about forty years of age he looked fifty. We spent the day together, and I only saw him one more time after that a few years later while sharing a holding cell with him at the Monterey County Courthouse as we both awaited our turn before the judge. When I thought of Jack later two things occurred to me: what a sad waste of a talented human life, and ... fifteen years down the road I could be him, if I lived that long.

Not completely without common sense, over the next ten years during which homelessness was the rule rather than the exception for me, most of the time I stayed in the southern tier of the United States where the climate is more conducive to living outdoors. The economies in the states of the Sunbelt were booming during those years too, and in my chosen line of work (construction and other types of manual labor) jobs were easy to find. If it looked like you had a strong back and it appeared that you could generally understand things, a job application was a mere formality. A good thing, because before too long it would have taken many pages to list all of my "Previous Experience." Too many times after getting paid on Friday, I'd head for a bar, a beer store or the drug dealer's house and begin a party which would last a week or so long, returning to the job again only if I had another paycheck coming.

Ashamed of letting down my boss and the company, it made no sense to go back otherwise after burning the bridge. In the years that followed, with full knowledge that the Lord's way was the only way for me, after hammering my head against the wall of substance abuse and my own self-will for a while, I'd make my way back to Salem Christian Commune and try to get back on the path again.

Once when allowed to return, I was put on probation and sent to the commune's other property in a town inland in the foothills of the coastal mountains. The nearby town was smaller, and except for the wife of the elder in charge there were only men at that property so that there would be less temptation for us. The land sat on the Salinas River, one of the largest underground rivers in the world, and one of the few in America that flow from south to north. Aside from a small house where meals were prepared and the elders lived, a bunkhouse and a sizeable chicken coop, there was not much on the property. Just as at the main campus, when we weren't doing migrant farm work or some other work off site, we were working on improvements to the buildings and land or in Bible studies. It was here that I gained a different and deeper respect for Wellington Howe, the Pastor and Co-Founder of Salem, when one day he called for all able hands to come down to the river. The riverbed was dry as it was for nine or ten months out of the year, but the rainy season was coming soon, and during these months the river came above ground and had been washing away our land in one area. The project that day was to build a flood wall to protect against further erosion. Our team of six or eight men had been working steadily for several hours when it started to rain. The Pastor announced that anyone who wanted to could head for cover, but when everyone else left, coming from a state where it rains frequently I didn't think twice about staying with him to finish the job. We needed to finish digging a trench for the readymade barriers and drop them into place before the water rose. Incredulous, I watched as the over sixty year old man matched me, a young buck in my early twenties and almost at the peak of my strength, shovel for shovel as we dug as fast as we could in order to beat the rain. After about an hour of gut wrenching work with the water beginning to rise around us, we climbed out of the riverbed having completed our mission.

Wellington (or Jacob as he was known) and his wife had donated the land where the original campus was, and were the backbone of the Salem. A number of the early members were elders and took an active part in managing and governing the community, but there was no doubt who the leader was. Jacob's family were prominent timber men in the big valley, the San Joaquin, and his tall straight body and leathery sun bitten features told of the years of hard physical labor and the life lessons it took to lead God's people. He claimed that he had been a "gangster" when he was younger and had purportedly robbed a gas station one time with a rifle, although no one was hurt. A stint in the Marine Corps did him some good and when he was mustered out, he didn't go back to his wild ways. Having distinguished himself as the military's All Asian Tae Kwon Do Champion, he soon learned some humility and got an interesting insight into the spiritual world at the same time. As Pastor Jacob told the story, one day during a demonstration match when he was to display his skills against an aged Asian Master, he looked across the mat at the shriveled up old man who was to be his opponent and snickered within himself that this would be a quick match. It was short. When the signal was given to begin, in a moment, before Jacob ever saw the man move he was rolled up in a ball in the corner of the mat. He had just had his first taste of the supernatural. The dragon, who is worshiped by some of those who practice eastern martial arts, is that same dragon mentioned in the Book of Revelation in the Bible—satan himself. He demonstrates his power in many ways, including to and through those who swear loyalty to him (as its suits his purposes). As far as Jacob could tell, the old man never moved or even touched him before he ended up prostrate on the ground.

Some years after Pastor Jacob was born again into God's family and was called into the ministry, he and his wife had a vision in which the Lord commissioned them to start the ministry at Salem, and gave them the foundational principals upon which He wanted it based. The old family house that was the center of the spiritual and social life of the commune now served not only as the meeting place for worship services, but also contained the kitchen where meals were prepared for the fifty or more people who lived at the main campus. A modest three bedroom wood frame house, it and the campfire in the middle of the large circular driveway in front of it were the places where you could often find kinship and a sympathetic ear. Right after dinner the Pastor would usually hold forth for a while on the front porch of the old house. Many of us young guys would head to the porch and he would answer our questions, often with a question of his own, and occasionally tell a story to illustrate a point. One night in answer to someone's inquiry about the Holy Spirit's gift of tongues (which some say ceased to exist along with most supernatural manifestations of God's power when the last of Christ's apostles died) he told of a time while serving as a traveling evangelist. When they arrived at an Indian Reservation where he'd been invited to preach, some hostility about the meeting had arisen because of resentment of "White Man's Religion" coming to the native people. In earlier American history, as the European and later American settlers wrested the land from the original inhabitants, sometimes brutally and deceitfully, Christian missionaries followed, and the natives unfortunately yet understandably associated Christianity with the hurtful practices related to territorial conquest. Jacob became concerned as a loud angry mob surrounded the building, and thought there might be violence. God showed up to save the day though ...when Pastor Jacob began to speak in tongues during worship, the Native Americans heard him in their own language! By the peaceful, miraculous power of God a disaster was avoided, the mob outside was soon dispersed and many came to Christ that day.

The Lord sent the perfect man to be my first pastor. Jacob was the kind of guy I could look up to. While not rude or unkind, he didn't jest or joke too much. He wasn't cold and distant though and knew how to be "just folks" too. When we talked with him, it was obvious to all that God's wisdom was with him, that he knew more than we did and that he wanted to bring understanding to us. He would challenge us to answer our own questions, and after we attempted to do so, he would either condone the speaker explaining why, or give us his answer, always based on the Bible, which would invariably strike true with me. Pastor, as does the Lord, called us to be in the world but not of the world, to be blameless in the eyes of unbelievers. We would have to be diligent and vigilant in order to accomplish this as it is much easier to yield to our natural desires and follow the world's mantra, "If it feels good, do it." Jacob must have had some New Yorker in him I thought, because the delineation between light and darkness, and good and evil was black or white to him ... there was no gray area. Like natives of New York City, thought by some to be hard or arrogant because of their brevity and forthrightness, he simply knew what he knew and without hesitation shared it and went on his way. He was a man secure and confident in his convictions. As I grew in Jesus Christ, I knew that the Pastor's confidence came from knowing our Lord and trusting completely that His Word is true and pure and does not change. Today, thanks to the tremendous work Jesus did in me through Pastor Jacob and many other mighty men and women of God I've been privileged to know, and the invaluable lessons in faith that He Himself taught me through life experiences, I have that confidence too. No matter the trials, storms and dangers of this life, my God's instruction book the Bible, guides me safely and surely.

Not long after building the retention wall beside the river, I had the priceless privilege of being used by the Lord to lead a teenager to Christ. It was a Saturday night (our night off) and I had walked in to town to hang out at a local coffee shop. Since I was almost always a stranger in town because of my cross country wanderings, coffee shops offered me a sense of community, of belonging somewhere. Having worked in about seven restaurants, a few of them coffee shops, I felt at home with the down to earth women who waited tables and the locals who hung out at these modern day "general stores." The friendly banter that passed between the staff and the regulars was a warm, welcoming backdrop as I read the newspaper while sipping steaming hot coffee, and often I benefited from transient friendships struck up while sitting at the old fashioned coffee counters. Such was the case that night, when a young man of about fifteen named Rich came and sat next to me. He was what my father refers to as "a lost soul." He said that he was on his way from his dad who lived in Southern California, to his mom who lived in the north. He was pretty sketchy on the details though and I expected that he was either abandoned or a runaway with a very difficult past. When I asked about his family, Rich told me among other things, that his father had Jimi Hendrix's guitar hidden under the floor boards of his house. Plainly the poor kid had concocted the story as a way of building up his dad and feeling good about a bad situation. We talked on and on well into the night and the Lord showed me that He wanted to save this kid. As the discussion turned to the Jesus, it came out that he knew almost nothing about the God of the Bible. Having grown up in a church going family, I figured that almost everyone in America must have some basic knowledge of the Bible. Rich knew the name of Jesus and had heard of Joseph and Mary, but had the Christmas story all jumbled up. Aside from that he knew nothing of Christianity. We talked about many things that night, yet the Lord always guided the conversation back to Himself. It's likely He had us touch on other subjects so the kid wouldn't be overwhelmed with the profound the principals of God, and to give him time to digest the spiritual truths which He was revealing to him. Even though I was a new to Christ, since I'd heard the entire Bible on tape by now and read some of it too, and as Jesus promised, He had sent the Holy Spirit to "teach you (me) all things, and bring to your (my) remembrance all things that I said to you" (John 14:26). I was able to lead the young man on the path to salvation.

Realizing that he did not have a place to sleep, I invited him back to Salem. As dawn was breaking and we were walking back to our land by the river's edge, Rich prayed asking Jesus to be his Lord and Savior! When we arrived back at the commune, I was in hot water for staying gone all night, but after the pastor met the boy and spoke with him, he did not reprimand me because he was convinced that not only was the boy saved, but that one day he would be a pastor. A number of times since then I've had the privilege of leading someone to Christ, but I'll never forget the joy of being used by the Lord that night.

# CHAPTER 16

Even though still in the throes of addiction, every now and then when not at the commune, I managed to get off the street for a while. The YMCA used to have a residence for men in downtown Dallas where they rented rooms for $128 a month with air conditioning and maid service included! Even for the early 1980s that was quite a bargain. Trying hard to get my life back on track, I had wangled myself a job as a security guard (there was a serious labor shortage at the time!) and enrolled again in college. Though it wasn't to end successfully, things went well for a while and I enjoyed school as always. My guard position entailed a long overnight shift protecting the old Dallas Times Herald newspaper production plant before the company went belly up. Beginning at four in the afternoon and ending at six in the morning, I watched as the reporters, editors and pressmen left at the end of the day and returned to work in the morning. It so happened that a chap who had worked my post recently had cracked up one night, and the next morning as the staff arrived for work, he began waving his pistol at them. This understandably upset management and it was decided they no longer wanted the guard to be armed. Therefore, my job consisted of sitting in front of an open door all night long in the downtown area of a the 10$^{th}$ largest city in America. Although there were occasional breaks in order to walk rounds (which I really needed because it kept me from falling asleep) for the most part I sat at a desk waiting to see who the night would bring through the door. Once, a guy decked out something like a 1920's gangster including a long fancy coat with a fur collar and lots of gold jewelry walked in with a woman on either arm and announced that he was there to visit a "friend." Though he named the guy (who I had no way of knowing), no doubt his friend was really a "customer" and the businessman who was addressing me likely had either a gun or knife or both concealed on his person. Shrewdly, I let him pass ... and never did see him leave.

My time at school was particularly enriching. Since I had managed to maintain a 4.0 average at the college before, I was allowed to enroll in an honors level writing class. Along with a stimulating US History course, if it hadn't been for the fact that I drank instead of sleeping when I had the opportunity, I would have thrived. Our writing professor announced one day that the following week we would travel as a class by bus to another campus to hear a couple of famous authors speak—Larry McMurtry and Ken Kesey. As a self-proclaimed hippie, I'd read about Kesey's legendary cross country trip in the book *Electric Kool-Aid Acid Test* by Tom Wolfe and couldn't wait for the day to arrive. Keeping long hours though, the day of the event I overslept and missed the bus from school and had to improvise. After scrambling about, I realized that the only way I'd likely get there on time was by taxi. Though I could ill afford it, I wasn't going to miss my chance at meeting Kesey. Arriving at the college too late, I learned that the authors had already left, but were at Brousssard's a local restaurant for lunch. "Step on it!" I barked at the cab driver, and I arrived in time to see a large table full of guests in a back room. After inquiring which one was

Ken Kesey, oddly enough the seat right next to him was open. The bad news was, within less than two minutes the whole gang wiped their mouths and were off before I had a chance to say anything but , "Hi." Deflated and angry that I'd wasted the money for the cab, I walked out to the road and stuck my thumb out to hitchhike back to town. Almost immediately a late model sedan pulled over right next to me. The car was almost full with several "suits" from the college ... and Ken Kesey! Kesey was dressed in slacks and an Indian print shirt, just as I might have expected of a by-golly, for real hippie.

"I'm Neil Leary, Ken ... pleased to meet you!" I volunteered while taking the seat next to him.

Kesey returned the pleasantry, and I explained my adventure in trying to catch up with them, and he smiled in appreciation. I then offered to get some good reefer if he wanted some. Before he could answer, one of the college guys, wanting to prove that he had done his homework on the celebrity, bragged:

"I can get that for you too! What do you want some Acapulco Gold or Columbian, or some Sinsemilla maybe?"

Kesey turned and we smiled at each other because the suit had mispronounced Sinsemilla, giving away the fact the he had no idea what he was talking about. "I prefer just plain old Mexican dirt weed." he said. "It's a nice mellow high, kind of like Tequila." Ken said.

"Would you like to go hang out and party Ken?" I asked.

"Well, they're taking me to the hotel." he said glancing kind of doubtfully in the direction of his escorts.

"We could hang out in your room for a while." I offered.

"Everybody knows me" Ken said, " ... it's probably not a good idea."

"We'd be up in the room!"

"They'd see us walking through the lobby. I'm sorry, maybe another time."

I could tell he would have liked to have had some fun, hippie fellowship and was at the moment regretting his celebrity, but such is life.

Soon we reached the fork in the road that I needed to take to get back to Dallas, and I thanked them for the ride, shook Ken's hand and watched him wave as the car pulled away.

# CHAPTER 17

Many of the most important lessons I've learned in my walk with Christ were impressed upon me while in extreme circumstances. While orbiting through Dallas another time I stumbled and fell hard. This time it meant another trip to the East Dallas half-way house for low end drunks which lacked air conditioning and was replete with cockroaches ... please understand that it beat living outdoors and I was grateful for it! The second week I was there a guy who was starting a courier business made the fateful mistake of choosing me to drive his delivery car so that he could drum up more customers while I was making deliveries. His business was shuttling dental appliances (dentures etc.) between dental labs and dentist's offices. Simple enough it would seem, but not with a yet to be rehabilitated Neil in the picture. Things went well for a few days, but one night after work I got thirsty and started to drink again. After swilling down beer late into the night with some complete strangers, unable to find the brand new car he had entrusted to me, I crawled into a unlocked maintenance closet at a nearby apartment complex and partook of some much needed rest. Upon waking up I was eventually able to reorient myself and find the car. Starting it up and heading onto the street, I soon realized that I was still pretty drunk and decided to park it. Turning into the parking lot of the apartment clubhouse, a jogger darted in front of me and I slammed the breaks on to keep from hitting him, then proceeded to park the car. Just then some forward thinking young folks gathered around my car to investigate the situation, and before I knew it, they had taken my car keys and called the apartment security guard who then called the police. Not one of them believed my story of selfless virtue (which happened to be true this time!) and the cop carted me off to jail.

Normally another trip to jail would simply have been a short lived and difficult nuisance to me, but recently Mothers Against Drunk Drivers had arrived on the scene here in America. One of their main purposes is to raise public awareness of the myriad tragedies inflicted upon innocent people by drunk drivers, and to motivate government entities to enact laws to mete out much stricter penalties for the crime. I had read part of an article or two about the strict new laws, yet had not given it much thought until now ... after all, I didn't own a car! As I sat in the back of the squad car on my way to the Dallas County Jail, I thought of the fifty or sixty public intoxication charges already on my record and once again began fearfully contemplating a trip to prison.

My jail experience was regrettably typical. There was a batty old man in the tank with us who was slow to get in line when food was served one day. One of the more astute bullies noticed this and went back and got a second tray of food before the old guy made it into the line. When he finally went for his tray there were none left—the food was all gone. I called the bully on his trick and the old man did get his food, but ten minutes later I got a punch in the mouth for my efforts. When he saw that his blow hadn't fazed me and that I simply cursed him and gave him a dire warning, he backed off and I requested a transfer to another cell. After a similar incident in the next cell block, they transferred me again, this time to the brand new Lew Sterrett Justice Center. Since I had already been involved in a couple of "incidents" they put me in a tank for "special" prisoners. It was designed with a large rectangular shaped common area in the center with tables and a TV set, and individual cells on two sides of the outer perimeter which actually had doors on them which you could close and lock at night, theoretically protecting you from your fellow inmates. The other two walls were half steel and half bullet-proof glass and looked out on hallways—guard walkways. My cell, bed and sheets were clean and new, and the place reminded me more of a hospital than a jail.

The comfort of the setting didn't last long though—the tank was dominated by a bigger, uglier bully than I had come across yet. As he cursed, mocked and badgered us constantly it was taking all the self-control I could muster to keep my mouth shut. The guy was very aggressive and potentially violent and was at least a half a foot taller me, very muscular, and much heavier, which made another a fight a rather unpleasant prospect. Though I was in very good physical condition due to my early athletic training and relatively unbroken years of construction and farm work, it was still a scary prospect. The fact that I had a lot of natural energy and pent up anger and had beaten men larger than him before didn't ease my dread of fighting this guy ... he seemed dangerous. It seemed that there could only be one of two conclusions to a fight—either he would kill me or I would kill him, landing me in prison. Neither prospect excited me much, and the strain of keeping my mouth and temper in check was stressing me to the breaking point.

In jail, although the guards are somewhat helpful and even polite sometimes, it can never be mistaken for a hotel. Days passed, and though I had asked jailers several times to check to see what I

184

was charged with and if a court date had been set for me, the same jailer never came back twice nor did an answer come. If I just knew when my time in court would come ... just having that target to aim for would have helped me endure the torment. It occurred to me that I might not make it out of there alive, and I began praying more and more fervently. One day when everyone else was in their cells, I went into the common area and reached up to turn the channel on the TV. Just then a bloodcurdling scream emanated from King Kong's cell as he unleashed a string of profanities at me for daring to change the channel. Literally shaking with anger, I turned and walked back to my cell without saying a word. How much could I take before I snapped, cursed back at the guy and all hell broke loose? Later that day in an empty cell I noticed a piece of paper on the floor and bent over to pick it up. It was one page out of a Bible— a Gideons pocket New Testament—from the Gospel of Mark. Reading it, I realized that this was no accident ... the page had been dropped there for me. It read:

"And when He (Jesus) came to the disciples, He saw a great multitude around them, and scribes disputing with them. Immediately, when they saw Him, all the people were greatly amazed, and running to Him, greeted Him. And He asked the scribes, 'What are you discussing with them?' Then one of the crowd answered and said, 'Teacher, I brought You my son, who has a mute spirit. And wherever it seizes him, it throws him down; he foams at the mouth, gnashes his teeth, and becomes rigid. So I spoke to Your disciples, that they should cast it out, but they could not.' He answered him and said, 'O faithless generation, how long shall I be with you? How long shall I bear with you? Bring him to Me.' Then they brought him to Him. And when he saw Him, immediately the spirit convulsed him, and he fell on the ground and wallowed, foaming at the mouth. So He asked his father, 'How long has this been happening to him?' And he said, 'From childhood. And often he has thrown him both into the fire and into the water to destroy him. But if You can do anything, have compassion on us and help us.' Jesus said to him, 'If you can believe, all things are possible to him who believes.' Immediately the father of the child cried out and said with tears, 'Lord, I believe; help my unbelief!' When Jesus saw that the people came running together, He rebuked the unclean spirit, saying to it, 'Deaf and dumb spirit, I command you, come out of him and enter him no more!' Then the spirit cried out, convulsed him greatly, and came out of him. And he became as one dead, so that many said, 'He is dead.' But Jesus took him by the hand and lifted him up, and he arose" (Mark 9:14-27).

For the rest of the day I thought about that passage. Up until that point in my life if there was an issue or situation which seemed impossible, for which I didn't see any way out nor have the faith to believe for an answer to prayer, I would not pray about it because I did not want to displease the Lord. Scriptures from James and Hebrews would come to my mind: "But let him ask in faith, with no doubting, for he who doubts is like a wave of the sea driven and tossed by the wind. For let not that man suppose that he will receive anything from the Lord; he is a double-minded man, unstable in all his ways" (James 1:6-8), and "But without faith it is impossible to please Him, for he who comes to God must believe that He is, and that He is a rewarder of those who diligently seek Him" (Hebrews 11:6). My time in the schoolyard growing up and my tenure on the streets had taught me that despite the great number of faults and shortcomings people have, calling someone a liar was like throwing down the gauntlet ... they are fighting words. Although I had an understanding of the Lord and knew Him to be a kind and loving and merciful God, I also knew that He was holy, mighty and powerful and that He has and will execute judgment upon the world. Taking these things into consideration, for me to ask Him for something and not trust Him to give it to me (after He promised us in many ways in His Word that He would supply all of our needs) was the equivalent of calling Him a liar. Picking a fight with God was not on my list of "wise things to do." Now though, push had come to shove ... I desperately needed an answer to prayer. It seemed that the Lord had put that page from scripture in my path to grow my faith, to teach me that He not only required us to exercise the faith we have, but is willing to give us more when what we have isn't enough.

When night fell and everyone else in the tank was asleep, back in my cell I sought the Lord. My thoughts focused on the man in the story, so desperate for his son who needed God's favor—just as I desperately needed it at that moment. Someone older and wiser taught me to begin my time with God by praising Him and by thanking Him for all He has done for me, and to repent of my sins before praying, and so I did.

Then, following the example of King David and many others before me I prayed, quoting God's Word to Him, "Lord, you said that if you abide in Me and My words abide in you, anything you ask in My Name I will give you. You said that if you have faith and do not doubt ... if you say to this mountain, 'Be removed and be cast into the sea,' it will be done and that nothing shall be impossible to you. You said that if you ask and believe and do not doubt you shall receive. Jesus, you told us, 'Ask and you shall receive, seek and you shall find, knock and it shall be opened to you. For everyone who asks shall receive, everyone who seeks shall find, and to everyone who knocks, it shall be opened unto him.' Lord, you know my situation—I need to get out of this jail SOON. I believe that you want to do this thing for me, but part of me cannot believe. Please Lord, help my unbelief!" (John 15:7, Matthew 17:20, Matthew 21:21, Mark 11:23, Matthew 7:7-8).

Getting up off of my knees I climbed into bed. Not wanting doubt to creep into my head, I began to quietly sing hymns and praise songs, hoping expectantly that He would do what seemed impossible. Within a very few minutes an announcement came over the intercom system, "Jones and Leary you're going to court in the morning!" and I could barely keep from shouting!

"Praise you Lord! Thank you Lord! Hallelujah! Thank you Jesus!" I said as loudly as a person can under their breath (not wanting to disturb the 800 pound gorilla in the cell around the corner). My prayer was being answered, I knew it!

Since there is always so much to do in jail, as usual they woke us at 5:30 A.M. for breakfast. With excited anticipation I ate my food, waiting for the call to go to court. The jailer came within an hour, and after being shuttled from hallway to hallway, from one holding cell to another, and then to another building across town (praying the whole time), I was finally seated in a consultation room adjacent to the courtroom to wait for my court appointed attorney. He arrived shortly carrying a folder, and after introducing himself sat down and looked at the paperwork. "So what are you here for?" he asked as he leafed through the papers.

"Driving While Intoxicated I think. I've got to get out of this place. I'm afraid with my record they'll send me to prison."

"Is this your first offense?" the lawyer asked.

"Yes, but I have about fifty or sixty public intoxication charges."

"That shouldn't matter. They shouldn't give you too long on a first offense."

He paused at something he read.

"What? The DA is recommending six months in jail, a $5,000 fine and $117 court costs. What did you do?"

I almost jumped out of the chair. "You've got to be kidding me!" I almost yelled, "I can't do it! There no way I can make it that long!"

He could see that I was shaken, and said, "Take it easy now. I don't understand why they asked for that much. It must be a mistake. Let me go talk with the DA."

After what seemed like an hour, he came back, "The DA said that you tried to run a guy over in the parking lot."

"No way!" I almost shouted, "The guy was jogging and ran out in front of my car, and I slammed the brakes on to keep from running him over!"

Attempting to calm me, the attorney said that he would go talk to the DA again, and ages passed until he returned.

"The DA said he'd recommend three months in jail, a $3,000 fine and $117 court costs."

"You've got to be kidding me man! I'll never make it!"

Sensing my desperation, the lawyer said, "Calm down, it's okay. The judge can do anything he wants to. Just tell him what happened when he asks."

So, I waited and prayed some more. Thank God I was one of the first cases to be called, and as the judge read the charges, I stood like a statue before the bench waiting for the axe to fall.

"The police report says that you tried to run over a man ... what was that about?" he said.

As calmly and coherently as possible, I explained what happened, then held my breath as the judge looked down for a moment. If someone had dropped a quarter in that courtroom I probably would have jumped three feet in the air!

At last he spoke: accepting my guilty plea, he proclaimed, "Two weeks in jail, a $500 fine and $117 court costs." BANG went his gavel!

Floating out of the courtroom and back to the holding tank, my mind reeled at what had just taken place! Since they gave monetary credit for time served in jail for poor folks who can't pay their fines, calculating in the time I'd already served it would take me about three weeks to serve out the sentence and to pay out the fine and court costs at the current rate of $25 dollars a day. Beaming with joy, over and over again in my head and under my breath I said "Thank you Jesus! Thank you Lord!" If the Lord thought that I could do a few weeks in jail with that gorilla, then I could! Overflowing with gratitude, I praised Him all the way as we wended our way back to the other jail. Arriving just in time for lunch, afterward I laid down in my bunk for a nap. Still full of joy, still working to get my arms around what had happened, it was as if electricity shot through my body when within a few short minutes a voice crackled over the loudspeaker,

"Leary get your stuff together, you're getting out!"

AMAZING! My joy reached a crescendo and I was able to ride its crest for the next ten or twelve hours as I was shuttled from cell to hallway to cell working my way through the elaborate process necessary to be released. (They put you in jail very quickly ... getting OUT is another story!) At about 11:00 P.M. that night, less than twenty-four hours after I'd prayed, I walked out the door and down the steps of the Lew Sterrett Justice Center which face eastward towards the Dallas skyline. A huge skyscraper completely outlined with green lights filled the sky and I felt like the Lion, the

Tin Man, the Scare Crow and Dorothy glimpsing the Emerald City for the first time. Freedom had never felt so good! Not only was I free from the lockup, the threat of the bully and the incredible stress related to him, but more importantly I now had a deeper and more real understanding of the love of my God and His readiness and willingness to demonstrate that love to me!

"What a mighty God we serve!" I thought. "What power He has and what blessings He's showered upon me ... a terrible sinner like me!"

What love, what awesome goodness and mercy He possesses! Even though I never doubted that He could do anything at any time, why would He do this for a man like me? Through extreme adversity, I had learned another profound lesson in His mercy and grace. As I reflected upon what had happened, the conclusion was unmistakable: not only does God give us whatever faith we have as a free gift: "For by grace you have been saved through faith, and that not of yourselves; it is the gift of God, not of works, lest anyone should boast" (Ephesians 2:8-9), but He also gives us more faith to meet challenges as they arise. As He taught me from Mark 9 and also in Luke 17:4-6 where Jesus did not rebuke His disciples when they asked Him to, "Increase our faith!" through this and many other sensational lessons of love, my Lord Jesus has showed me that He will freely give us all that we need in all circumstances ... not, as some falsely teach, all that we WANT, but certainly all that we NEED!

# CHAPTER 18

Another short hiatus from the streets began in 1980 after I had done what appeared to my Dad to have been an honest effort at turning my life around. In fact, I did that every month but always failed miserably … sooner or later the living quicksand of addiction swallowed me up each time. This particular go 'round though convinced my Dad to come alongside and assist me for a while, so he kindly bankrolled me to go back to college again. Bearing in mind my recent scholastic record, on the suggestion of a friend of his, the plan was to enroll me in Austin Community College to begin, then later transfer to the University of Texas at Austin to complete a degree.

The venture began auspiciously as learning and schoolwork have always come easily to me, and I carried a 4.0 average well into the semester. The dorm that my Dad had arranged for me was really nice. Newly remodeled, it was situated on the side of a small hill not far from the UT campus, and in the middle of frat row. The crowd at our dorm was a mixed one. Since it was neither university nor fraternity owned, it was naturally populated by people from many different segments of society, and there was some animosity between the guys in the dorm and the "conformist, preppie" guys at the frat houses surrounding us. My extracurricular activities (consuming booze and drugs) as usual began dominating more and more of my time and eventually began overlapping with the times when I should have been studying or in school. One incident should have been a loud wake up call for me. The crowd I'd been hanging with was a bunch of bright young guys and good students who also liked to party and have fun too. It was Rob's nineteenth birthday and five or six of us piled into his pickup truck to celebrate. We headed to the drive in movie with a couple of cases of beer to begin the night. The movie wasn't very good, but as usual I found the beer interesting enough and proceeded to entertain my friends as well. The night seemed to be off to an excellent start as we left the theater and Rob guided the truck back to our dorm. Just as we pulled next to our building and he maneuvered for a parking space, I felt it necessary to toss my empty beer bottle into the air. Unfortunately, it landed on the back windshield of a parked car which happened to belong to one of the frat guys from across the street.

Since it was a Friday or Saturday night the neighborhood was hopping with activity, with cars and people moving about like moths circling a street lamp on the warm autumn night. My flying beer bottle was immediately noticed, and the simmering feeling of anger that hung in the air between the "frats and the dorm rats" burst into flame and grew into a bonfire. The owner of the car was in Rob's face, and the two argued loudly toe to toe as guys from both sides poured into the street in front of our dorm. Having had more than my share of trouble in my young life, I made a retreat into the dorm and sat down in front of the big screen TV in the lobby. Within five minutes a fellow came by and said,

"There's a riot about to start outside!"

I jumped to my feet and went to the door. Sure enough, the street was full of people, hundreds of them! From the vantage point of the porch, the two antagonists could be seen in the middle of the crowd still toe to toe, but now standing next to a police car as some cops were attempting to mediate. Feeling awful that poor Rob was having to deal with this because of my mistake, I made a command decision. Working my way through the crowd, I inserted myself between Rob, the prep and the cops, and in my most eloquent manner exclaimed,

"Officer I'm perfectly drunk, let me explain everything!" The crowd became quiet and of course I had the officer's attention as well.

"It was me, not Rob, who carelessly hurled the offending beer bottle. I am to blame for the entire conflagration."

When witnesses corroborated my story, the cops saw an easy way out and arrested me. It's striking what one good arrest will do to a crowd of rowdy young men. As unlikely as it seems, that night I had single-handedly nearly started a riot, and single-handedly ended it! Just before the handcuffs came out and the crowd began to disperse, realizing that I had some marijuana in my pocket and I pulled it out and dropped it on the ground. One of the weasels from across the street reached down and picked it up and said, "Look what he dropped officer!" Seeing him for who he was, the cop was not interested. Still, once again I was being escorted into custody by a couple of armed chauffeurs. A rare and singular thing happened next—a collection was taken up by some of the guys at the dorm and I was bailed out of jail in fairly short order. It had been years since I'd been bailed out, and it would happen only one more time in the years to follow.

Despite that generosity, the incident used up just about all of the good will I had engendered at the dormitory and soon things went from bad to worse. The familiar pattern fell into place whereby my increasingly erratic and obnoxious behavior alienated me from all of my friends, and even my more hardcore drinking and drugging buddies began avoiding me. This ultimately drove me to heavier and heavier consumption of booze and drugs as I sought to medicate the pain I was causing for myself and blot out any thoughts of guilt, or fear of the looming crisis that would surely soon be upon me. More and more of my time was spent down on "The Drag" the name the locals called the road and the strip of businesses on the street bordering the west side of the University of Texas campus. Although some of the businesses on The Drag were legitimate, some were pretty seedy. The Dungeon fell into the latter category. It was a typical "drink all you can while you can" bar with loud music and as few rules as possible. In fact, I was the only person that I knew of to get thrown out of the place during my time there, and in that circumstance it was for one of my more innocuous offenses. While having a particularly good time one night,

I screamed out at the top of my lungs, "An de lay, an de lay, viva, viva, an de lay … AH, HA HA, HA!" then I let out an Indian war woop (or at least what I thought was one according to what I had learned in old western movies), "WOO, WOO , WOO, WOO, WOO, WOO, WOO, WOOOO!", a sound produced by fanning my hand over my mouth. The first time brought chuckles from my friends and a few scowls from others sitting nearby. The second time brought more scowls and a warning from the bartender, and the third time (yes, I'd always push the limits) got me tossed out. By shifting from the dorm crowd to The Dungeon bunch I'd once again moved my alliances from a more respectable "party as a hobby" crowd to the "live to get high, get high to live" crowd.

In the course of my wanderings up and down The Drag, I ran into a real live witch. There was a coffee shop just north of The

Dungeon on the other side of the street, and one day as I sat drinking a hot cup of coffee, smoking and reading the paper, I looked up to see a woman who looked exactly like a gypsy. As if she had just stepped off a Hollywood set, she wore a bandana, hoop earrings, heavy eye markup, a peasant blouse, and long dark skirt with a sash around her waist. Whether because of what I'd learned since coming to Jesus or it was the Holy Spirit, I guessed as she sat reading Tarot cards at the next table, that she was on the opposing team. You cannot judge a book by its cover though, so simply because she seemed like a caricature of someone from the dark side, there wasn't proof … so I struck up a conversation with her to find out.

"What are you doing?"

"I'm reading the cards." she replied.

"How can you tell what they mean?"

"By what the card says, and how they fall. Would you like me to read yours?"

"No thank you." I said. "I'm Neil, what's your name?

"Madge."

In the course of a fairly short but pleasant conversation she explained what several of the cards stood for, and what they meant when they fell in a particular pattern. I learned that she was a witch and she learned that I was a Christian. We exchanged a few other pleasantries and parted, but from time to time we'd run into to each other on The Drag, often at the coffee shop. Although she was considerably older than I, we liked each other and always chatted for a minute or two when we met. The deep dark circles under her eyes which added years to her appearance, were likely etched there as she spent the dark hours of the day communing with spirits.

During this period of rapid decline, I became stuck in yet another web that the enemy had woven for me which almost ended in my demise. My usual behavior while drunk or stoned—talking way too much and asking too many questions—drew the suspicion and ire of the locals, and word got out on the street that I was a narc (an undercover narcotics police officer) which I didn't find out until it was almost too late. One night while at The Dungeon I made the acquaintance of a guy, and after talking with him for a while I learned that he was homeless (or so he said). Since I had driven my roommate away by this time and had an extra bed in my room, I invited him to spend the night.

He obviously didn't expect this and his countenance changed toward me, "You don't have to, it's okay!" Later I realized that it was not something he had anticipated ... almost as if he expected quite a different outcome for the evening. After protesting again though, he accepted, and as we walked to the dorm under the inky dark autumn sky as a brisk wind rattled the few remaining leaves on the tress, our conversation turned more personal in nature as we talked about family and home. Jake was a short guy, an older hippie (or biker) and probably in his mid to late forties if not older. He was a likable, and after talking all the way back to the room we both turned in right away since it was almost three in the morning. When we awoke the next day, we both had to get on our way pretty quickly, but before he left, Jake looked me in the eye and said,

"Don't ever invite a stranger to your house again like that."

"Jake, you're no stranger!"

"You just met me last night. Don't do it."

He then handed me a card. It was about the size of a business card and he proffered it that way, yet it had no name, address or telephone number on it. There was simply a picture of a hearse in the middle of the card and underneath it was a poem which in effect said that the next time a hearse goes by, you may be in it. When he could see that I read it, he looked me in the eye as if to say, "Do you get my message?" nodded his head and left. With only a few hours of sleep and a bit hung over, it took me a few moments for it to sink in. The message he was trying to convey was that he was sent to kill me, but after spending some time with me decided that whoever hired him was wrong! This was pretty unsettling, especially since I had yet to figure out the narc angle. Plenty of people had wanted to do me bodily harm or even kill me at the spur of the moment out of anger, but never had I been the target of premeditated murder before (as far as I knew). Knowing the Lord, I trusted the matter into His hands and was able to continue sleeping at night.

Not many nights after that, as the crowd at The Dungeon spilled out onto the sidewalk at closing time, I found myself standing next to Madge the witch. As the crowd milled around us and I chatted with her, suddenly Madge raised her eyebrows and said, "What is this? A gathering of the brotherhood?"

Four or five guys, all dressed in black or dark clothing and who could have been either hippies or bikers were standing in a tight circle around us. At her words they all reacted with the pained looks of those whose plans had been foiled. Each, as if on command, turned around and walked away. It appeared that Almighty God chose that night to use the witch to save my life. Before the week was over, I learned that the word was out on the street that I was a narc and that night was supposed to be my last.

My guard was up from that point on, and now I had even more reason to retreat into the dreamland of drugs and booze. This of course left me even more open to danger ... only the Lord could have preserved me during that time. In short order as I spiraled deeper into to a maelstrom of drug and booze induced chaos, my anti-social behavior landed me an invitation to move out of the dormitory. A new shipment of LSD had just come in, and adding the effects of the last few months of heavy drinking and other drug use, and the usual malnutrition and sleep deprivation into the mix, I soon lost touch with reality again and the devil took me on a real trip. Within a few days I was nuttier than a fruitcake. All of a sudden, the world was coming to an end and conspiracy was swirling all around me. In my crazed mind, the enemy whispered that I was an angel or prophet of doom with a specific and integral part to play as the final curtain fell upon mankind. About to step out of a convenience store after buying some cigarettes, the news story flashed from a radio that John Lennon had been killed in New York City that day. "Where have all of our heroes gone!" someone lamented.

"Another sign!" I thought as apocalyptic images flitted through my mind like birds scattering at a loud noise.

Because of the intense partying, my school attendance had dropped drastically and the 4.0 average I had carried most of the semester was about to come crashing down. With an inflated view of my capacities, I attempted to make up for one of my foundering classes by testing out of Biology through challenge by examination. After a few quizzical and worried glances from the staff of the school's science department, I sat down to begin the exam. My fevered brain failed me and I was surprised that although I'd once known the material pretty well, the terms, facts and relationships were all jumbled in my head, so after about fifteen minutes I walked out a little less sure (at least momentarily) of my superior abilities.

Finding housing then became my top priority, for upon my last circuit through the dormitory the manager reminded me that my deadline to move out was almost up. Money as always was an issue. Recently back in the good graces of my dad, I went back to the well one more time but came up dry this time—he wouldn't do it. I then hit upon a scheme (how brutal of me) to sell the sterling silver set of forks, knives and spoons which my grandmother had left me to raise the necessary rent money. Knowing that my dad wouldn't allow that, yet counting on his innate sense of fairness (they were after all mine), I explained my plan to him and he bought them from me for $500 to keep them from going out of the family. After arranging for a local banker friend to give me the money in his stead, with a pocketful of cash I set about finding a place to sleep that night, exuding an air of power and authority.

By now though the demons were zeroing in for "the kill." There was a room for rent nearby and I talked with the landlord, but lost my focus and never made it back to close the deal. With vast resources now at my disposal, it was time to treat myself … nothing but the best for this guy! Walking into one of the finest hotels in town I booked a suite for $250 a night (in 1980 that was a LOT of money). After surveying the place, I returned to the lobby restaurant for some dinner … again nothing but the best! The best steak on the menu and lobster tail fit me well that night, and to wash it down I asked for two bottles of Château Lafite Rothschild 1927 which, according to my many hours of research watching television, was among the most expensive wine on the planet. When they could not produce it, I feigned outrage and asked to speak with the manager who assured me that the best wine they had was $90 a bottle which I grudgingly accepted and bought two of. When I had polished off the food and one of the bottles and grandiosely tipped and thanked the waitress, I retired to my palatial quarters for the night.

Once there, the enemy switched tactics on me and started hammering home the point that I was in fact quite lonely and friendless, and really had a very dim future. Quickly drinking the second bottle of champagne while watching a re-run of the classic movie "The Bridge on the River Kwai" I compared my worthless life with those of the valiant World War II heroes on the TV and decided that I could not bear live to anymore—it was time to end it all. How was the question. In a bit of a hurry, the best plan I could come up with was to lie in a hot bathtub and slit my wrists. Providentially the only implement I could find to do the cutting with was a disposable razor blade. Having broken the tiny razor blade out from the handle, it was impossible to grasp it tightly enough to cut very deeply into my wrist and I abandoned the project in disgust, noting that I couldn't even kill myself successfully. Quickly dressing, I gathered my few belongings and walked out of the hotel into the night, no doubt driven by demons. My $500 was gone, my spirit devastated, and I didn't even get one night of sleep! I'm reminded of the words of Jesus, "The thief does not come except to steal, and to kill, and to destroy" (John 10:10). The devil helped me out of that money like a polished con artist taking candy from a baby!

The doors of my mind were blown wide open now and it was truly the devil's playground. Still intoxicated by the apocalyptic vision, off I went into the night. Upon seeing the Texas State Capitol building with its golden dome lit up on display for visitors and citizens alike, although I knew what is was materially, I perceived it to be a symbol of the New World Order (as yet unannounced by Mikhail Gorbachev and George H. W. Bush) and that this was not really Austin, Texas, but somehow I had been transported to Jerusalem! It only made sense to my fevered mind, since end times scenarios are all played out in and near that great city. As the day dawned, I viewed the passersby as poor deluded folks who hadn't a clue as to the momentous events that were upon them. The hands of time were winding down, Christ's return was imminent, and yet they were going about their business oblivious to the whole thing! A tremendous sense of paranoia then hit me ... surely among these children of the darkness I must stick out like a sore thumb. As soon as they recognized me, they would capture me and inflict a painful death upon me! It must have been quite a sight to see me darting from one side of the street to another, glancing furtively around like an escaped convict. Entering an upscale restaurant during lunchtime, I requested a glass of water. My odd behavior must have caught their attention, because as I lingered in my confusion and drank the water, I noticed the wait staff giving me odd glances. They had spotted me as an outcast Christian! As they continued to glance my way and whisper to each other, I figured it was time to leave. As soon as I set foot out the door a squad car pulled up, and I was on my way to jail again.

This was to be trip a like no other. Convinced I was a high priority, one of a kind prisoner due to the fact that I alone on the face of the earth was not serving the Anti-Christ, I heard innuendos in every word spoken by the cops and the guards at the jail. At one point, I believed that the steel encased jail cell I was being held in had actually been prepared especially for me, and was in fact part of a space ship. The plan I believed was to launch me into outer space, to isolate me from the rest of the population which was under the spell of Satan. It even seemed to me that the ship was launched! My behavior and mutterings must have been bizarre indeed, because before too long I was moved to the local branch of the State Mental Hospital. After being administered a regime of psychotropic drugs and getting much needed food and rest, and *not* getting any more booze and street drugs, I slowly came back to earth. Not before I had one final flight into psychosis. One of my fellow patients was an Asian who also happened to be a believer in the Bible. We struck up a friendship, and after talking we arrived at the idea that angels or a helicopter or something was going to swoop into the enclosed exercise yard of the hospital and airlift us to freedom a la James Bond. Preparing for this event, we sat back to back on top of a manhole cover in the middle of the yard (at just the right moment of course) and waited for our deliverers to snatch us away to freedom. After five or ten minutes we realized that our calculations were in error and gave up the plan for the time being, awaiting further instructions.

After hand writing a Writ of Habeas Corpus (where and when I learned the proper text for that I don't know) they released me, even though my final draft was rife with crossed out words and rewrites. Evidently the medical staff no longer considered me a danger to myself or others since I was coherent enough to write the thing. Once again Neil Leary was let loose on the unsuspecting populace. Having worn out Austin, back on the streets, I hitchhiked on to my next stop.

Another excursion into the world of the unreal brought about by my destructive lifestyle began before a trip home for Christmas. Though not often welcome at his house, my dad had once again blessed me with some frequent flier miles so I could see my mom, and with a plane ticket to New York in hand, I partied hard in preparation for the trip (of course in those days I partied hard in preparation for breakfast, lunch and dinner as well!). Wandering around Dallas as the temperatures hovered around freezing and wearing only my standard uniform of combat boots, jeans and a one pocket tee shirt with a pack of cigarettes in the pocket (if it was a good day), I was oblivious to the cold. With a goofy grin on my face, I stopped by the low bottom half-way house I occasionally lived at to give them a cheery hello in my trek across town. My cousin Conn's house was on the way to the airport too, so I popped in to say hi there. Recognizing my disconnected state, he kindly gave me a thick, wool US Navy issue pea coat before I went on my way—a good thing too, because it was quite a bit colder in New York than Dallas! By the time I boarded the plane that day I was flying pretty high and did nothing that would tend to bring me down to earth in the days that ensued. When we were airborne it came to me that the whole trip was a carefully orchestrated homecoming for me, and that my years of suffering and being misunderstood were about to end. I was convinced that the flight attendants and others were aware of the plans and that when we landed, along with an entourage of old friends and admirers, my love April Anne would be waiting to reunite with me. Oddly, I was not very taken aback when the welcoming party was not at the gate. Assuming that the plans needed to be altered slightly, I simply kept a keen eye out for the reception committee.

Thankfully for her, my mom had a reason to be elsewhere when I arrived, and my Aunt Cornelia and Uncle Roy graciously offered to allow me to stay at their home upstate in Kinderhook. After arriving safely, it was great to see the home folks again and we shared a time of pleasant reminiscence. The beautiful old house seemed to welcome me, though the ever present sense of unease that pervaded in my life in those days prevented me from feeling the joy I'd always known in the past. The house was strangely empty and lifeless without my cousins, sisters and parents. The theme of The Moody Blues song "Lost in a Lost World" seemed to aptly fit my mood. Being with my aunt and uncle and Robert their servant (who had long been family) and sharing a few meals in their lovely dining room helped bring a little bit of the serenity and sense of home which was always present years before. One beautiful, snowy afternoon Aunt Cornelia asked me to read some Shakespeare aloud to her and Uncle Roy. As we sat in the living room of that beautiful old house surrounded by the lawns blanketed by deep, white snow and guarded by the towering giants of oak, chestnut, maple and pine, and with the crackling of the fire in the hearth and the tunes of the classical masters gentling caressing our ears, a glimmer of happier times soothed my tired, aching mind and soul ... if only for a little while.

The arrival of a few guests lightened my spirits as well. One afternoon as Aunt Cornelia and I sat with Emma, a friend of my cousin Conn's who had dropped in, the conversation turned to California. The annual celebration of Christ's birthday had just passed and our thoughts turned to years gone by. A fond moment from a previous Christmas came to mind, and I shared,

The old Mission in downtown San Luis Obispo is one of my favorite spots which I never miss when in town. One day as I approached the plaza in front of the old church, I noticed that a big crowd was gathered, and someone told me it was a Christmas festival! There were microphones set up at the top of the steps leading to the entrance to the church, and it was serving as a stage for the entertainers who faced the open plaza. A small group was performing some "seasonal" music which was well done yet secular in nature. Just then a love-filled surge of the true Christmas spirit, the Holy Spirit, inspired me to sing some *real* Christmas songs ... carols which glorify the Christ of Christmas! Locating someone on staff I asked if anyone could perform, and he said yes, it was an open mike. Stage fright hit for a moment, then I stepped up to the microphone and began to sing. Although nervous, I'd been singing Christmas carols ever since childhood and was able to sing two or three verses from half a dozen carols … and the crowd applauded and cheered when I finished!

To my amazement Emma said, "I was there! I saw you! I heard you sing!"

Just as when I stumbled upon my boyhood friends in Haight Ashbury a few years before three thousand miles from home—I came full circle, to California and back!

The next day, my cousin Kerry and her daughter Kyla came to visit. Kerry is the oldest of my cousins and we didn't have much opportunity to get to know each other when we were younger because of the twelve-year difference in our ages and because she left home quite young. There seemed to be a special affinity between Kerry and me since we were the blackest of the black sheep in our respective families. When younger, in addition to all of the usual crazy things some people did in the 1960s and 70s, I later learned from Conn that she used to race her husband's car at a local stock car track—an activity not common for a woman today, but almost unheard of then! She was a stunning beauty, and as we talked I looked at her with wonder and admiration. A strong, bright woman, I pondered what motivated her. They left after a while, and just before they drove off, I hurried out the front door and handed her a Bible through the car window, "I think Jesus wants you to have this!"

"Thanks." she said. As she reached to take it, a sweet smile crossing her lips.

As the car crunched through the snow down the driveway and onto the street, Aunt Cornelia, who had said goodbye earlier came out on the front porch and asked, "What did you just hand her?"

"A Bible." I replied.

Stunned, she said, "She would never take one from anybody

before!"

That may have been the sole purpose for my trip that year.

Without money (as usual) and in a state of constant pining and craving for my "medicine", angst drove me to my old tricks as I connived and manipulated to get my hands on more drugs and booze. Once successful I consumed it ferociously, like a starving man might attack his first plate of food in a month. The resulting chaos was inexorable. As I descended into the usual downward vortex, my dear aunt was at a breaking point. Not wanting to damage our relationship any further, I announced plans to go skiing. She and my uncle were hesitant to let me go hitchhiking off into the bitter cold winter of upstate New York, but after assuring them of my sturdiness and ability to survive in the outdoors under any circumstances, my Uncle Roy drove me to the New York State Thruway. Armed with a check from Aunt Cornelia (a belated Christmas present) hitchhiking, I made it to Hunter Mountain in record time. Surprisingly I was able to cash the third party check and furnish myself with skis, boots, poles and a lift ticket. True to my tendency to spend every nickel I had as soon as possible, I paid the entry fee to race in a NASTAR ski race with the last of the money. Not having skied in years I had a blast, so much so that I missed the race! As the afternoon wore on and knowing that my mother had wisely stayed gone, it occurred to me that I'd better think about where I'd be spending the night. Surely one of my old friends from Pleasantville would put me up!

After turning the equipment in to the rental place, I walked out the entrance of the ski area and stuck my thumb out. By the grace of God, a station wagon full of young guys from New York City soon pulled over and took me right to Pleasantville. As much as I had assured my aunt and uncle of my ability to survive the cold, I may well have died of hypothermia that day if the good Lord hadn't arranged for such prompt rides for me.

It was my first time back in Pleasantville in years, and although it was good to be home, home wasn't quite the same. Gone was the warm comfortable house with the well-stocked refrigerator. Gone was the feeling of security and belonging I'd felt as a boy. After calling a few friends and reaching none of them, I began a lonely vigil outside of a bar that was (or used to be) the main hangout for my crowd. Even tightly buttoned up in the almost half inch thick woolen Navy pea coat with a windbreaker, a flannel shirt and thermal underwear underneath, and topped off in a thick woolen ski cap, the bitterly cold night air nipped at me as I paced back and forth in front of the bar, hoping that one of my pals would get my message and meet me there. After a long time and beginning to doubt that anyone would show up, I looked over my shoulder saw a couple of guys standing by the entrance, laughing and looking my way. As they persisted, I approached them and one called me by name.

"Don't you recognize me?" The taller one said chuckling.

"No." more snickering.

"It's Dave!"

" ... and Frank!"

My former running back and wide receiver from high school both wore full beards now and in my dazed state I may have not guessed for a while.

It wasn't the reunion I had hoped for though, for after they teased me and questioned me a bit, instead of inviting me into the warm bar for a cold beer, Dave assured me that it wasn't a good idea for me to go inside and offered to take me somewhere in his car. Kindly, he'd probably spared me from a confrontation with some former upperclassmen who hated me. When we parked in front of his house a short while later, he said, "So where are you going to spend the night?"

"How about your place?" I said sheepishly.

"Nah, I'm sorry. My wife (another former classmate who knew me pretty well) would not want me to do that."

"Are you sure?" I said.

"Nah."

A long time before that, almost everyone in town, in *any* town in which I was known, decided they didn't want me around because of my wild behavior when drinking and using. My hopes of receiving a hero's welcome in Pleasantville, as an old warrior might receive after returning home from many campaigns, were now completely dashed. Dave kindly offered a sleeping bag and pointed towards the woods as a possible resting place for the night, but the terrain was rather steep and the night very cold, so I declined and asked for a ride downtown. Dave did give me a little pot to smoke (which was more than he would have done in the past) and I was touched … but the high didn't last long. As I walked the streets of downtown Pleasantville a bit in despair and trying to figure out what to do next, as a final insult my suitcase broke open. I crammed its contents into a trash barrel in disgust and left the case on the sidewalk next to it.

It was very late now and the cold was burrowing into my bones. Any thought I might have had of knocking on doors looking for help quickly evaporated in the rare night air … it was far too late for an unexpected out-of-town guest. Here I was on Bedford Road in my hometown … how many times had I walked up and down this street in more carefree days … belonging, hopeful and expectant, looking ahead eagerly to a full and happy life! Now I had nowhere to turn. A few more steps took me to Wheeler Avenue. Wandering in the direction of the train station, the direction years which years before would have taken me home, I noticed the Police Station. Surely they'd help me!

"Is Detective Ritelli here?" I asked the startled desk sergeant.

"No. What do you want?" he asked, eyeing me somewhat suspiciously.

"I used to live here in Pleasantville and he was my friend. Can you call him or something?"

"He's retired." replied the officer.

"Oh ... I just came to town to visit and I have nowhere to sleep. Is there a place around here I could stay, a shelter or something?"

"No, nothing like that."

I looked around, thinking quickly. "Could I sleep in one of the jail cells?"

"No, you can't do that."

Another officer had joined us while we were talking, and told me to wait a minute as they left the room. When they came back, he said he'd take me to a place where I could stay. A few minutes later a squad car pulled up front and the patrolman came in and told me to grab my stuff (what was left of it) and come with him. From the warmth of the police station to the warm car and a promise of a place to stay, I began to feel better.

After a little while I asked, "Where are we going?"

"These people will take care of you." He said without looking over his shoulder.

His indirect answer gave me pause. Soon we were wheeling in to the driveway in front of a large multi-story building, a part of a complex of buildings.

"What is this place?" I asked.

"Grasslands Hospital." was his clipped response. Then quickly,

"These people will help you."

Waiting to talk with the intake staff, I realized that he'd dropped me at the mental health unit! Quite disoriented when I left Texas, but not necessarily psychotic at the moment (or so I thought), paranoia seized me. I decided to put on my best face and hope they didn't throw a net over me. When the psychiatrist and nurse interviewed me, I must have made a good show of it because they said that they would give me a place to sleep and have someone talk to me in the morning about getting some help to get back to Texas. An orderly took me to what looked like a dorm room in an adjacent building and left me, saying that someone would come and get me in the morning. Down the hallway at a communal restroom, a guy I met told me that this was a dormitory for employees, then he fixed me with a quizzical look and said:

"Are you here for brain surgery?"

I froze in my tracks. "No, I just needed a place to spend the night, and the cops brought me over here."

"Hum. They have always used that room for Dr. Kildare's surgery patients, since they start so early in the morning, they put them there overnight. Are you sure that you're not here for brain surgery?" he asked.

"I'm sure!"

Fear stole over me as I walked back to my room, and paranoid thoughts of conspiracy crept into my head again. What if they tricked me? What if they plan on giving me a lobotomy like the guy in "One Flew Over the Cuckoo's Nest"? I wrestled with that one for a while, but exhausted, turned it over to the Lord and drifted off to sleep.

Upon waking, thankfully I wasn't wrapped in a straitjacket or ushered into a surgery prep room, but to a social worker who listened to my sad story and was able to arrange a trip back to Texas for me, replete with a plane ticket and a ride to the airport! My brain chemistry had never fully recovered from the past few weeks activity though, because things really started to become unglued for me again after I arrived at the airport. The plane was late taking off, which offered the gate attendants more time to observe my odd behavior. They became spooked and wouldn't let me on the plane (this was many years before 9/11, so I must have been pretty squirrely). Wandering about LaGuardia airport as it got later and later and the concourses emptied of people, I passed the night in a semi-psychotic stupor. Early the next morning, just after daybreak I boarded a plane bound for Cleveland, Ohio …with a boarding pass marked for Dallas, Texas from the day before!

I was flying in more than one sense of the word. Real or imagined, I was a true American hero that day having accomplished great things for my country. After a long flight (which I determined was far too long just to get to Cleveland) we circled in for a landing over a vast white expanse of what I later realized was Lake Erie. At the time though I was convinced that some mysterious "they" had purposely diverted me from boarding the flight to Dallas and had arranged this flight specially to take me to an isolated Arctic Air Force Base to be briefed on a secret government mission requiring my extraordinary prowess (must have sat through too many episodes of Mission Impossible!).

Reality set in to some degree as I deplaned and walked to downtown Cleveland. It was New Year's Day, and at 27 degrees below zero Fahrenheit with a strong wind blowing off the lake, even with my extra warm clothing I knew that I was in danger. The cold or the Lord or both made me come to my senses enough to seek help. No doubt guided by His hand, after walking just a short

212

distance I came to the local public psychiatric hospital and before long was admitted. A day or two later I was starting to come down and stabilize, but one evening after hanging out with another patient all day long things turned dicey. We were talking foolishly, rambling on about some nonsensical things just to have fun and pass the time, but our game was misinterpreted. Without us knowing it, the staff became very concerned about us and called the doctor. One minute we were sitting there talking, and the next minute a bunch of aides approached and informed us that we needed to come with them. They led him into one room and me into another and said that we were going to be restrained (read tied to a bed)! Try as I might to talk my way out of it, there was no way.

Whether it was claustrophobia or not, I became mighty uncomfortable as they restrained me, one limb at a time to the steel frame bed. It was a misunderstanding, which made it all the more difficult to accept. My partner in crime and I began shouting to each other through the wall since our rooms were adjacent. Something I said upset him, and he began screaming vehemently at me. He must have freed one of his hands, because the next thing I knew, he was pounding on the wall with his fist, and punched right through the wall! Now I was scared, and not just a little. We had been yelling back and forth to each other for ten minutes and that had not brought any kind of response from the staff. Now, as the anger crazed guy in the next room continued to smash the wall and reach through trying to get to me, I began to scream at the top of my lungs for help. Still fully restrained and completely unable to defend myself, if that guy got himself free there was no doubt in my mind that he'd come through the wall and kill me! Thank God they must have noticed the difference between our earlier yelling and my terrified pleas for help, because they showed up a minute or so later and took care of the situation. A day or two later after a chat with a social worker, I was on my way back to the airport headed for Dallas again, thanks to the good auspices of some government agency or charity. This time, I got on the right plane.

# CHAPTER 19

Back to earth after my wild trip to the north, I set about to pick up the pieces of my life and begin again. Although yet to figure out that my bouts of psychosis were directly related to my alcohol and drug binges, I would probably not have gone to the halfway house for psychiatric patients that they lined up for me in Dallas except for the fact that I'd have been homeless again otherwise. Looking back on my own experience and those of many friends and acquaintances who are or were classified as mental patients by the medical community, it's evident that more than one of us have used the system just to get off the streets. Though I ended up indoors and in the "system" this time, that wasn't my premeditated plan. There was a time though, when in downtown Fort Worth in the winter, that I saw the nut farm as a warm comfortable place to escape the rough consequences of my bad choices.

The Greyhound or Trailways Bus Stations, Denny's and other all night restaurants were regular stops of mine when on the streets. Back in the day, if you kept your head low in any of these place and didn't bother the "cash customers" you could stay out of the weather for a while and even eat or catch a few winks. As I wandered around inside the bus station that night, exhausted and hungry as usual, the comfortable psychiatric wards I had inhabited in days gone by came to mind. An idea struck me as to how I could exchange the cold and unfriendly street life for a warm clean bed and a few square meals. There was an off duty policeman guarding the Greyhound Station that night, and after getting myself "into character" I pleaded with him to shoot me. Putting on a performance that might have earned an Academy Award if I were being filmed, the cop was convinced that I really wanted him to put me out of my misery, suicide-by-cop as it's been referred to.

Instead of being shot dead, before too long I was firmly ensconced in a clean, fresh, fairly new and well-appointed room at a local mental hospital. My respite from the elements didn't last long though, and I was back out on the streets within a week, but it was a nice break. Two significant events took place while I was there. Although I had been following Jesus for a few years already, I had yet to begin attending church except to poke my head in once in a great while, nor had I begun reading the Bible with much regularity. Unaware of the existence of Christian radio (where there is a lot of good Bible teaching available), and lacking any other training, I was still a child in the faith and pretty defenseless when under attack. In those days the enemy of our souls would regularly vex me with the thought that my precious family was destined for Hell. Addressing that concern, the Lord sent some loving believers from a local Assembly of God congregation to minister to us on Sunday. A kind elderly man was among them, and took me aside to talk.

"Is there anything I can pray for you about?" he asked.

After I related to him the very real fear that my dear dad would end up in hell, the old man showed me the scripture where Paul and Silas comforted the Philippian jailer, "Believe on the Lord Jesus Christ, and you will be saved, you and your household" (Acts 16:31) and I've taken comfort in that since then. [Praise God that, many years later at the age of eighty-seven, my father expressed faith in the atoning death of Christ!]

The other notable experience was an encounter with some folks on the dark side … modern day idolaters. One day, after being there long enough for the other mental patients to know that I was a Christian, some self-proclaimed pagans revealed themselves to me. While sitting in a common area with three others, a young lady pulled something out of her pocket. The object was wrapped in cloth, and with a smirk on her face she pulled it out and set it on the coffee table in the middle of the small room.

"Do you know what that is?" she said as she glanced at her two friends who were also smirking at me.

A small black statuette adorned the table. "No." I said.

"It's OUR god!" She said triumphantly as they all leered in delight, waiting I suppose, for some sign of shock or despair on my part.

No doubt the demons who held sway over these poor folks were there in the room at the moment too, because a cold chill ran through me. Immediately taking stock of the fact that my GOD created these people and their "god" the fallen angel behind the statuette, I knew that in spite of my emotions I had nothing to fear. But fear is what the diabolical forces intended, as a heavy weight seemed to be resting on me trying to push me to the floor. The demons must have communicated their plan to the young lady and her friends, and they proceeded to taunt me and take great delight in the game. Eventually she suggested to her friends (without saying my name) that I would make a good sacrifice to their little god. As they gleefully agreed, I acted as if I did not realize that they were talking about me. In my few encounters with demon or satan worshippers I learned that a

217

common tactic in order to confuse and unnerve the intended victim of their evil games is to talk about them using personal pronouns and never their names. Regardless of the certainty that my Lord would protect me, I didn't get up and leave right away (which they may have mistaken for fear) but stayed and endured their wicked, childish game for another five minutes or so before politely saying goodbye and leaving. Back in my room, I prayed fervently for them.

Given my life as a low bottom, hardcore waster, I've been in the presence of truly evil people more often than most, yet I haven't been scared to the bone too many times. An exception occurred one night at Pirate's Cove. In the 1980s, Pirate's Cove was a refuge for nudists and whatever hippies still inhabited the Central Coast of California. Generally, hippies disdained any social convention and encouraged most types of non-conformism and even rebellion, so hanging out at a nudist beach was a good fit. The main attraction for me was that it was a beautiful beach, and due to the sheltering cliffs which also created a small natural harbor, the air and water were considerably warmer than anywhere else I'd found on the California coast. No matter what else you planned on doing there, it was a captivating place to enjoy a summer's day of sand, sun and surf.

To get to the beach you had to hike carefully down a steep hillside, a trip that took five or ten minutes. Occasionally Sheriff Deputies would come down the path or access the beach by riding on horseback at low tide around one of the cliffs which hemmed in the beach on both sides. Aside from those two access points, supposedly there was no way in or out. That pleased the nudists and the hippies who were both breaking one law or another … the hippies (who were often carrying drugs) spent more time watching the path than the nudists did. One day when the weather was particularly beautiful and reminiscent of the blissful beach days of my youth, I alternated between baking in the sun and cooling off in the blue Pacific. Like a supernova, the light of the day was set like a brilliant gem in the rich blue sky, shining from the heavens and sparkling like a million diamonds off of the dark green surf. Some tents had been set up against the cliffs, and one of the guys told me that some of the hippies stayed there all summer. It was so nice that as the day wore on, instead of heading back into town for the night I just stayed. A tremendous sunset was followed by a cool breeze, and before too long a half a dozen of us were huddled around a fire to stay warm. Earlier in the day I'd struck up a friendship with one of the guys whose name was Scott, and he, along with several others who had no tent or sleeping bag, sat up late into the night around the fire. Anywhere very far away from the fire was too cold, so we all took turns gathering wood to keep it going, and sleep was not an alternative. As the night wore on, the conversation around the fire grew scary. It regressed more and more until one of the guys spoke in a way that indicated he was a killer and would feel no remorse if he felt like one of us needed killing that night.

Earlier before the sun set, Scott had pulled a knife out of his pocket to show me—he was proud of it. "It's a wood carving knife!" he said. The blade was about four or five inches long and had an unusual shape, kind of like an elongated fish which not only narrowed and came to a point at the end, but also at the butt where it was attached to the handle ... and it was razor sharp. As we sat around the fire an almost tangible, fearful chill seemed to settle on me as the scary guy talked. The sound of the wind and the waves muffled my voice as I whispered to Scott, "Can I borrow your knife?" He gave me a questioning look, but consented and handed it to me. With the knife in my pocket I felt somewhat safer—if the scary guy tried anything, I'd be ready for him. Although evil and fear were intensely present at that moment, for some reason it didn't occur to me to leave, perhaps because we sat in a small circle of light surrounded by blackness and "out there" didn't look so inviting either. After a few minutes though, I asked Scott if he wanted to split and he agreed. He then showed me a "back door" out of the cove. Not far from us against the cliff wall and secreted by underbrush clinging to the wall of the cliff, hung a thick rope that he said was secured at the top. He grabbed a hold of it and began to work his way up the sheer face of the natural seawall and I followed. thirty or thirty-five feet later we grabbed a hold of the branches of the tough native shrub to which the rope was tied and scrambled over the edge onto flat ground. It was now very late at night (or rather very early in the morning) and as we made our way up the road, we happened upon a picnic bench that was on the lawn of a small apartment building.

As we sat down to rest, I asked him if he wanted to smoke some pot. "Sure!" he said.

There was a pretty stiff breeze blowing though, and after striking my last match and unable to light the pot, I said "Not to worry, I'll just knock on one of these apartment doors and borrow a match!"

Scott wasn't as stoned or as stupid as I was, and he was completely against it and got up and left.

Dismissing the idea that it was too late, I insisted upon banging upon a few doors, but to no avail. Well, it did have some affect … no sooner had I given up and walked out to the street than two squad cars pulled up and out jumped two cops and a police dog!

"What's wrong?" I asked.

"What do you think you're doing banging on people's door in the middle of the night?" scowled one of the cops.

"I was just trying to borrow some matches!" I protested. "My friend and I just came up from the beach, and we needed a light!"

"I don't see any friend! Where is he?"

"He took off in that direction about five minutes ago."

They then decided to search me and came upon the knife in my coat pocket, which by then I had forgotten about.

"You make one wrong move and I'll have this dog rip your face off!" snarled one of the cops.

"It's a wood carving knife that I borrowed from my friend!" I protested.

"I don't think there is any friend."

"He was with me! He took off that way just a little while ago!"

"We'll see!" he said.

They cuffed me and put me in the back of the one of the squad cars, and away we went. Encouraged when within a few blocks we came upon Scott, my hope didn't last long. They stopped and spoke to him for a long time, but he must have had all the right answers (except for admitting that the knife was his) and they let him go. They took me to jail, and I was charged with possession of a concealed weapon—a felony! As I sat in a holding cell all night repeating over and over to myself, and out loud, "Oh my God, my God, what have I done!" I was mortified at what had happened. In the face of all the really stupid things I'd done intentionally that could have landed me in prison or the grave but didn't, now it appeared I that might be going there over a minor error in judgment! More than almost anything on the dark side, I feared a trip to the penitentiary. The typical county jail in the USA is no hotel, but life hangs by a thread in prison and it was something that held more dread for me than death itself. After numerous trips to jail and hearing many stories from people who had been to prison, I knew that my life wouldn't be worth a plug nickel in there … I'd be dead within a year. According to the (likely true) horror stories I'd heard and read about, the abuse that often precedes death is worse than death itself. There are only two possible ways to survive time in the penitentiary I was told … join a gang or keep your mouth shut and stay out of everyone's way. For safety sake I'd always been a loner on the streets trusting no one, so gangs were not my style. Oh, I'd hang out with folks and party, but never align myself with clicks, groups or even individuals for more than a few hours. As to keeping a low profile, keeping my mouth shout for very long has always been a great challenge for me … keeping it in check in prison amongst a bunch of bullies seemed extremely unlikely.

The shock of my impending doom did not wear off when they moved me to the county jail, and for three days I was in torment hoping that God would hear my prayer yet again as I pleaded for mercy. Breaking the strain of it, while in the exercise yard one day I ran into an old friend from one of the halfway houses I'd been in. Gale, who was a nice, gentle young guy but a heroin addict, introduced me to his mother who had come to visit him. Like so many poor addicts, Gale didn't make it …a few years later he died of an overdose. On the third or fourth day of my captivity much to my relief, they came and told me to pack my stuff … they had dropped the felony weapons charge which left only a misdemeanor for disturbing the peace. "Time served." declared the jailer. Once again, my Gracious Lord rescued me.

# CHAPTER 20

One of the reasons I fell into unbelief when I was a child was that the religion into which I was born taught that the only people who will go to heaven are those who strictly follow their teaching and extra-Biblical traditions ... and even those have no assurance of getting there. It was hard for me to swallow the fact that my chums in town were all going to hell because they attended a different church across town. Some in that religion have broadened their view regarding that doctrine to allow that some other Christians might enter heaven as well, but I understand that the church's official stance remains the same.

Years later after being born again, a similar conflict bothered me. To my knowledge every evangelical denomination which is considered orthodox in their beliefs has a morbid prediction regarding the future of, for example, a native of a remote area or anyone else who lives and dies without ever hearing the name of Jesus Christ. That poor man or woman, along with legions of others in similar circumstances, is destined to spend an eternity in torment separated from God, burning in a lake of fire ... all because they had the bad fortune to be born in the wrong place at the wrong time, something they have no control over at all. These concepts were some of the main contributors to my decline into atheism, because the idea of a fair, just and loving God acting like that made no sense at all. Years later after being born again, I accepted the doctrine regarding the fate of those who had never heard the gospel to be true, because people I trusted agreed with it, although I purposed to talk to the Lord about that and some other concepts and doctrines which I had questions about, when the time was right.

Without waiting for me to ask, my Savior addressed that topic with me more than once, first when I was hitchhiking through a bad part of Dallas one dark, rainy night. Among the hundreds of rides that I was blessed with as a hitchhiker, that night would be the second and last time that a woman ever picked me up. A rainy night in one of the worst parts of town seemed an unlikely place to get a ride from anyone, yet as a hungry, tired homeless person I longed for a break. As a four-door car pulled to the curb I climbed in and was greeted by a cheerful smiling woman who appeared to be in her mid-forties. Completely at ease with helping a stranger in the barrio late at night, her joy filled the car as we chatted for the few minutes that I rode with her. Knowing that she was sent by the Lord, I naturally asked,

"Are you a Christian?"

With a smile she answered, "Yes!"

"What church do you go to?" (Surely it was a good one I thought.)

Her smile never fading, her bright glow not diminishing an iota, she said, "I am a Latter Day Saint." It didn't register at first, and seeing the quizzical look on my face, she said, "I'm a Mormon!"

Feigning a smile and I said, "Oh!"

I don't remember exactly what we talked about for the next minute or two as my mind was processing the situation—could she actually be saved? Her actions and words rang true with my understanding of what it is to be a Christian, about people who truly belong to Him, yet how could it be? Her church teaches ideas which are antithetical to those of the Bible. When she dropped me off at my destination (thankfully the rain had let up by then) I climbed out of the car full of gratitude.

The Lord was bringing me to the understanding that, for the same reason that in His mercy He would not condemn a person to hell forever because they had never heard the gospel and never had an opportunity to accept or reject Christ, neither would He expect a brainwashed person to readily and easily overcome something that was trained into them ever since they were a tiny child. A person who all of their lives was taught by those that they love and trust in to believe in a false religious system, cannot easily or readily accept that those they love would teach lies to them. The loved ones themselves were most likely simply victims of their own parents' confusion. Since false religions are constructed by the devil himself, that craftiest of liars, it makes sense that many are held under the sway of his lies for most—if not all—of their lives. Salvation though—where we stand with God—is not a matter of saying the right words or doing the right things (as if we could earn our way into God's favor) nor does it seem *necessarily* that we can miss salvation by believing certain wrong theology. "For the Lord does not see as man sees; for man looks at the outward appearance, but the Lord looks at the heart" (1 Samuel 16:7b).

Regarding the citizen of some corner of the world who is never exposed to the truth during his lifetime, Paul states in his letter to the Romans: "… because what may be known of God is manifest in them, for God has shown it to them. For since the creation of the world His invisible attributes are clearly seen, being understood by the things that are made, even His eternal power and Godhead"

(Romans 1:19-20).

And "… (for not the hearers of the law are just in the sight of God, but the doers of the law will be justified; for when Gentiles, who do not have the law, by nature do the things in the law, these, although not having the law, are a law to themselves, who show the work of the law written in their hearts, their conscience also bearing witness, and between themselves their thoughts accusing or else excusing them) in the day when God will judge the secrets of men by Jesus Christ, according to my gospel" (Romans2: 13-16).

And in speaking to the Jews for whom circumcision (*doing* the right things) was a sign of belonging to God, " For circumcision is indeed profitable if you keep the law; but if you are a breaker of the law, your circumcision has become uncircumcision. Therefore, if an uncircumcised man keeps the righteous requirements of the law, will not his uncircumcision be counted as circumcision? And will not the physically uncircumcised, if he fulfills the law, judge you who, even with your written code and circumcision, are a transgressor of the law? For he is not a Jew who is one outwardly, nor is circumcision that which is outward in the flesh; but he is a Jew who is one inwardly; and circumcision is that of the heart, in the Spirit, not in the letter; whose praise is not from men but from God" (Romans 2:25-29).

Based upon my experiences with the Mormon lady and later my native American friend Bill Williams over Christmas, and others (as well the result of sincere, heartfelt prayer on the subject, and of course God's merciful love) I learned the awesome truth of what the Bible teaches—that our God, the Father of our Lord Jesus Christ and Creator of the Universe will populate His heaven with whomever He pleases—and many of us will be surprised at who we meet there. Understanding our gullibility, weaknesses and prejudices, it may be that He is not so concerned with the fine points of our theology but conceivably only how we " ... love the Lord your God with all your heart, with all your soul, and with all your mind." and " ... love your neighbor as yourself." ... "On these two commandments (Jesus said) hang all the Law and the Prophets" (Matthew 22:37–40).

And, "Then the King will say to those on His right hand, 'Come, you blessed of My Father, inherit the kingdom prepared for you from the foundation of the world: for I was hungry and you gave Me food; I was thirsty and you gave Me drink; I was a stranger and you took Me in; I was naked and you clothed Me; I was sick and you visited Me; I was in prison and you came to Me'" (Matthew 25:34-36).

Truly man looks at the outside, but God looks at the heart!

# CHAPTER 21

Although California Highway 1 is one of the most beautiful routes in the country, fatigue and discouragement had taken the shine off of it for me as I headed north from Malibu late one night. Whatever I'd been doing until that point had once again taken me to a state of nearly total exhaustion, and as I stood along that isolated stretch of road with my thumb out, hypothermia began to set in. It was not very cold, but malnourishment and extended abuse of my usually strong and healthy body had brought me to a state of near collapse ... the magnificent machine which God made to house my spirit and soul was giving out. It's hard to imagine one dying of hypothermia less than a quarter mile from the ocean in Southern California, yet from the signs I was exhibiting it was clearly a danger. Since it was the middle of the night cars were few and far between, and there were few signs of civilization. Needing to get off the road and find shelter soon, I began hitchhiking with a passion, jerking my thumb vigorously, doing my best to display my salient need to the few cars that approached. It's doubtful they could see the pain and urgency on my face as every ten or fifteen minutes one sped past in the dark—they probably didn't even see me until they were within a fifteen or twenty yards. Sensing that death was near and after praying fervently for a while and getting no results, I took matters into my own hands and began to stand in the middle of the road flagging my arms frantically at each approaching car, moving out of the way only at the last second to keep from getting run over. None of them even slowed down. At the very least I hoped that they would call the sheriff who would take me to a nice warm jail. Yet my actions availed nothing.

Something (or rather some One) called my attention to the industrial facility across the street not far from where I was standing. A Chevron sign hung on the fence that surrounded the small compound which was about a city block long and sat between the road and the seashore. The place was surrounded by a tall cyclone fence, on the other side of which was a hedgerow of dark evergreen bushes which topped the fence by five feet or so. As I drew closer, it appeared to be a pumping station related to the oil rigs which were just off the coast. The gates were open, but as I walked onto the property there were no signs of life; no cars or lights on in any of the half dozen or so one story dark green, wooden clapboard buildings scattered about the property. About twenty yards in just off to the left was a very small building not much bigger than an old fashioned outhouse, replete with a door, windows and roof. Walking closer and peering in the door which was open about eighteen inches, for joy I could hardly believe my eyes ... flames! Though my mental state was anything but sharp at the time, the small building was built around a loop of ten or twelve inch diameter pipe which rose from the ground and went right back into it. In the middle of the riser about waist high was a section which ballooned into what looked like a small furnace with a glass pane in the front where a door would have been if it had been a furnace ... behind the glass pane flames danced! Ostensibly its purpose was to allow unwanted gases to burn off from the pipeline which was bringing crude oil in from the rigs. Standing as close as I could to the oven like pipe, I soaked in the warmth for a long, long time, thanking and praising God over and over again for saving my wretched life ... once again.

The wisdom in the recovery community and Twelve-Step meetings—where I spent much of my time for about six years—was that if you think you can control your drinking or drug abuse, try stopping after one or two. Try it more than once. Only once in my life did I start drinking or using without the express purpose of getting as high as I could for as long as possible. What was the point of starting otherwise!

When my wanderings took me back through Dallas one year, I landed a job with a plumbing outfit which was building new apartments out in Keller, Texas. The night before my 25$^{th}$ birthday I had been drinking hard liquor and had a giant hangover the next morning. Not really up to carrying heavy cast iron bath tubs up two and three flights of stairs to set for the installation crew that was following us, I barely made it through the hot, humid spring morning. When I complained to a co-worker, he offered to smoke a joint of marijuana with me as a cure. My spirits, health and outlook on life took a turn for the better. When cancer patients and other seriously ill people smoke pot, I've heard that it helps with nausea— it helped mine a bit, enough to get me through the day. Able to buy a few more joints from my friend before leaving work, I also realized that the world class hangover which by now was wrapping its sickening tentacles around me again, would only get better one way, as the country boys put it, " ... by the hair of the dog that bit you." I needed some booze to cure me. The trouble was that my Dad was expecting me for dinner at his house that night to celebrate my birthday. By this time everybody knew that it was not a good idea to be around me when I was drinking, and I didn't want to spoil dinner with my dad. With that in mind I bought just one "Tall Boy", a quart size can of beer. Drinking it slowly, I threw out the can and didn't drink one more drop that day. I did it! I had successfully exercised the ability to control my drinking ... and it was easy! When considering my feat, I conveniently overlooked the fact that after dinner (immediately after dinner at an awkward time, and in spite of my dad's protests) I took a long walk and smoked more of the pot. When I came back through the door my dad immediately realized what I'd done, and effectively the evening was spoiled anyway. But just one experience "controlling" my drinking was enough to keep me going down that hellish path for five more years. The wisdom in the program said to try controlling your drinking or use more than once ... except for that one night, I never did it before or again, nor did I try.

It was about this time that Jesus showed me the depth of His boundless love for us in a way that I'll never forget. It was an experience which brought me a profound, new understanding of the power and effectiveness of Christ's atoning death for us on the cross. During the years I wandered in the wilderness after being born again, often I thought about why the Lord didn't deliver me immediately from the obsession to use drugs and booze. That He could, I had no doubt ... and I desperately wanted me to be free. Was it because I was a house divided, still strongly drawn to the things of the world? Did God have a higher purpose for my ongoing suffering? Eventually I realized that during the almost ten years that I spent in limbo between defeat and victory, He taught me two invaluable lessons which I could not have learned any other way.

The first lesson was about His love. About five years after I received my new life and five years before the day that He broke the chains of addiction which bound me, the Lord taught me an incredible lesson in His love that I never could have learned had He set me free immediately. As an atheist, I carried very little guilt about my wicked, immoral behavior—I honestly didn't think that there was a God or any gods or spirits, or *anything* beyond the physical world. In my understanding we were just cosmic coincidences and when we died, we'd go back to the dirt from which we sprang. As long as I didn't purposely hurt anyone emotionally or physically my conscience was relatively clear.

In line with the teachings of the day, any poor behavior on my part was the result of environmental factors such as a difficult childhood or a chemical imbalance, and any subsequent feelings of guilt were to be blamed upon preconditioning inflicted by erroneous societal norms and were easily dismissed. Like Robin Hood, robbing from the rich and giving to the poor (me) did not constitute hurting folks as long as those from whom I was gaining could afford it. Regarding my consistent lying to avoid pain or to get gain, frankly I must have performed quick mental sleights of hand to justify the offenses … I don't remember feeling guilt over most of that at the time. Things were quite different now though; now I *knew* that God was real, that He wrote the Bible, and that all of its teachings are true. Denying it or feigning ignorance wouldn't work. Yet because of the chaotic and anarchistic effects that the massive doses of drugs and booze had on my mind, every sin which I had committed before coming to the knowledge of Christ, I committed again afterward—a hundred times over. My ugly sin followed me around from episode to episode, and guilt hung over my head like a guillotine. Set up to fall into a trap, one night satan sprung a deadly one on me. The bold and wicked deceiver that he is, he does not hesitate to use God's own Holy Word in his twisted plots to try to destroy us. Step by step he planted doubt and fear in my mind using scriptures … one by one building an airtight case against me.

Waiting for the best time to launch his assault, after another of my many "slips" back into alcohol and drug abuse when I was physically and emotionally worn out, he attacked: "Therefore, if anyone is in Christ, he is a new creation; old things have passed away; behold, all things have become new"(2 Corinthians 5:17), he whispered into my heart. "Neil there is nothing new about you! You're the same old lying, filthy, thieving sinner you always were! Nothing has changed!"

Then … " 'They honor me with their lips, but their heart is far from me.' (Matthew 15:8b) That's you!' "

The devil went on, "You're a con man Neil. When you were an atheist you had nothing to fear because you didn't believe in God. Now that you know that hell is real, you're trying to con God! Forget about it! He doesn't believe you! He knows what a liar you are!"

And again, his arrows flew, " A dog returns to his own vomit, and a sow, having washed, to her wallowing in the mire' (2 Peter 2:22b), so Neil, you go back to your sins!"

And pounding the final nail in, sealing the coffin shut, he said, "For it is impossible for those who were once enlightened, and have tasted the heavenly gift, and have become partakers of the Holy Spirit, and have tasted the good word of God and the powers of the age to come, if they fall away, to renew them again to repentance" (Hebrews 6:4-6a).

Skillfully satan hammered away at me until I believed his lie … the lie that I was bound for hell. He pounded me using God's own

Word as a cruel hammer to convince me that I was of the very worst kind and too wicked to receive the Lord's grace. Once he had me fooled, he bludgeoned me again and again with the ghastly lie until I walked into another drink, another drug binge, and soon found myself back in the bad part of town again, in a cockroach infested halfway house. But that was by no means the worst part ... I was going to hell. So convinced of his lie, I felt like a walking dead man. People who know me would very likely classify me as a "Type-A" personality—high strung, brimming over with energy, even hyperactive. Yet for about forty-five days, I walked the earth with my head hung low, hardly speaking to anyone—I was morose. My eyes rarely left the ground and I probably found every penny folks had dropped along my path during those days. Though quite familiar with low times, even contemplating and attempting suicide both before and after coming to know the Lord, nothing I'd been through before compared to this: I knew for sure that hell was real ... and I was going.

After a couple of weeks of this terrible suffering, an interesting series of events began to unfold. One day the thought crossed my mind that the Peak and Eastside Church of Christ on Columbia Avenue in East Dallas where I had attended years before, was only a few miles away ... I could walk there. Remembering how kind the folks there were, it seemed appealing for a moment. But now? It seemed absurd. Surely I was headed for hell. What would be the purpose? The idea wouldn't go away though, so after putting it off for a while I eventually went. Never before (or since) a "back row Baptist", my usual favorite spot in a church is right up front and center where I cannot be easily distracted by the crowd and can focus best on the teaching and worship. However, in the middle of this damnable nightmare I sat way in the back and could not so much as lift up my head, let alone raise my voice in song or prayer. This congregation believed that musical instruments shouldn't be included in worship since they are not mentioned in the New Testament, yet their a cappella singing was some of the most beautiful music I've ever heard. Normally there are very few things on this earth that I'd rather do than sing praise songs to my Lord, but I was mute and empty, unable to join in the lovely hymns and wondered why I was there. Yet for some reason I went three Sundays in a row.

Having hitchhiked many tens of thousands of miles by then it was natural for me to hitchhike even within a city, for I'd yet to develop much patience for waiting for the bus or anything else, and usually had no money anyway. While hitchhiking a short time after my first trip to church, a Christian picked me up. In fact, each time I hitched for the next few weeks, a born again believer stopped. In every case not only did the ride take me where I needed to go, but the love of God was extended to me through these precious people. They asked me home to dinner, invited me to church and genuinely reached out in love and cared about me, each relating that Jesus was at the center of their lives and the reason for their kindness.

Walking back to the halfway house after the last of four or five rides dropped me off, I marveled,

"EVERY ride I've gotten in the last few weeks has been from a Christian! Jesus said that, '... narrow is the gate and difficult is the way which leads to life, and there are few who find it' (Matthew 7:14). How could it be that EVERY time I hitchhike a believer picks me up?! The odds against that must be ASTRONOMICAL!"

At that moment the Lord spoke to my heart as He did on the night that I was born again, just as if He had stepped down from His throne and joined me as I was walking ... I felt the most beautiful feeing of love, like warm oil, hit me on the top of my head and fill my body.

"Neil, I LOVE you and I FORGIVE you and NOTHING CAN CHANGE THAT!" He spoke to my heart.

The guilt, fear and heaviness of the last month and a half fell away from me like heavy chains, crashing to the ground and shattering like so much glass. A tremendous joy and freedom filled me as the love of God lifted me from the hell on earth that had filled me, and it felt as if I was floating those last fifty yards or so back to the halfway house! Once again, my whole life had been revolutionized. It was as if I had been born again all over again! The incredible understanding of the depth of His love for us is something that I never could have experienced had I not remained in chains for all those years after coming to know Jesus as my Savior, falling again and again into the deepest depths of sin and depravity. His amazing love! The power of the atoning blood of Christ is limitless! There are "Christian" religions which teach that we are saved by a combination of the grace of God as demonstrated by the sacrificial death of Jesus Christ on the cross as a substitute for us AND our own good works—they teach that we, in our own self-righteousness, play an important role in securing our salvation. My experience with the Lord that day on the sidewalk in East Dallas, and subsequent Bible study and learning from many wise, godly teachers taught me that His love for us and His perfect complete atonement for our sins is <u>all sufficient and complete</u>, needing no help from us puny, powerless men and women. We have but a small inkling of His incredible love for us! That He would lower Himself to save a wretched worm like me, one who chronically, continually *ran* to sin, is an astounding testimony of the unfathomable extent of His awesome love and mercy! The teaching that our good works are required in order to secure our salvation only feeds the human pride and ego and invites us to think that we as individuals deserve to be saved ... which could not be farther from the truth. It's clear that there was no better way I could have learned these things with such assurance without having sunk again and again into the very worst sin *after* knowing that God is real, and that His Bible is true from cover to cover. To me, the heinous sins which I committed as an atheist might have seemed excusable in the eyes of a merciful God ... transgressions by an ignorant fool seem much smaller than those of the son of a judge, well familiar with the law. To do what I did with my eyes wide open, and *then* be forgiven? The lesson was poignant and unforgettable!

The second invaluable lesson those ten long years taught me was about how Jesus intended to shine His love through me to others by using those prolonged years of suffering and then redemption as an object lesson for others. Remembering that He had allowed me to suffer and yes, even sin in so many ways, so that I could "walk a mile in their moccasins" in order to be able to minister to as many people as possible, it occurred to me that even the extended suffering was a part of His training. The other great lesson that I could have never learned without those tortuous 10 years was how to patiently and hopefully love the most hopeless and helpless addicts and alcoholics in the world, as well as others suffering under other types of bondage, sin and oppression. The additional years in that vile trap enabled me to empathize with and have compassion for all others who truly want to escape their grievous sin yet cannot until God sets them free. As badly as I wanted to shrug off the chains that held me I COULD NOT ... only God in His mercy can free sinners from sin. Today with a bright smile on my face I can point others back to the milestones which I passed along that rocky road and say, "I have been there too, Jesus helped me and I know He wants to help you!" and "See how great His love and mercy is for us! See how completely He is ready to forgive our sins!" Had it not been for the long years in that lonely and difficult school, had I not been among the most hopeless, I would not have been prepared for the work that He has honored me with since then.

# CHAPTER 22

When not at Salem my days were usually full of misery, though occasionally joy and splendor entered my life. Hitchhiking often took me through mundane and colorless landscapes, but sometimes brought me to scenes of unspeakable magnificence. Big Sur along the Central Coast of California is such a place, and my travels took me up and down that stretch of highway many times. The coastal mountains join the sea for mile after mile as the almost sheer face of the mountains meet the crashing waves below in a spectacular intersection of land, sea and sky. To see this place is a privilege few can forget. Although my trips there were all memorable, a couple stand out as best capturing the sense of its awesome beauty and the masterful creativity which God demonstrated when He shaped this rugged section of His universe.

Here the slim ribbon of California Highway 1 clings tenaciously to the edge of the mountains sending a twofold message. First, man's tiny insignificant effort to obtain a glimpse of this wild corner of God's creation is contrasted by this amazing example of His handiwork. Scratched out of the edge of these massive sentinels guarding the west cost of America, the little road seems to hold on ever so tenuously to the foothold it has gained on this ragged edge of the world. Indeed, powerful storms have often quickly swatted away sections of the road as if it were so much dust. Cars wending and winding their way along its twisted path seem like little birds perched precariously on the back of a rampaging buffalo, holding on for dear life. On the other hand, the little road is also a testimony to man's God given ingenuity and tenacity—first the Herculean effort it took to build the road in the first place, and then the dogged determination to repair it every time a portion of it is swept off the edge into the sea. A few times witness to the effects of those powerful storms, I marveled at the force it took to wreak such destruction.

Hitchhiking back to Salem Christian Commune after an abortive trip to northern California one year brought me face to face with one of those storms, and gave me a chance to know such power firsthand. The sky was threatening when a guy picked me up south of Carmel just as it was getting dark. As was most often the case, I had only the clothes on my back and didn't look forward to the idea of spending a night in Big Sur without a place to stay or any camping gear, especially with rain blowing in from the Pacific. My relief at getting a ride soon left though, because not long after entering a section of the road dotted liberally with hairpin turns and cliffs overhanging the ocean, my patron questioned if life was really worth living! It had begun to rain heavily, and as the guy negotiated the road at a fairly high rate of speed it occurred to me how many cars may have gone over the cliffs accidentally … and that he may just drive off!

I launched into my best amateur psychologist imitation and reassured him "Sure it is!" Alternately thinking furiously of what to say and do and praying fervently for safety and the right words or actions, I tried to maintain a completely unruffled exterior so as not to set the guy off. Talking about the Lord, I attempted to be as

Pollyanna as possible, but he was not buying any of it. He told me that he had thought about the bright side many times, but was now thoroughly convinced that he would be better off dead. Surely it was the Lord that reminded me that somewhere along this stretch of road there was a natural spring which ran down the side of one of the mountains and had been funneled into a drinking fountain which hung off the sheer face of the cliff into which the road had been dug. Cautiously carrying on a soothing conversation with the guy (I dared not leave him alone with his demons) I eyed the cliff wall carefully looking for the spring. Praise God there it was!

"Do you mind stopping so that I can get a drink!" I chirped cheerily.

Mercifully he stopped. After stepping out get a long cold drink, I walked back to the car and announced that I would stay there.

"Are you sure?" he asked. (On the side of a cliff? In the rain, at night?)

"No problem!" I proclaimed, "I like it here!"

Offering no further argument, he drove off as I heaved a sigh of relief, and said a prayer for him.

My relief didn't last long though as I realized that the rain was falling even more heavily now, the wind was blowing much harder, and it was cold too. There are few enclaves of civilization on the hours long drive along this most beautiful yet treacherous area called Big Sur, and most of the cars which traverse the route are tourists who do so by day in order to drink in and photograph the fantastic scenery. Even if there was any traffic at night (in a storm) experience had taught me that getting a ride while hitchhiking at night was a very low win proposition. The dark, cold, wind-driven rain was swirling around me, seemingly closing in on me. I'd heard tales of the ferocity of the storms of the Pacific Northwest which battered this section of the coast, and had seen the aftermath of some of them … huge piers swept away with hardly a trace remaining, barrier islands cut in half by ferocious towering waves, winds blowing structures away as if they were so much straw. For a few moments, fear clutched me as it seemed that this tempest just might sweep me off the side of the mountain and into the black, raging sea below.

The Lord heard my prayers though and a peace came upon me, almost like warm arms surrounding me. Shortly after that a car wheeled around the corner and the guy stopped, let me in and gave me a ride all the way to Salem. As I sat in the warm dry car thanking the Lord while the windshield wipers rhythmically clapped away the miles, I prayed fervently for the man who drove ahead of us, trusting the same Good God who saved me off of those cliffs to save him too. Looking back, the second chap who picked me up was very pleasant and friendly and not at all talkative … he may well have been an angel.

The second noteworthy Big Sur trip occurred when I was on a leisurely excursion one time with no particular destination. On the streets in Southern California I had heard of a place called Hobo Heaven which was supposed to be one of the best spots on earth for a hippie/hobo/bum, like me to live. While hitchhiking north I decided to try and find it. The word was that it could be found high above the Pfeiffer Big Sur State Park, and I reached my jumping off point that day excited about hiking up the ravine to the top of the mountain and being rewarded not only with a fantastic view, but Hobo Heaven! Still stuck in the swamp of addiction, I also hoped and expected that some booze and Big Sur (un)Holy Weed which I'd heard was some of the best marijuana on the planet, would be waiting for me. The park service had built a trail up a lovely ravine, down which a pristine, narrow mountain stream flowed. Realizing that the headwaters of the little stream were probably near the top of the mountain, I hiked to the end of the path then continued onward and upward. The going was not very difficult because although it was relatively steep, the footing was solid and relatively free from obstructions. The forest consisted primarily of new growth redwoods, and the combination of the canopy which the treetops formed and the fact that the mountain itself kept out all but the late afternoon and evening sun, discouraged the growth of any significant underbrush. The fragrance was unforgettable! The fallen redwood needles which lined the ground on either side of the stream gave off one of the most refreshing, clean, natural smells I can remember. As I climbed higher and higher, I came upon the burned out remains of one of the ancient giants, marveling at the gigantic diameter of what remained of the great tree. Even some of the "new" growth trees were five or six feet across! Up and up I went, drinking in every delicious breath of air, every new sight! The only sounds were those of the mountain stream gurgling and babbling down the ravine, the occasional lonely birdsong echoing through the halls of this massive cathedral, and my own footsteps and heavy breathing as I tramped on. The Lord must have called me to my senses and reminded me that the evening was fast approaching and that I had no food, equipment or supplies to help me survive a night on the mountain. My search was a bit quixotic in nature. I didn't have very solid information to go on in my search for this Hobo Heaven! Somewhat let down, though blessed even in failure by my extraordinary surroundings, I turned and descended to the floor of the park. In spite of not reaching my goal I had indeed tasted a bit of heaven on earth. Upon returning to Highway 1 the sign at the park entrance read "Julia Pfeiffer Burns State Park"—I had hiked up the wrong ravine in the first place. Though similar in name, it was miles south of Pfeiffer Big Sur State Park which is where I *should have* begun my hike. Thank God I didn't continue upward as it would have been futile if not dangerous.

# CHAPTER 23

My stays at Salem Christian Commune were always enriching, but there was much work that the Lord still needed to do in me, and for the most part the only way I learned was the hard way. During each stay at Salem it wasn't long before I slid back in to drug and alcohol abuse and was kicked out again. On those occasions sometimes I'd head back to Texas or another far flung destination, sometimes I'd stay in California and sometimes I would just go. On one such foray I hitched a ride to Washington DC where my sister Pam was living. A graduate of Georgetown University, she'd landed a job in the area and was kind enough to put me up for a few days. Deciding to head back to California after that, I'd made it as far as Alexandria, Virginia when a torrential rain began. Soaked to the bone by the time an old van pulled over and the driver opened the door, I asked, "Where are you headed?"

"Florida." the thin grizzled man replied.

"Me too!" I said with enthusiasm.

"It will likely stop raining by the time we get there!" I thought to myself with a grin.

Mac was a friendly sort it turned out, and probably welcomed the company as many folks on the road do. There is a kinship that often springs up easily among people who travel the highways, probably because we are all a long way from home and looking for a friend to share the time with. In any case, Mac and I gabbed for hours as we rolled down I-95 headed south. He was carpet layer and offered to teach me the trade when we arrived in Florida. Planning on staying with his ex-wife, he was sure that she wouldn't mind putting me up for a while too. It sounded like a weird arrangement to me and I was pretty uneasy about it, but was willing to see how it worked out. After all I had no money and nowhere to stay, what did I have to lose?

When we arrived at the small tract house north of Miami it was spring time, and the steamy sub-tropical heat was in full force. The household which welcomed us now consisted of the lady, her young child, a couple of her grown children, the live in boyfriend of one of them, Mac and I. Add to that mix, five dogs, seven cats, and subtract air conditioning and any substantial means of support (one or two of the adult kids worked but I don't recollect anyone else doing it) and it was one big mess! Sharing a room with Mac and another guy, it was so hot in the house that each morning when I woke, the hammock I slept in was soaked from my perspiration. Mac did not find any work soon and as the days passed my housemates became more and more aware of the number of their cigarettes I was smoking and the amount of their food I was eating. It didn't look like Mac was going to be teaching me to lay carpet anytime soon and my welcome was wearing thin, so I struck out to look for work one day. Before noon I came upon a place where they mounted fish that the tourists had caught in the Atlantic, and they were hiring. The manager showed me through the production line and I learned that the "mounting" of the fish was done by taking an impression of the fish, chucking the fish, and painting the now molded fiberglass creature to look like the "trophy" caught from the deep blue sea (leaping from the water no doubt!) ... the actual fish probably ended up being eaten by cats in the alley out back. I was flabbergasted! After all, wasn't the whole point to show off the "big one" that didn't get away!

"Is that how they all do it?" I asked the man interviewing me.

"That's the only way it's done." he assured me.

After touring the rest of the plant, he hired me on the spot to start the next day. Walking away a bit disillusioned about the fact that the "real" trophy fish were phony, I also had second thoughts about deep breathing all the chemicals used in their production process *and* the tropical house overflowing with animals and people. It occurred to me that South Florida in the spring (without air conditioning) wasn't my bag, so as soon as I made it back to the house, I packed my things and headed back to the Interstate singing yet another chorus of Willie Nelson's "On the Road Again."

Interstate 95 intersects with Interstate ten in Jacksonville and from there it's a straight shot to California. This was only my second time on this stretch of highway and it felt good to be back on the open road. The trip was somewhat uneventful until I reached San Antonio, Texas. Arriving there after dark, I got sidetracked off the Interstate. The good sense of direction God gave me must have been dulled by fatigue because before realizing it I was right in the middle of the barrio. Though I'd never had any bad experiences with Mexicans, I had heard some unpleasant stories about the barrio and was anxious to get out of there as soon as possible. It must have been a Friday or Saturday night because I could hear Hispanic music and the sound of talking and laughing drifting towards me through the balmy South Texas air from every direction. That relaxed me a bit, yet I was still relieved when a car pulled up and offered me a ride. Explaining what had happened to the dark haired, dark eyed young man that picked me, he told me that I was miles from Interstate 10 and offered to take me there. He was smoking and I asked him for a cigarette. After searching my pockets for a light, I asked him for one of those as well. He looked at me kind of hard, then clicked his lighter and held it up to my smoke, and then asked some questions of me as we got acquainted. Pablo seemed like a nice enough guy, and as we talked a rapport developed between us.

"Do mind if we stop out at my ranch before I take you to the highway?" he asked.

"Sure. Who knows how long it would have taken me if you hadn't picked me up!" I said. I'd be on my west again soon, and a slight detour was okay.

As we headed away from the city into the dark rolling scrubland, Pablo told me that he was the head of the largest gang in San Antonio which had 300 members. His girlfriend had defected to a rival gang and had turned him in to the federal government. Preparing to prosecute him, they had put a lien on everything he owned and seized it as evidence. All Pablo had left for now was this older car and the ranch that we were driving to. As he talked, he

snapped off his words with a hiss, and the angry bitterness he was wrestling with hung heavily in the air. He told me that he was going to rally his gang, arm them with M-16's and kill all seventy members of the rival gang!

Pablo must have seen the doubt in my eyes, because he said, "I'm out on bond now, and the Feds follow me everywhere."

By now we were on a desolate country road and he said, "Look behind us."

I did.

"Do you see that car?"

On the dark, lonely country road there was a car about a quarter of a mile behind us.

"Now watch ... when we stop, they will stop."

Sure enough, I could see that not only did the car stop when we did, but they turned off the headlights as they pulled over and waited for our next move.

"This may not be a fairy tale." I thought.

No light showed through the windows as we pulled in to the yard in front of what appeared to be a ramshackle old ranch house. We entered the house which was dimly lit by candle light and were greeted by an older Mexican man, who glanced at me as my new friend greeted him in Spanish. Pablo turned to me and told me that Emilio had been a friend of his father's and had saved his life one time ... and that he was very good with a knife. My friend must have explained to him what he was going to tell me, because when he spoke to me Emilio's face lit up with a big smile as he looked at me. I grinned and nodded wanting to show the proper amount of respect, and certainly not any fear. The next 15 or twenty minutes were spent as the three of us conversed, with Pablo acting as the interpreter. All of a sudden the older man pulled out his knife and hurled it in my direction, sticking it deeply into the wall behind me just next to my head.

The two men laughed uproariously, and Pablo said, "See, I told you he was good with a knife!"

"I see!" I said as we all laughed together this time.

Emilio came to my aid when all the rest of my gang abandoned me for fear of going to jail "... he will stand with me when we seek revenge on our enemies!"

It seemed as if everything he had told me was true.

After we talked a while longer, we said goodbye to Pablo's

comrade and I bowed slightly from waist, dropping my head to show my respect to him, and we went back to the car. Before we pulled off I asked Pablo for another cigarette. He handed me one and this time lit it without me asking.

Pablo paused a moment and said, "When I gave you a light earlier, that was the first time in my life I ever lit a cigarette for a man."

I nodded my head. Though I didn't yet understand very much about Mexican-American culture, I understood that he respected me and had done me an honor. Ignorant of his world and what it meant to be the leader of a gang, in our short time together I'd developed a respect for Pablo, Emilio and the circumstances of their lives … I also realized that the Lord had sent me to them. As Pablo drove me back to the Interstate, after praying I counseled him,

"Pablo, you're still a young man, you have your whole life ahead of you. Your anger at being betrayed is very understandable, but the Lord had something much better for you than the fiery end which must surely come if you pursue your plan. You might be successful, but do you think the cops are going to just look the other way if you kill seventy men! You'll either be killed or spend the rest of your life in prison!"

Then I shared another way, the Way of the Cross with him. Pablo listened carefully and nodded his head. "Praise God!" I thought, "He's thinking about it."

When he dropped me at the on ramp to the Interstate, I bid my new friend goodbye … and prayed for him for many days after that.

# CHAPTER 24

Hitchhiking was most often a great lesson in patience, but occasionally a cliffhanger would spice things up. One such event occurred while I was heading south between the two Salem Christian Commune properties one sunny Central California afternoon. An older man in a four door sedan picked me up at the top of a steep mountain pass through which the road descended about 2,000 feet in just a few miles. The road clung to the side of one of the mountains that formed the pass, and the passenger side of the car was just a few feet away from a drop off of hundreds of feet to the ravine below. Shortly after we began our descent the man greeted me in a louder than usual voice,

"Where are you from boy?" he boomed out in a stentorian voice.

"Well, I'm from New York, but I live at a Christian commune over by the coast. We do migrant farm work mostly, and have some fishing boats in the harbor as well."

He became very animated as he almost shouted, "So, you fish for Leroy eh!"

I timidly corrected him saying that the boats belonged to the commune, yet he insisted, "Ah! Leroy!" with the same volume and strident tone as before.

He began to drive faster and faster, and as I turned to look at him, to my horror his face was contorted as if in pain, his head twisted slightly to the left and down, and his eyes were CLOSED as we plummeted down the steep grade … and I was just a few feet from certain death in the ravine. After saying a quick prayer, it seemed prudent to try to distract him from whatever it was that gripped him, so I asked him where he was from. He didn't seem to hear me, and when I asked again his only response was, "So, you fish for Leroy eh!" This time I was mute, and simply hung on for dear life as another spasm grabbed him, causing him writhe and squeeze his eyes shut.

Alternately praying and carefully watching our position on the road, I considered whether grabbing the steering wheel would be a wise move. Venturing a look to my right I was relieved to see that we had reached the bottom safely. Noticing an exit coming up and trying not to sound anxious, I told him that this was my street. He didn't seem to comprehend at first, but began to slow to a stop after I repeated myself. WOW! Some people pay money to jump out of planes, climb sheer cliffs and perform other death defying stunts for the sake of obtaining thrills … I got them for free!

In the 1970s and '80s you could hitchhike almost anywhere in California except on the freeways. A sign was religiously posted at each on ramp just before it merged with the highway warning, "Pedestrians, bicycles, and motor driven cycles are prohibited" and they meant it. No matter where I was no matter what time of the day, if I became frustrated by standing on a low traffic onramp for too long and set foot on the shoulder of the main road, those black and white cars with the gold shields driven by the California Highway Patrol would appear seemingly out of thin air and immediately warn me off the freeway. One bright, sunny summer day on the desert about thirty miles west of Indio on Interstate 10, a ride had dropped me off at a road that as far as I could see, shot like an arrow straight into the distance and seemed to lead to nowhere. Besides the road itself and sparse traffic on the highway there was no sign of civilization, and the horizon was distorted and shimmered with the heat radiating from the desert floor. Gauging from my years living outdoors, it felt as if the temperature was approaching 120 degrees Fahrenheit. As I stood lawfully on the ramp and felt the intense heat begin to bake in to me, I realized that the likelihood that a car would come anytime soon was extremely low. Even if one came there was no guarantee that they'd pick me up, so I walked down the embankment to the highway and into the shade created by the overpass and stuck out my thumb. Presto! A Highway Patrolman pulled over and wrote me a ticket. It was the only time I got more than a warning in all the years I hitchhiked in the Golden State. The cop said that if he saw me back on the freeway, he'd take me to jail. Sheepishly I went back to the top of the ramp. After another fifteen or twenty minutes of baking in the sun and staring at nothingness, I decided that I'd be better off living in a nice cool jail cell in town than dying of heat stroke there on the ramp, so back I went under the bridge and awaited my fate. Within a few minutes another hitchhiker appeared seemingly out of nowhere. Even more surprisingly, within a just few more minutes a Volkswagen van pulled over and picked us both up! It's usually very hard for two guys to get a ride while hitchhiking together as people are wary of being robbed. The guy in the van (an officer in the military) was surely sent from God, because not only did he rescue me from the heat and the cops, but also took me from that spot all the way to the doorstep of my father's house in Dallas.

A couple of years later, that trip would come back to bite me.

My stays at the commune were always good for me, as each time I learned more about the Lord and grew closer to Him. Because the miracle of deliverance hadn't happened yet though, with sickening regularity I'd fall off the wagon and they'd have to throw me out. A few times though, I actually left of my own accord. One of the first gifts God gave me after being born again was that both of my parents had allowed me back into their lives ... ever so carefully. Christmas was approaching and I thought that it would be nice to spend the holiday with my mom in New York, and she consented. About a week before Christmas, after getting permission from the leadership at Salem, I set off to hitchhike home. Making good time until some deputies in Santa Barbara stopped me for questioning, for some reason it took an inordinately long time for them to check my background. This made both them and me kind of edgy—them because I could possibly have been a bad guy using an alias, me because it's no fun being around edgy, nervous people with guns! Eventually the report came back showing my record was okay except for the relatively minor charge of failure to appear in court for the time I was ticketed by the California Highway Patrol for hitchhiking on a limited access highway ... a warrant for my arrest had been issued. They were actually pretty nice guys and offered to let me go on the promise that I'd take care of it soon. For some strange reason I declared that I wanted to get my record straight right then—I wanted to go to jail! Maybe it was because of an old movie I'd watched where a penitent crook decided to come clean and pay his debt to society, but in moment of madness, instead of availing myself of their generous offer to let me go, I stuck out my wrists voluntarily and was cuffed and hauled off to jail.

My Christmas trip to New York was now in serious jeopardy. In days gone by much of my stupid behavior could have landed me in jail, some for a long, long time, but thank God I was only slapped on the wrist most of the time if I got caught at all. However, the petty offense of hitchhiking where I shouldn't have been ended up costing me over a week in jail, and was another harrowing adventure. Shortly after the deputies dutifully booked me into the Santa Barbara County Jail, I was placed in a cellblock with a tall black man named Conrad, a Mexican named Nacho, and a short white guy named Frank, and began what was to be a most unusual jail stay. A few times while incarcerated I had made a friend or two, but most of the time it was a sad story of tension, fear and violence. The four of us were locked up right after Santa Barbara had opened their brand new county jail and it was very clean and bright and most importantly not close to being full—in fact section we four occupied was meant to hold sixteen people. Most jails that I'd been in up to that point were very dark, dank, smelly, hot, overcrowded and downright depressive. This place was a model of the humanity of the American justice system. As opposed to the tomb like steel cages that were formerly the norm, the clean brightly painted rooms and corridors, and the absence of bars was a welcome change. Instead of bars there were giant thick panes of bullet proof glass that took up the upper half of at least one wall of most of the cells and common areas, and the steel which the rest of the wall consisted of was painted a light pastel color instead of battleship gray or some other dark, depressing color which was the standard.

Usually there is not much constructive to do in jail unless there are books available. When not an outright nightmare, routine life in jail for me included eating, sleeping, television and occasionally (best of all) reading. Though my stay in Santa Barbara was meant to be brief while waiting to be transferred to the custody of the county which issued the warrant for me, in my short time there

Conrad, Nacho, Frank and I became friends. We talked a lot … about our lives, about current events and other topics, and several times even had involved philosophical discussions. My plan was to be in New York for Christmas and in the back of my mind that was nagging at me, but in the meantime I was actually enjoying myself—in jail! One day after playing a card game, we decided to have wrestling matches. The likelihood of that happening in a jail without it ending up in a fight possibly to the death, would normally have been infinitesimal, but wrestle we did. There were plastic mats in the cellblock meant for exercise or more likely for the day when it would overflow with men and all the bunks would be filled, forcing some to sleep on the floor. We turned them in to wrestling mats, and two at a time we went at it. Conrad was by far the tallest and heaviest of us so he dominated the matches, though we gave him a good run for his money. Though we all got beaten by Conrad at least once if not most of the time, due to the dynamics of wrestling, little Frank didn't stand a chance. He was feisty though and didn't give up easily. The second to last match Frank simply couldn't accept defeat, and after much urging talked Conrad into one more match. He fared no better, and in his zeal to win became furious. In the end we all decided that wrestling should be a game of the past.

The camaraderie we shared for those few days was rich. Sailors on a small ship fishing for a week in the coastal waters, or soldiers at a desolate outpost might have bonded as we did then. We were a captive audience for each other, and thankfully our personalities meshed. For hours on end, some combination of us would talk, play card games or watch TV, taking unscheduled rotations back to our bunks to read or nap. Jesus was a recurring topic of our conversations as well … oddly the closest thing I can compare the feeling of this experience is to a church men's retreat. Incredible as it may seem, it almost felt like a vacation! A problem that developed not in our area but with the guys in the next cellblock, brought reality crashing in though. We must have been having too much fun one day, because one day the guys from the next block screamed obscenities at us and told us to shut up. Usually more subdued in jail because of the likelihood of there being violent or even murderous people there, the presence of the steel walls and thick bullet-proof glass which separated us must have emboldened me, because I screamed back at him and told them where to go. This happened several times, and finally my protagonist promised to kill me if he had a chance. Given the situation his words didn't faze me too much, but then one day, contrary to the routine we'd been through up to this point, we were told that we would be leaving the block to go to the dining hall ... my blood ran cold. What if we went at the same time that they did! Stories I'd read or heard about or seen on TV or in an old movie of convicts being stabbed to death while gathered in the exercise yard or dining hall raced through my mind. Soon I called Conrad aside and asked him what to do. He promised to stand with me and the other guys did too. It was the only time I was ever in danger in jail and had anyone stand with me, and it was somewhat reassuring. Just the same, I was as keyed up as I'd ever been by the time we lined up and walked to the chow hall.

Sure enough, the guys from the other block filed into the room the dining hall shortly after we were seated. My enemies sat directly across the table and looked at each other and grinned devious grins ... the moment had come! The table and benches were steel and anchored to the floor, and I was glad that my new friends Conrad, Nacho and Frank were on either side of me, yet the scarcity of guards and the tangible feeling of violence which hung over the room kept me at maximum ready, like a bowstring about to release an arrow. It must have been the Lord who showed me to keep one hand below the table at all times, meaning to give the impression that I had a weapon. Whatever held them in check, fifteen minutes later we all filed back out of the dining hall in an orderly manner and went back to our respective cell blocks. The rest of my time in the Santa Barbara County Jail was a similar to what had preceded the incident, but I could not feel entirely at ease until I was safely far away from my murderous adversary. Eventually they came to transport me to the other jurisdiction and I was provided an armed escort beyond his grasp. Unhappily though, it was out of the frying pan for me and into the fire.

Although my ultimate destiny was a jail in the Mojave Desert, they needed to transport me in stages, so my first stop was a jail in the greater Los Angeles area. Part of the sprawling megalopolis which covers a large part of Southern California, the jail had the feeling of the inner city. The place was taut with tension ... death and hatred seemed to hang in the air like a malevolent fog. While being booked in, I noticed that that most if not all the sheriff's deputies that served as jailers had tattoos notifying the world of their allegiance to among other groups, the Ku Klux Klan and the Nazi Party. They were as you can imagine, humorless men who processed us through as if we were cattle. For over twenty four hours I waited in a holding cell directly across from the booking desk before being moved to a cellblock. This place bore no resemblance to the cozy tank in Santa Barbara. Instead of the clean, bright, freshly painted walls and floors with lots of bullet proof glass to allow light in, there were the more typical bars and low, dark, steel ceilings and walls, and filth was visible everywhere. Dirt absorbs light rather than reflecting it, so in spite of the somewhat adequate lighting it was a permanent dusk inside. There were likely 120 men in the cellblock that had probably been designed for less than half that many. At night, since all the bunks were full, almost the entire floor was covered with sleeping men and all the tables became makeshift beds as well. When I first arrived in the tank (as cellblocks are sometimes referred to) I noticed that just as in the stories I'd heard of prison, the crowd was divided along racial lines. A short white guy with long hair called to me and I went over and started talking with him. The guy was trying to get up a game of cards and I joined. The game, and any semblance of peace I was to have for the next couple of days was very short lived though. It seemed that their way of socializing was to roughly joke with each other, and part of that was to mockingly call each other vulgar names, including the slang for a homosexual. I'm not sure how that would be taken today in jail, after the decades long, full-fledged campaign by the leftists in American politics, media and academia to normalize that behavior, but back then (except apparently in this odd microcosm of society) when one man accused another of being a homosexual, they were meant to be fighting words. When the short guy addressed me in that manner and I responded with a crude expletive, the guy slammed his cards down and rose up to fight.

"What's the matter!" I exclaimed, "You were the one that started it!" I yelled as I jumped up and took two quick steps back preparing for battle. He didn't hit me just then, but that was the end of my smooth ride on this jail trip. As I made my way as far from that guy as I could (which wasn't very far) I braced for a siege.

The cell block was divided into two sections, a day room where the tables were, and a bunk room where supposedly everyone was to sleep. After considering what to do next, I tried to get a bunk which would put some more distance between me and the combative guy. Walking into the bunk room I struck up a conversation with a Chicano guy, who suggested that I might be able to sleep in an empty bunk in their section of the room. "Sure" I said, and he went off to ask the head man if it was okay. The two of them came over and the "boss man" checked me out, then told me that if I acted right, I could stay. Assuming that meant as long as I didn't make any trouble, I settled in. Before too long the boss came over and asked me to clean up the area. That didn't seem unreasonable at the time so I did it. When he came back to check on my work and tried to give me another assignment, I realized that his idea of acting right meant being an indentured servant. There was no way of telling where that might have led, so I opted out right then and went back out to the day room. To my dismay, the short white guy persistently baited me and things only got worse. After spending the night sitting up with my back up against the bars where the jailer walked by (ever so infrequently) I was spent the next day in the same place alternately trying to get some sleep and warily watching for my antagonist who would come by with some regularity to taunt and hurl insults at me.

Although praying almost constantly, by the time night began approaching again I was a wreck. Without sleep and under pressure for thirty-six hours now, I was pushed to the limit. If it was just a matter of fighting this guy I would have reluctantly done it, but in this prison like setting where each racial group stuck together like glue in violent bands, if a fight ensued the rest of the gang would likely jump me … it would have been dangerous if not deadly. The night would bring peace I hoped, if not sleep. The tank started to quiet down as one by one the multitude went to sleep, but my nemesis did not, and instead came by to make one more attempt to draw me in to violent combat. I broke, but not in the way either of us expected. Turning my back to him, I got on my knees, clasped my hands and began to pray. This infuriated him even more and he bent over and put his face next to mine and started pouring blasphemous sewage out of his mouth, raging to the point that I knew any minute he'd hit me. Aside from meal times we rarely saw a guard, but like an angel one appeared just as the man was venting his hatred on me. He yelled at the guy to stop and immediately took me out of the cell. Hell itself could not hold much more demonic terror than I experienced in that cell block. The clean white sheets on the bunk the jailer took me to in the medical ward couldn't have been more welcome, and after a nice hot shower I must have slept twelve hours, at last secure enough to rest.

Within a day, they called me out for transport again, and after finally arriving in the city where I was to face the judge, thankfully there was no more trouble. Anti-climactically, after another good night's sleep the judge ordered me released with no further penalty. Thanks to God's grace I survived that ordeal and walked away with a deeper understanding of how that poor, broken segment of our population known as convicts spend their lives.

# CHAPTER 25

Another frustrated journey home from California to New York for Christmas resulted in an educational experience of a different kind. Rides were not coming easily and progress was painfully slow. It was Christmas Eve and I wasn't even out of California yet, and by the time I reached the desert town east of Los Angeles it was sundown and I was really stuck. The place, situated in some small hills on Interstate 10 was a one or two exit town isolated from its neighbors by miles of desert. One car after another swung onto the road picking up speed to head east with no indication of stopping, as I stood on the ramp late into the night and watched. The Lord reminded me it was a special night, and with God's brilliant starlit desert sky sparkling above I sang all the Christmas carols that I had learned as a child. Memories of crunching through the snow, walking from house to house with my family caroling the Good News of Christmas welled up within me. Hoping for a Christmas answer to prayer, that some kind soul sent by the Lord would whisk me away for a belated trip home, I pressed on through the night alternately singing then whistling each carol. As dawn began to break on Christmas morning, exhausted and hungry I gave up and walked to a nearby 24 hour coffee shop. Famished by now and opposed to using some other tactics, I immediately asked for the manager.

"Do you have some work for me? I'd like to do enough work to earn two steak and egg breakfasts." I said.

After some hesitation, he invited me back to the kitchen and put me to work scrubbing the kitchen floor by hand. It was a grimy job but I went about it with vigor, with visions of beefsteaks dancing in my head. The guy was a real softy though, because after less than an hour he came back and told me to come on out and eat. Cautious, I made sure he understood that I wanted *two* steak and egg breakfasts and assured him that I was ready to work as long as necessary. He said it was alright, and I sat at the counter eagerly waiting for my feast. Half way through the second plate I struck up a conversation with the guy on the stool next to me. A nice chap who also knew Jesus, I soon discovered he was a Native American as well. Actually, he was half Native American—the other half of his bloodline was Northern European. Bill Williams, who was probably in his mid-sixties at the time was a brilliant and likeable guy, and after talking for a long time about a number of different subjects including his tribe and local history, he invited me to his place to sleep before I headed east again. Talking with older, wiser and more experienced people has always been one of my favorite things to do and Bill was all three, so I jumped at the opportunity.

After convincing him to purchase a six pack of beer for us (which as was invariably the case, drank primarily by me) we ended up talking through most of the night. Rarely at a loss for words, when I drank even a little, words flowed even more freely. Not only was Bill brilliant, more than that he'd had a fascinating life. Born the son of white man and a Native American woman, he grew up in a rough part of Chicago and was raised as a Quaker. The neighborhood he grew up in was pretty colorful and was home to among other things, ethnic street gangs. Bill had a strong intellectual bent and concentrated on his studies trying to stay away from trouble. As he carried loads of books back and forth from school, the combination of his different racial background and his atypical propensity for learning set him up as a target for the gangs. Although a peace loving Quaker, he often had to fight his way home after school. At the outbreak of World War II he was drafted into the U.S. Navy but on religious grounds was given a non-combat role. This period of our history has always fascinated me, and I asked him one question after another regarding his war time experiences. Minutes wore into hours as we talked about many, many different subjects. After the war, Bill went on to become a physicist, and since physics is one of my favorite subjects, we returned to that over and over again. The other subject we circled back around to again and again was the Lord and spiritual things. He had embraced the Quaker religion of his father, and later also learned the traditions and beliefs of his mother's people who were indigenous to the Mojave Desert. He had even become a medicine man. Familiar with the writings of Carlos Castaneda and others, and with the understanding that most of the religions of the world are demonically inspired, I questioned him politely but warily as to his spiritual beliefs, probing as to where they might contradict any teaching from the Bible.

Bill was an accommodating and patient man. Even though he was tired and told me so, he could see that I was really thirsty and anxious to learn and continued to answer my questions and allow me to explore his world. Because of exhaustion I should have been flat on my back for at least fourteen hours, but the combination of the booze, this brilliant man, and the new intellectual and spiritual frontiers I was exploring kept me talking well into the night, questioning and challenging. My understanding of God, the Bible, and orthodox Christian doctrine was new and not yet very deep, but I did know that there were many wolves in sheep's clothing and many false religions masquerading as Christianity. Also, since I was not yet convinced that the two spiritual systems which Bill was involved in could co-exist without being mutually exclusive, it seemed wise to be sure before I slept, that I wouldn't end up a ritual sacrifice before morning.

Late into the night Bill became inspired to make a point. Sensing my tentativeness regarding his native religion, he told me that he wanted to show me something outside. Pulling on his jacket he opened the door and led me to a spot a few dozen yards from his trailer and said, "Look between my fingers." as he held them in front of his body as if grasping something like a small ball.

"I don't see anything." I said, expecting that he wanted to show me a rock trick, as one might roll coins over their knuckles or something to that effect.

"It's not dark enough here." Bill said, stepping further away from the trailer. "Here, look." he said.

"I still don't see anything!"

"Look between the tips of my fingers."

Then I saw it ... between the tips of the fingers of his left hand and his right hand were what appeared to be faint beams of light, like a holographic projection.

"What is it!" I exclaimed.

"It's my spirit." Bill said. "Now look between your own fingers."

I did and noticed the same phenomenon, only the light was fainter. "Why is mine dimmer?" I asked.

"Because you are not as aware of your spirit."

Though it was pretty freaky, I could not deny the evidence in front of me. I'd only known the Lord for a short time and Bill had known him for many years, so I continued to listen. He mentioned that there was a place on his land not far from where we were standing, that was like a door to the spirit world. We walked over there and didn't see or feel anything out of the ordinary, and Bill explained that spiritual things are not always the same nor are they predictable. Back at the trailer, I finally stopped talking and let Bill drift off to sleep. Pondering what I had learned and what had happened, I thought, "Surely Bill has been kind and hospitable and done nothing to make me think that he is anything but a generous Christian man."

I remembered that Jesus said, "Then the King will say to those on his right, 'Come, you who are blessed by my Father; take your inheritance, the kingdom prepared for you since the creation of the world. For I was hungry and you gave me something to eat, I was thirsty and you gave me something to drink, I was a stranger and you invited me in'" (Matthew 25:34-35).

"Surely Bill has been a living Bible to me," I reasoned. "How could he anything but a true believer?"

My Lord also said, "Therefore by their fruits you will know them" (Matthew 7:20).

"Yes," I thought, "this was something very new and different that I learned tonight, but nothing about it seems to point to the enemy."

The Lord chose His special people Israel and set them apart to Himself forever, thousands of years ago. Yet knowing how great His love is for *all* of us, it did not seem unreasonable to believe that He would sprinkle some light around the globe far from the Promised Land until such time as He would reveal the full truth everywhere. Indeed the prophet said that Jesus was to be, " ... a light to the Gentiles" (Isaiah 42 : 6b). Jesus Himself said, "And other sheep I have which are not of this fold; them also I must bring, and they will hear My voice; and there will be one flock and one shepherd" (John 10:15-17). As I mentioned earlier, one of the reasons I became an atheist was because in the religion of my youth, we were taught that anyone who didn't follow our exact path was destined for Hell. I could accept that for the scoffers, for those who hated God or knew the true gospel and rejected it, but how about the natives in the jungles of Borneo or others who had simply never been exposed to the truth? Would our gracious, loving heavenly Father condemn them to Hell for sheer ignorance of the way? It made no sense! That prior to worldwide propagation of the gospel, the merciful God of the universe would show some of His light to the Native Americans and every nation not near the Holy Land makes perfect sense! Coming to a peace about what I had heard and seen, I was then comfortable enough to go to sleep on this most unusual Christmas. Before drifting off, it occurred to me that this was well worth being late to home.

# CHAPTER 26

Once again riding my thumb to another adventure, hitchhiking east out of Dallas with the intention of going to visit my mother in New York, things weren't going well. Progress was slow and I was grateful when a Christian family picked me up near Greenville, Texas. It was late in the day and I was so tired … they had compassion on me and offered to let me stay the night at their home. After feeding me a great home cooked meal, they gave me a safe comfortable place to sleep for the night. It was a restful break to spend a few hours in their peaceful home, and the next morning they bought me a bus ticket to New York … their Christlike love was unforgettable. Waving goodbye to them through the window of the bus, the thought of a nice easy trip to New York was a welcome change. As was the case so often in those days though, I found a way to blow it. The toxic brew of my own sin and stupidity, and the demons who were out to destroy me were once again about to spoil the soup.

The first place where the bus stopped for more than a few minutes was a medium sized country town. Conveniently located across the parking lot from the Greyhound station was a bar, and I walked over there with a couple of guys from the bus to get tanked up for the long trip to New York. After drinking as much as we could in the short time we had, we made our way to a nearby liquor store to lay in a supply for the road. On previous trips I had never ridden with a savvy bus driver, but this time when we approached the bus to board it, he called down from his seat, "No way! You're not coming on my bus with booze!" We protested innocence, but he wasn't buying it and so we shrugged and walked away. Figuring we'd catch the next eastbound bus, we each headed in a different direction to pass the time. Walking through the nearby neighborhood looking for a good place to sit down and drink, and finding none, I soon and began to get thirsty and snuck under the high, raised porch of a house that was open on one side and closed in on the other with lattice work. Opening the bottle of 151 proof rum I had secured for the trip, all of a sudden paranoia hit me and I became afraid that someone may have seen me duck under the porch, so I swilled down the bottle in two or three quick gulps, and made way back to the sidewalk. Though I still had a very high tolerance for alcohol at this time, since I'd already consumed a generous amount of beer, downing the pint of high potency rum in less than two minutes sent me for a loop.

As the powerful poison quickly took effect, I was a new man— not better, but not at all the same either. Brimming with confidence now and at ease with the world, I sauntered over to a nearby Mercedes-Benz dealership and pretended to be in the market for a high end car. Honing my acting skills (lying) was a fun diversion for me in those days, and playing the part of a big wig shopping for a luxury car was a gas. The salesman spending his time with me was probably not as amused, and was one of the many casualties and collateral damage of my reckless, self-centered lifestyle. By the end of that charade I was in a bit of a fog and I'm not exactly sure of what transpired for some time. By the time night had fallen, while walking through a residential area WHAM someone hit me in the face with a two by four. By the grace of God it didn't knock me out, and I struggled with the guy for a minute slugging him a few times before he gave up and ran away. Stunned, I stood there a moment and took stock of the situation. Though in a drunken stupor, it seemed a good idea to get back on the bus. Anesthetized from the booze though, I failed to notice the blood all over my face. When I walked in to the bus station to check on the next eastbound bus, without tipping me off they immediately called the police.

I protested lamely as they hauled me off to the jail, and after escorting me into the courthouse the two policemen stood at the booking desk chatting with the duty officer. Astutely, I noticed that the door we had just come through was wide open. The arrangement was this: booking desk, two officers, me, the door. It was too good to pass up and out the door I ran at top speed. Although I'd been pretty fast in my football days just a few years before, I failed to take into account the fact that it's hard to run with your hands cuffed behind your back. About fifty yards from door one of the cops tackled me. He flipped me over, and having seen WAY too many old western movies and still under the sway of the 151 rum, I looked him in the eye and said, "If it's the last thing I ever do, I'll track you down and kill you." With that he jerked me to my feet and made sure I was safely inside the jail.

When I awoke the next morning, at first I had forgotten where I was and how I had gotten there. It started to come back to me, and then I felt my nose throbbing. It was swollen terribly, and having had my nose broken twice before I realized that this was number three. My nose was pushed way over to the side, and based upon my experience with the promptness of any type of help in jail including medical attention, either I'd set my own nose or it would heal crooked. Mustering up all the moxie I could, I proceeded to push my nose back into place, making it as straight as possible— any mistake would require someone to break it again to set it right!

Then it was time to wait. There is no place in the world better to develop patience than jail. Not only do you wait, but you usually wait with no idea of how long you'll wait. The next day they took me to be arraigned though, and when the bailiff read the charges, for a moment the world stopped spinning. Public Intoxication, a misdemeanor and THREE felony counts! The day I had been dreading had come! They had charged me with Assaulting a Police Officer, Terrorist Threat Against a Police Officer and one other that I cannot remember. My mind reeled as they took me back to my cell ... I was almost paralyzed with fear. The word on the street was that southern penitentiaries were the worst in the nation. Not only did it look like my greatest fear would come to pass, but in the worst possible way! On the streets it is common knowledge that if you commit a serious crime and get caught you'll go to prison, but if the crime is against a policeman they'll throw away the key! Contrary to the norm I learned my court date right away and it was only three days away. Praying constantly yet still fighting off stress day and night, it didn't help any that I was never given an opportunity to speak to an attorney before my moment of reckoning.

In the three days leading up to my court appearance, I was probably quieter than almost any time in my life before or after. I prayed and anguished and prayed and prayed. My father had long since stopped bailing me out, but even if I was the President's son it seemed very unlikely that anyone but God Himself could get me out of this ... it was a seemingly impossible situation. The day came and they escorted me into the courtroom with the other prisoners, and I took my place on the front row, numb with fear. The old courtroom looked like what you might imagine the courtroom in "To Kill a Mockingbird" would look ... hardwood floors, clean white walls and ceiling, and lit mostly by giant paned glass windows framing tall, stately trees. Quite beautiful if it didn't represent an execution chamber for me! Unable to look at anyone, I stared alternately at the floor and then the ceiling, praying fervently the whole time. The judge entered and began the proceedings, and I split my mind between praying and listening attentively to hear my name called. When he called it and read the charges, the words sounded ugly and menacing as they echoed off the bare walls and ceiling of the old country courthouse. Astoundingly, no sooner had the words left his lips than the District Attorney (not the Public Defender) jumped to his feet and said, "Your Honor, we recommend leniency in this case!" As far as I know, nobody that I knew was aware of my circumstances. Yet as I sat there dumbfounded, the judge dismissed all the charges against me except Public Intoxication! This was not a case of some high powered lawyer intervening, or some other big shot somewhere pulling strings for me ... it was the hand of Almighty God! Wrapped in a cloud of grace and love, I served out my time and walked out of jail two days later with an even deeper understanding of God's mercy and grace.

# CHAPTER 27

The devil is such a sly and devious liar. The "freedom" of the hippie movement, the drug culture and the sexual revolution of the 1960s and 1970s was merely a sham to lure people in to idol worship. In centuries past many were duped in to worshipping gold, silver, wood, clay, and stone statues of false deities. We in the modern western world are (for the most part) far too sophisticated for that, so satan tricked us into worshipping our appetites and *ourselves*. "If it feels good, do it!" was an enduring mantra of the times. Freedom, and ultimately personal freedom were put on the highest pedestal, and that lie has grown to be a religion in our present day. In America, the enemy craftily twisted our inclination to venerate the principles of our country's founding fathers and the early patriots who had sacrificed greatly and fought bravely to free us from the tyranny of an unjust government, into worshipping individual freedom as the highest form of morality. Today in our country, there are many who would say that the worst transgression a person can commit is to do or say anything that would imply that it is wrong to do or say *anything*! That now widely held belief makes no sense at all. Case in point, "I like to chop people into small pieces!" may be one person's choice of an "alternate lifestyle." Even the New York Times would object to that way of life. So, there are *some* absolute morals … the question is whose?

Being a child of the '60s I often sang the words of Janis Joplin, "Freedom's just another word for nothin' left to lose, nothin' I mean nothing honey if it ain't free!" Yes, I was solidly in the iron grasp of alcohol and drugs, but one of the things that drove me back and forth across the country was the battle cry of "Freedom!" Calling to mind Richie Havens' powerful anthem at Woodstock, as he called out again and again, "Freedom, freedom, freedom, freedom, ..." and " … sometimes, I feel like a motherless child. Sometimes, I feel like a motherless child … A long way from my home." How often during those days of "finding myself" did I and so many others on the same path feel like a motherless child? How many times did I forlornly sing chorus after chorus of "500 Hundred Miles Away from Home" as I wasted away by the side of the road, hoping that at the end of it would be something worth finding.

Non-conformity was a hallmark of the times, and though I was not so much against conformity to the existing mores of society, or the government of the United States in particular, I was against conformity in general. From my point of view after observing people, it appeared that people often did things not because they thought it out and concluded that a particular course of action or way of thinking was the best, but were drawn into it by others, by the need to comply (people don't do that … everyone is doing it, etc.). Though peer pressure, the "herd instinct" may well serve some positive purposes in helping to maintain cohesiveness in society and has acted as a glue for civilization to an extent, great evil has been inflicted upon humanity because people have simply followed the crowd, either blindly or out of fear. For those reasons I have deliberately avoided doing things simply because the crowd is. After careful observation and consideration, I've joined the majority in some act or opinion if it seemed to be meritorious, though it has become manifestly evident to me over time that the crowd is more often wrong than right. It's not necessarily true that everything that people have done in the past was wrong, but simply that we should live purposefully, carefully choosing a direction at each crossroads rather than do things because, " ... this is how it is done." When lobbying my mother to join my friends in some questionable event or practice, she'd often say, "If everyone jumps off of a bridge, are you going to do that too?" There is value in repetition, and I'm so glad that she repeated that! Not cutting my hair for many years was an outward sign of non-conformity which I hoped would cause people to stop and think. When at eighteen, I cut it, it was by no means a betrayal of my ideals (inside I was always " ... letting my freak flag fly"), but since I was often carrying illegal drugs it seemed best to go underground in order to avoid attracting the attention of law enforcement. As an adult they could put me away for a long time and I wanted to do everything in my power to avoid that. For years I was an undercover hippie. To my shame, to some degree I've also marched to the beat of a different drummer as an act of pride, simply to prove that I was bold and smart enough not to be like others ... and ended up the loser.

Aside from the more important physiological and spiritual aspects of addiction, and addiction to sin, considering the hippie mindset which was so deeply entrenched in me may explain to some extent how I remained dependent upon mind altering substances so long, and had not seen that I didn't have drugs and booze, but they had me. After all, the freedom of the open road, new adventures and new places, the freedom to do whatever I wanted from day to day was an alluring proposition. No doubt it was also a delightful distraction to a guy who just lost his job, or his place to live, or just got out of the county jail, to just take off for points yonder. How quickly my mood would shift from deep dejection to excitement while heading towards the nearest Interstate for some distant shore or mountain range. No wonder that I was a little taken aback when the Lord spoke to me one day while standing in line at the Santa Barbara Rescue Mission. Waiting for a free meal, a warm shower, and a clean comfortable place to sleep, I shifted my weight from foot to foot, occasionally glancing to see if the door had opened yet. My attention was drawn to the extremely filthy, ragged condition of the old alcoholic in front of me. When I turned around and realized that that the guy behind me was in the same shape, I stood sideways to try to avoid touching either guy, concerned about lice or … who knows what!

"Yuck" I thought, "The poor old bums!"

At that moment Jesus silently spoke to me, "Neil, do you see the bum in front of you?"

"Yes Lord."

"And do you see the bum behind you?"

"Yes Lord." I replied.

"Guess what? YOU'RE a bum!"

At first, I was taken aback. ME? Wasn't I part of the elite intelligentsia who recognized the futility of life in establishment America? Wasn't I one of the avant-garde leading the way to a more enlightened world? No, I was a bum. I was a drain on society, a leech. While reaping many of the benefits of living in one of the richest, most secure and comfortable countries in the history of the world, I was contributing nothing, only taking. That revelation brought upon a paradigm shift for me, and once again I saw the world in a new light. From the day that I was born again the Holy Spirit began peeling back the layers of false ideas that the devil had been brainwashing me with for years, and God has continued to do so ever since as I have been ready to receive it, and sometimes in spite of my resistance. In fact, God has promised that, " … He who has begun a good work in you will complete it until the day of Jesus Christ …" (Philippians 1:6). That is one of the most comforting and exciting truths in the Bible! Thankfully the Word says "He" started the work and "He" will complete it … we cannot mess it up. We are His project!

# CHAPTER 28

After getting thrown out of Salem Christian Commune once again, one evening I was standing by US 101 at the top of an on ramp on the northbound lane in a town not far from Salem, and satan was hard on my heels. Up to my old tricks, having recently consumed massive quantities of drugs and booze, with no sleep, water or food, my weary brain was again a playground for the enemy of our souls. The enemy's theme once again was the last days and the apocalyptic time described in the Book of Revelation. Although I'd read it, I had not up until that point paid particular attention to that book of the Bible. My thought was then and still is to a degree, that the exact way the end of time unfolds is in God's hands and not well understood by men. How I will be affected by it or play a part in it will be determined by the Lord. My responsibility to the Lord is to seek the Him with all of my heart and strength on a daily basis. If indeed I live to see the advent of those days, Jesus will order my steps then. Considering my casual attitude towards the subject, it would seem that I was an unlikely candidate for the specific psychotic trip that satan was about to take me on. Even so, as evident by the number messianic complexes recorded throughout history it appears as if it's a favorite trick of the enemy to leverage the dramatic end time events and our uncertainty about aspects of how they will unfold, in order to sidetrack us. He often plays another favorite card of his during such assaults, the pride card, exploiting our desire to feel important by insinuating that we will play a key part in the climactic struggles.

Knowing that with all my many sins I would never fall for the idea that I was the Pure and Holy Son of God (the more common Messianic complex) … satan proffered a lie which I could buy, as he did once before … that I was an angel declaring doom to the world (the word angel means messenger or one who is sent, so does not necessarily mean a heavenly being). As I stood waiting for a car to wave my thumb at and gazing to the southwest, words boomed in my head and seemed to be emanating from me, "WOE, WOE, WOE, YAY, WOE!" Repeating this three times, it seemed as if I, by God's direction, was declaring the final curtain call upon a lost and dying world. There was so much force behind the words as I seemed to be fulfilling the grave duty, that I could do it without even needing to move my lips! Then, after what seemed like a few minutes of repeating this announcement to the world, an astounding thing happened. Whether a trick of the devil to reinforce his twisted charade, or the effects of psychosis I don't know, but as I looked, the sun which had moments before been hanging low next to a mountain about ten or fifteen degrees above the horizon suddenly dropped below it, like an apple falling off a tree. Of course it did not, but the effect on me was quite a shock and it brought me out of my reverie. A kid who was playing down the street with some others came over to me and said,

"Do you know how long you've been standing there?" as if to imply a long time.

Stunned by the whole experience, I struggled to think up an answer, "Fifteen or twenty minutes." I said nonchalantly, though I could only guess.

"Yeah, about that." he said as he slowly walked away, glancing over his shoulder, question marks in his eyes.

In fact, the sun had undoubtedly dropped as slowly as it always does as I stood like a statue, though it had appeared to me to be a fantastic miracle coinciding with the "world shaking proclamation" I had been "commissioned" to utter.

Mulling all of this over in an acute mental fog, I stood there for a while longer. Realizing that particular on ramp was probably one of the least traveled in town and that it was getting dark, I changed plans and directions and walked over to the most heavily traveled ramp heading south. I'm not sure where I was headed, but by now I had hitchhiked in and out of this area so many times that I was probably on auto-pilot. By the time it was nine or ten o'clock I had gone no more than thirty miles. A Denny's restaurant was once again strategically nearby, and I made my way to the coffee counter with hopes of either catching a ride or at the least passing the night in a warm safe place.

The demons were circling closely around me though, and I found neither a refuge nor a ride that night as the devilish hoard played the paranoia card on me and drove me back into the night. As I stood on the freeway ramp with the Apocalyptic stage set in my head, the night seemed to grow darker and darker and the cars fewer and fewer. The devil convinced me that the darkness was the final curtain being drawn closed on the universe … even the headlights on the oncoming cars seemed to be swallowed up by the darkness, showing only a pale orange.

"These cars are some of the few brave souls fleeing to distant Los Angeles or San Francisco on some desperate mission in these final hours!" I thought.

280

Feeling as if catastrophe had come upon the world, I felt justified in taking extraordinary measures to secure a ride. As the next few cars approached (which now seemed to be going in slow motion) I walked into the middle of US 101 and waved my arms from overhead to my side, as if flagging down help for an emergency. Since the drivers could likely not see me until they were almost upon me, the only reaction I got was blaring horns and violent maneuvers to avoid hitting me. Since even that tactic was unsuccessful, I retreated back up the ramp and headed in to town.

My brain was overheated like an old car low on oil and coolant as I headed down the main street in to town and came upon a nice clean motel. "With the world coming to an end as it is, maybe the proprietors of this place would extend the courtesy of a room for the night." I thought. As I approached the entrance and entered the lobby, a little gray haired old man and his wife were standing at the check-in counter. As he turned to look at me with sad eyes, his face resembled that of my father's father. My fevered brain (no doubt on the suggestion of a devious spirit) somehow determined that this was indeed my own father, shrunken and withered with age (I quickly assumed that time had become telescoped in this fantastic end time scenario).

"Dad?" I called to him.

He gave me a startled look and turned first to his wife, who appeared equally startled and frightened, then to the motel clerk.

"Dad?" I said again, this time with a hint of pleading in my voice.

Now the man and his wife backed away from me, huddling close to the front desk. Walking back out the glass front doors and down the sidewalk in front of the motel, I stopped to reassess the situation. Unknown to me, my bizarre behavior had alarmed them enough that the front desk clerk immediately called the police. Equally likely was that someone from the highway had called to report my behavior there, because less than a minute after exiting the motel five or six police officers materialized out of nowhere. In a flash they wrestled me to the ground and into straitjacket. After a short stay in the Emergency Room of the local hospital I was whisked away in an ambulance for what seemed like a very long ride to the regional mental facility. Before long I was in the proverbial padded room, and two burly guys arrived with a hypodermic needle with my name on it. Normally not afraid of needles, in my paranoid state I tried to get away from them. Notwithstanding my great physical strength and talent for wrestling, they were expert in their trade, and with surprising ease the two of them quickly subdued me and gave me the injection.

It must have been mighty strong stuff, because the next thing I knew, my eyes opened to the scene of a beautiful bright blue sky with a few lovely white clouds floating in the frame of a window. At first, I couldn't remember where I was or how I got there. Then the events of the previous night came back to me with the realization that I had been on a fantastic psychotic trip, and that it was over. Although I am far from being a proponent of psychotropic drugs, I must admit that if nothing else, the injection they gave me the night before enabled me to sleep long enough for my raging brain chemistry to settle down. Only at the hospital for a few days, my stay was unremarkable except for one interesting episode. A pretty young woman, a patient whom I had befriended when talking one afternoon, left the room and after a few minutes came back with something in her hand. With a sparkle in her eye and a somewhat mischievous smile on her beautiful face she said,

"It's a very special ring ... and you're supposed to have it."

She opened her hand to reveal what looked like a very old ring in the shape of a dragon biting its tail. I am not a jewelry person, and except for my wedding ring I've rarely worn jewelry in my life. In spite of the beauty of this attractive young lady and her gentle persuasion I could not be convinced to put it on though.

"It's a great honor." she said, "It's very important that you put it on and always wear it from now on."

No way was I going to do that. As I had learned relative to martial arts and other teachings, the dragon (satan) possessed the ability to endow a person with supernatural abilities and was to be worshipped. I sensed that whoever it was that wanted me to wear that ring (a person or demon who had put her up to this) did not have my best interests in mind. To put it on would have been like accepting a signet ring from a king …. it would make me a prince in his kingdom but at the same time a vassal, and would shackle me to the "dragon" putting myself under his authority and his power.

The devil knows my weaknesses, and denying the beautiful young lady was difficult for me—I even offered to take the ring from her but not wear it, but that wasn't in the plan and so she left in a huff. Having just come down from a psychotic episode, I thought about what had just happened—it seemed much more real than the fantasy world I'd been in the day before. Whether my speculation regarding the ramifications of the wearing the ring were correct or not, in the last few days I'd had some uncomfortably close encounters with death *and* the enemy of our souls.

# CHAPTER 29

Not enough can be said of the tremendous patience and love with which my dear family dealt with me during those terrible years. If a person has cancer or diabetes or some other dreadful malady people feel sorry for them, but when they are an alcoholic or addict eventually if not immediately, everybody, even those who love them the most are repulsed and flee. My dad and mom blessed me in countless ways during that time and did their best to endure, yet often had to shut me out of their lives just to maintain their sanity. Two though, my dear sister Pam and my beloved Aunt Cornelia, would always take a phone call from me ... I will never forget how much their kindness meant during those darkest days of my life!

An illustration of the great capacity for kindness of my precious sister Pam and her husband Duncan happened when I showed up at their door in Westwood, a wealthy enclave near Beverly Hills and Hollywood, California. They lived in a high rise which was populated by luminaries and others who could afford the rent in that chic neighborhood. After a particularly rough desert crossing from Texas I was dirty, dusty and sunburned, so much that my nose was cracked and bleeding. When I announced myself, the doorman said that they were out for the evening. Having nowhere else to go I waited. Hearkening back to my first visit there, I speculated as to what kind of reception I'd get when they showed up. A year or two before when they'd been kind enough to put me up for a few days, things went well until they both needed to travel on business. In short order I began to take advantage of their generous bar, and by the time they returned the other residents of the exclusive building where ready to vote them out because of my shenanigans. When Pam and Duncan finally showed up that night dressed in formal attire, the look on her face said it all. She asked Duncan to go upstairs then read me the riot act which continued as we entered the elevator to ascend to their apartment. I've never seen her so mad and thought that she may kill me! But ... true to her nature, she allowed me to stay the night rather than turning me away. The next morning after she drove me to the freeway so I could hitchhike north to Salem Christian Commune, she reached into her purse and handed me all of the cash she had, about seventy-three dollars. To me it was a fortune, but more importantly it was a sign of her deep love and tender, generous spirit!

# CHAPTER 30

When the brutal routine got to be too much, if I didn't go to Salem I'd head to a rescue mission, a drug or alcohol treatment program, a mental hospital or just down to the Interstate to find a fresh batch of people who didn't know me, and would attempt to get on my feet again. How I made the gradual shift from mental patient to addict/alcoholic is uncertain, but I ended up in the substance abuse program that used to exist at Terrell State Hospital in Terrell, Texas. The first time there I came to the conclusion that I was an alcoholic, but not a drug abuser. The second time I concluded that I was a drug addict, but not an alcoholic. On the second day of my third stay there, I decided to smoke pot right on the front porch of the place, and as you can imagine it was a short stay. For quite some time I bounced back and forth between Texas and the California coast with an occasional trip to other parts of the country. My usual destination on the west coast was Salem Christian Commune, but I had many and varied other roosts out there as well as favorite spots in other parts of the country.

At about twenty-three, I got wind of a program in Dallas called Palmer Drug Abuse Program (PDAP). It was geared towards teenagers and I was one of the older participants, but it was a good place for me to begin learning the utility of a "Twelve-Step

Program." As far as I know, most secular drug and alcohol recovery programs base themselves on some variation of the twelve steps, and PDAP was a variation which included the bright idea of using the natural tendency of young people to conform to the mores and manners of their peers to a positive effect. Using the group as a moral guide, yardstick and a big brother figure, and engendering a "one for all, all for one" philosophy (We'll either hang together or we'll all hang separately!) the PDAP Program was a tight knit community. Those who had some sobriety and clean time would pool their resources and rent apartments, then allow the newcomers to sleep on couches or the floor for free, supplying food as well until the newcomers were able to gain some clean and sober time and then establish themselves. The "sponsors" would also make sure we got to the community meetings every day. The meetings made me think of an Amway rally because of the rah, rah sessions which included singing and chanting slogans … it also resembled a high school pep rally a bit. Like other Twelve-Step groups they not only recognized significant accomplishments like thirty, sixty, and ninety days clean and sober but smaller ones too, and unlike other programs they did so at every meeting—a good idea considering the fragile egos of teenagers. Though grateful for their help, I was unable to stay with the program for long, as one day I stumbled across a party at the apartment complex pool (although it was the dead of winter). Wandering back to my benefactors apartment hours later, full of booze, pot and LSD, they noticed right away and asked me to leave.

"Here we go again!" I muttered to myself as I walked out, cursing my ongoing stupidity. Jumping the fence behind the complex, I slipped and slid down the steep, snow and ice covered embankment carrying all of my belongings in a matching set of designer luggage—two large black plastic garbage bags. Crossing LBJ Freeway quickly due to the relatively light traffic (back then you could still do that without getting run over) and climbing up the other side, I headed for one of my favorite way stations, Denny's Restaurant. Denny's and other 24 hour coffee shops across the country were lifesavers for me often as they gave me a place to regroup, get warm, drink a little coffee and sometimes get a bite to eat. Many an otherwise long night I passed sitting at the counter, nursing one cup of coffee after another until the sun dawned on a new day. The kind waitresses usually surmised my plight and kept my cup full without asking any questions. Once in a great while one of those sympathetic ladies or their managers would buy me a plate of food.

This night would be different though. Panhandling fifty cents for a cup of coffee from a patron who was leaving the place, I stashed my bags behind the cigarette machine in the foyer and stepped in. Unlike the sleepy atmosphere I often encountered, it must have been Friday or Saturday because Denny's was packed that night. All the tables seemed to be full and every seat at the counter except one was occupied. Slipping into the last open seat and hoping no one would pay any attention to me, after settling in I noticed that the guy next to me was reading a Bible. "Interesting." I thought. He was an odd looking duck, with thick glasses, bushy red hair and a long bushy red beard to match. We struck up a conversation and before long we were chatting away like a couple of magpies. Mack and I probably talked for a couple of hours and I knew that the Lord had sent him my way. Not only to did he offer to let me stay with him for a few days but said that he thought his friend Biff would take me in after that. After some more coffee and talk, true to his word we headed to his place. He said that Biff would be at a Wednesday night Bible Study he usually attended and promised to call him ahead of time and apprise him of my circumstances. On Wednesday night we drove to the Bible Study and it was great! We ate good food, enjoyed good company, had a great time singing praise songs to Jesus and were then taught from God's Word. At the end when everyone was beginning to file out, I remembered my need and turned to Mack, "How about Biff? Are you going to introduce me to him?"

Just then Biff stepped into the door way and Mack said, "Hey Biff, this is the guy I told you about. He needs a place to stay."

"Oh sure!" Biff said with a big smile and stuck out his hand.

I took his hand and introduced myself and asked, "Would it be okay if I stayed with you for a while until I get on my feet?"

"Yes, sure! But no drugs or alcohol."

"No of course not!" I responded with all the sincerity I could muster.

Mack said he'd run me by Biff's house the next day, and everything was set. When he dropped me at the comfortable looking house in a nice neighborhood in the Lake Highlands section of Dallas, it seemed too good to be true. Like something out of a movie, Biff showed me to a large room on the second floor with its own bathroom. It was the most luxurious place I stayed in years! He was an easygoing, likeable sort and it seemed as if this would be a great chance to get started again down the right path. He too had struggled mightily with booze but the Lord had set him free, and he now attended a Twelve-Step Group which he briefly told me some about. The Lord got me a good job right away and I was excited about my prospects. One evening, Biff offered to give me a lift somewhere and our route took us by the place where he attended the Twelve Step Group meetings which helped him stay sober. He pointed it out and told me that an older guy named Buck took care of the place and was there often, especially in the mornings. Biff said I would be welcome there anytime. I thanked him, but shrugged it off at the time unconvinced there was any value in it.

The "good" job may have been good from a pay and work standpoint, but it was only one of two jobs that I ever worked where drinking on the job was acceptable. The idea was just too novel for me and I felt compelled to participate in a big way. The other guys were no doubt used to knocking down a few beers during lunch and going back to work … I was used to knocking down quite a few beers and NOT going back to work, so when they finally coaxed me out of the truck, I wasn't much good for anything and the job ended rather abruptly. A few days later while preparing to go to a rock concert, Biff questioned me about the wisdom of doing that. Though I'm sure he was suspicious that I was off the wagon again, it was only after I returned from the concert coked to the gills that he gave me my walking papers. In the middle of the run though, just before I had to move out, I had a revelation. While heading back to the apartment complex where the PDAP people lived (since that was my last known source of drugs) as I crossed a parking lot and headed toward the north bound lane of the main street to begin hitchhiking, I felt like a piece of seaweed going out with the tide. Not a nice clean sun-bleached piece of driftwood, but a dark green, dead, slimy piece of seaweed—lifeless and worthless and going where I didn't really want to go—but going anyway. Just then I looked up and saw the building where Biff said the Twelve Step group met. Remembering how he spoke about it in a cheerful light, I stopped for a moment and thought,

"I'm completely beyond hope. I don't know what good this or anything else will do, but what the heck."

290

Like a sleepwalker I drifted across the street, climbed up the stairs ... and began a new chapter in my life.

The Buena Vida Group was a tremendous collection of folks from many different walks of life. Each one seemed larger than life. They appeared so to me I suppose because God had sent me there manning the place with just the type of folks I could respect and learn from. Although I had quite a bit of experience with group therapy in a clinical setting, I had never encountered the raw honesty of a closed Twelve Step discussion meeting. The setting was very refreshing and stimulating, and a good catalyst for the changes that needed to take place in me. Buck, the caretaker of the place came in every morning, opened up, made a pot of coffee and cleaned up. He was a retired guy with a very kind smile and welcoming spirit, and was as regular as clockwork ... something I really needed in my life at that time. Another thing I needed was to be unconditionally accepted. Neil Leary was to test the patience of these good people to the maximum in the next three years, but there was a core group that never gave up on me, including Biff. Though they may have shaken their heads many times and expressed unbelief at my unique and unrelenting stupidity, they stuck with me and kept telling me to "keep coming back."

For three years, I walked through the doors of that place almost every day. Truly determined to stay sober, it occurred to me right away that I couldn't buy booze or drugs there, so every day after work and all day long every weekend there I sat. *Almost* every day and every weekend, because for three long years, I could never racked up more than two to four to six weeks sober and clean time in a row. Somehow, some way that old serpent the devil would trick me in to thinking, with an excited glint in my eye, "It's time to party!" Time and again, I dragged myself back through the doors of the Buena Vida Group ashamed and beaten, but with the dogged determination of a man who had taken his last stand. Because I had been told by more than one mental health professional that I was a certified nut (one lettered lady said that I was a "psychiatrist's dream") I often doubted that the a Twelve Step program or anything else could set me straight. Since lying was a way of life for me, I also feared that I had gotten myself so knotted up in dishonesty that I might not be able to dig my way out. A book used as the basis for one of the Twelve Step programs talks about people who are "constitutionally incapable of being honest with themselves." Oftentimes it seemed that between my diagnosed mental problems, the damage that massive quantities of alcohol, LSD and other drugs had done to my brain, and the web of deceit I'd been spinning for years, that I was probably beyond help.

New hope dawned though after about a year of attending meetings there religiously. The main speaker at the meeting one night looked like a reject from the old TV show "Hee Haw." He was a rolly polly guy with a big smile on his face, denim bib overalls and a red and white checked shirt—the only thing missing was a straw hat. For 45 minutes I sat glued to my chair as he told the story of his weird and incredible life as an alcoholic. The stories of every other speaker I'd heard until then, no matter how far their substance abuse had taken them, paled in comparison to the wild life that I had led. This guy was different. When drinking and using he was a NUT with a capital N, and there he stood before us," … clothed and in his right mind" (Luke 8:35).

"If he was able to get better," I thought, "there may be hope for me too!"

From that point on I was filled with new resolve … there just may be light at the end of the tunnel! In spite of slipping off the wagon *so* many times, by the mercy of God I wasn't killed and didn't overdose or die from other related causes. I just kept coming back ... besides going back to the commune where else could I go?

Though satan and his minions are never far from us, I believe that one of their most dangerous characteristics is their ability to remain unnoticed as they go about their devious work. The opportunity to see them in action or at least recognize that they are at work in a situation has been rare for me except in hindsight, when regrettably the damage was already done. Such was not the case shortly after my 25 birthday. Since I'd started attending the Buena Vida Group, more often than not living on the streets was behind me. Working more regularly in those days, I had recently rented a nice room from a lovely older couple in northeast Dallas and had just purchased my first car, a relatively good looking but falling apart mechanically 1970s sedan which required that I feed it a quart of oil every few days.

Outwardly things had been going fairly well, but the chains of drugs and booze still held tight, so it was just a matter of time before disaster struck. Once I began partying, my style of drinking was never that of a maintenance drinker (all day long every day, always slightly drunk) rather my routine was to get very high or drunk for as long as possible, then sooner or later I'd either end up in jail for a spell or simply have to go to sleep for a few days before resuming the party. Because of that, although experiencing horrendous hangovers on occasion, I never drank long enough to be physically addicted and so had yet to experience delirium tremens, the sometimes fatal effects of withdrawal from alcohol.

One night shortly after my birthday though, my young and otherwise healthy body was getting tired of the abuse. After drinking only two or three days I went to bed in my comfortably furnished bedroom in a state of extreme agitation. My whole body seemed like a tightly coiled spring. As my heart raced in my chest, I tossed and turned trying to relax and fall asleep which was usually took very little time, especially after a days-long drinking bout. Vibrating from head to toe as if I'd had too much caffeine or methamphetamine, I became quite concerned about this state which I neither understood nor had experienced before. I prayed that the Lord would help me fall asleep, hoping to wake up better. Eventually I did.

What happened before that though was terrifying. Dreaming, yet feeling as if my experience was as true as any waking moment, I "awoke" to find myself lying flat on my back, completely paralyzed. Diabolical laughter came to my ears, and although able to open my eyes, I was unable to move another muscle as many gargoyle-like creatures pawed at my body, grabbing a hold to take me somewhere.

Cackling, one of them said, "We've got him now!"

Without having any frame of reference, somehow I knew that they were demons, that I had died, and they were attempting to take me to Hell! The feeling of their fiendish hands on my body made me want to jump out of my skin, yet I couldn't move an inch. Sensing movement as their efforts to take me were slowly having an effect, terrified I called out to God, begging Him to help me.

Within a few moments, a light skinned being with long, very dark hair (I only caught a glance of his or her face) seemed to fly to me, snatching me out of their grasp and away to safety. "An angel!" I thought. My joy and relief were short lived though, since moments later I was back in the clutches of the demons being dragged away. It suddenly occurred to me that I was asleep and that I needed to wake up which would allow me to escape. Fighting my way to consciousness (or so I thought) as I looked around at my room, I saw all of the furniture in its normal place and the door and the window where they should have been, but something was just not right. The whole scene had a strange, sepia look to it like an old photograph. Dread shot through me as it occurred to me that I was being deceived into thinking that I had woken up so that I would relax and fall back asleep (or into unconsciousness as was probably the case) and back into the grip of the demons! Shaken by this realization I fought violently to awaken, and sure enough, I then actually opened my eyes and saw the room in reality. Sitting up in a cold sweat and swinging my feet to the floor to ensure that I wouldn't again enter into that nightmarish battle, I knew that the intense stress of marathon drinking and the subsequent withdrawals had caused my heart to stop, and that what I had experienced that night was literal redemption from the hordes of hell.

# CHAPTER 31

Since becoming born again I was drawn to church, God's operating arm on this earth. However, during each tentative visit, I felt like Jack the Ripper at a Sunday School picnic. Slithering in under the front door, and slithering back out after the service was over, a low life such as me just didn't fit in with the "nice" church folks or so the devil told me. Back in the early 1980s church parking lots where I lived were mostly full of shiny new cars, and all the men wore suits and the ladies dresses, their Sunday best. My Sunday best was what I wore the other six days of the week ... blue jeans, combat boots and a one pocket tee shirt with a pack of Kool Filter King cigarettes in the pocket (if I had money that day). The small talk at church would go something like this:

"Hello, I'm Bob! Are you new here?" And "What do you do for a living?" And "Where do you live?"

To which I would have to answer, "Yes." and ..."I'm looking for work." And "I just got out of jail and live in a halfway house, how about you?"

My honest responses just wouldn't fit in with the patter, and my plans when going to church certainly didn't include lying about anything. If it wasn't my low self-esteem or fear of someone finding out about my past that the enemy took advantage of, he would swing me all the way in the other direction and delude me into thinking I was *better* than them! Reminding me that the people back at Salem Christian Commune had given everything, their whole lives for the sake of Christ, he'd suggest that these folks were merely Sunday and perhaps Wednesday Christians at best and were just playing church. One visit in particular galvanized my view at the time that the most churches were populated with barely committed people. As the service unfolded the scene seemed like a sardonic parody from television: we sang a hymn or two with the accompaniment a fifty-person choir bedecked in robes, a soloist sang a song or two, one of the ministers got up and made a whole bunch of social announcements, along with a lame joke or two, ("Is this place country club or what?" I thought.), then a duet sang a number ("Is this The Lawrence Welk Show or what?"). The minister then began his sermon with a joke or two, with jokes interspersed throughout the rest of it—the world was going to hell around us and he thought it was comedy hour! Please understand that I do not mean to denigrate a particular style of church or worship service, but coming from my background this was fantastic! Compared to the solemn liturgical services of my childhood and then the old fashion Pentecostal meetings at Salem Christian Commune, lasting two or three hours every night and filled with very impassioned pleas for mercy, holiness and grace, this service seemed like a "B" movie meant to be a mockery of true Christianity. It's likely that there were a bunch of people there who really loved Jesus, but the cultural differences colored by the jaundiced twist which the devil was putting on the whole thing, combined to do the job of keeping me away. During the first nine years after being born again, each time I set foot in a church, different versions of this scene unfolded, and aside from my somewhat brief stays at Salem it was just me and

Jesus.

In absence of that positive influence and convinced that the Twelve-Step meetings were a path towards a new life, I attended steadfastly, hanging on like a pit bull dog. As might be expected, my endless months of stumbling along were wearing out my welcome with the Buena Vida Group. Given the aim of the program and the broadly negative background of most of the attendees, it wouldn't seem likely that many people are thrown out of Twelve Step groups, but I was one of the few people that almost made the list. The meeting place was actually a private club consisting of recovering alcoholics which rented the hall where the Buena Vida Group Twelve Step meetings took place. One night the club members had a group conscious meeting to determine whether or not they should ban me from the facility. The premise for the sake of civility was that I was not getting better and that somewhere else (anywhere else!) would be better for me. By God's grace enough of the participants present at the meeting voted in favor of letting me stay. Eventually though, the bad blood I had engendered there made it fairly uncomfortable, and the next time I fell off the wagon I hitchhiked to Shreveport, Louisiana.

While at a halfway house in Longview, Texas a year before, I'd heard that Shreveport had one of the oldest and best alcohol treatment programs in the country, and as things looked, I probably needed the very best help that was available. From what I learned during the intake interview, it seemed to be a very well thought out program. Most of the substance abuse programs which I was aware of in those days were meant to be specifically focused on alcoholism, but most drunks of my generation also used drugs regularly too, and we dual addicts understood the need to de-emphasize the drug aspect if we hoped to be admitted to many of the established rehabilitation programs. Considering my history of drug abuse and psychiatric treatment they almost didn't accept me, but soon I was settled in one of two nice residential homes that they had purchased in the countryside miles from downtown. There was a house for men and one for women, and most of us were in our twenties. The setting was rustic and restful and the program was the best secular program I was ever in. During our free time I read my Gideons Pocket New Testament which was always with me in those days. Things went well for a few weeks and I felt on pretty solid ground. Evidently this sentiment was not shared by all. In our group discussion meeting one day, one of the leaders encouraged everyone to call out, "Be real Neil!" whenever they thought I was not being completely honest or transparent. This became a fun distraction for them it seems, because it soon happened almost every time I opened my mouth, and it began to wear on me. To this day I think the whole thing was off base ... although often wordy, as part of my solid determination to change, I was completely committed to being ruthlessly honest with myself and others. Remembering the warning from the Twelve Step book that there are those who seem to be " ... constitutionally incapable of being honest with themselves" and they may not make it, I worked very hard to make a complete change and be honest at all times. Just as the best map in the world can only help a person find their way if they know where they are on that map, a person trying to find their way in life can only do so if they know the truth about who and where they are now ... we must know our starting point. We must start with reality, know our goal and then follow the path which will take us to our goal. Without complete honesty, our starting point is an unknown and hence a reliable path to the desired destination cannot be charted and followed.

Doing my very best to conform to their wishes and to participate enthusiastically in all the activities there (my goal was for this to be my last trip to a treatment center) I did everything in my power to cooperate, and prayed regularly for success and for the ability to conform to the program. It was not meant to be. The head residential counselor in the men's house and I had a personality conflict. We'd never had any serious confrontations though, so I was shocked when they called me into the office one day and said that they were throwing me out of the program.

"You've got to be kidding me!" I said. "What did I do!" A bad attitude was their response. They were about to drive into town and asked where I would like to be dropped off. I was flabbergasted. After forty-five days clean and sober, the longest I'd ever had (voluntarily) since I was twelve years old, and they were throwing me out on to the street! Quickly, I packed my trusty Army duffle bag and steamed quietly as my nemesis drove me to Interstate 20 in Shreveport. Fortunately it was a long drive, and after praying I was able to reciprocate when he kindly wished me the best as I climbed out of the van. Before walking over to shoulder of the highway to stick out my thumb, I stopped to pray and ask the Lord how I'd let Him down and what He now had in store for me.

"Do you want me to stay in Shreveport Lord, or go back to Dallas?" I asked.

After praying some more to seek His guidance and trying to hitchhike west for a while, I noticed that it was getting close to sunset. Since it was very unlikely to get picked up after dark, I prayed,

"Lord, if I don't get a ride towards Dallas by sunset, I'll assume that You want me to stay here," and I left it in His hands.

Within minutes of praying, an almost new, bronze colored

Lincoln Continental pulled over and let me in. It was a man and his wife and child and they were going all the way to Dallas! As the sedan sped through the countryside, although I was still unsure what God had planned for me with this abrupt and seemingly odd change of course, I thanked Him that I'd be back in familiar territory before too long. The man was an amiable chap and a good conversationalist, yet in response to my question regarding his livelihood, he told me that he was involved in an operation which regularly flew cocaine into an airport in Dallas. That it was being done was no big news, but I wondered at his nonchalance about it and why he told me. After listening a while longer, he seemed to be mentally stable so I kept riding, and ended up sharing Jesus with him and his family. Then something happened that was indelible proof to me, not only that the Lord had indeed heard my prayer and had directed me to Dallas, but that in spite of what I may or may not have done wrong at the program in Shreveport, on that night I was right where God wanted me to be.

The gentlemen's travel plans "coincidentally" took him right through the part of Dallas where I had recently been living, and after bidding him thanks and farewell, I hefted my duffle bag onto my shoulder and walked down the off ramp. Once again, a Denny's Restaurant would be my pivot point—this one sat next to LBJ Freeway in Garland near the border of Dallas. As I crossed the road and began to traverse the parking lot towards the restaurant, crossing at a complementary angle to mine was Skeeter! Skeeter was transformed from the last time I had seen him. He had been the manager of a low bottom halfway house where I had lived in the bad part of East Dallas when our paths had first crossed. He had dressed like a biker then, covered with leather and festooned with chains. He was pretty stoic and tight lipped then, and carried himself with an air of cool indifference. This night he was dressed as if getting ready for a high school yearbook photo in the early 1970s—slacks, loafers and a blazer all neatly in place. Instead of the aloof, self-confidant attitude he had before, he seemed scared and jumpy, his eyes darting back and forth glancing around as he walked through the parking lot with his elderly parents. "Skeeter!" I called out. Giving me a blank stare at first, a slight smile of recognition crossed his face, and after introducing me to his parents, we talked as we walked. After entering the Denny's, he told his parents that he'd join them in a minute and asked if we could sit down at the counter and talk. The Lord immediately made an opening for me to share the gospel with him, and though we only had a few minutes, I knew that the Holy Spirit had arranged our meeting. The Lord gave me powerful, poignant words for him and I could see they were striking home. When Skeeter and I parted, he was well on his way to a new life in Jesus Christ!

Overwhelmed with joy as I stepped out into the warm evening air, a revelation hit me like a bright light: in spite of my all too regular fallibility, my Holy God loved me and had purposed to use *me* to share His glorious Good News with Skeeter. By getting thrown out of the program on that day and arriving at the Denny's parking lot at precisely the moment when my path would intersect Skeeter's, God demonstrated His love for him *and* me! Though without meaning to, my behavior may have contributed to me being jettisoned from the program, yet at that moment I was right exactly in the center of God's perfect will for me! Once again, the Lord had proven that He truly cares for me and all of us even in the smallest details. His expert orchestration of the events of that day not only reinforced the truth of His marvelous love for us, but of His awesome power and complete sovereignty … His ability to put us both exactly where we needed to be at exactly the right time, for His glory and our own good!

Another example of how the Lord stepped into my life at the exact moment I needed Him was when I had once again dragged myself back to the Buena Vida Group after a fall. It was a particularly hard fall and I'd gone there to rustle up enough money for a good meal as I hadn't had anything to eat for a long time. It was toward the sad end of my time there and it was becoming difficult to find a sympathetic ear, so I was glad when Joe walked in. Joe supposedly had been in the Mafia, and although everyone in the program remains anonymous to a greater or lesser degree, the word was that he went by an alias since he still had some baggage from the past to clean up. It was difficult to believe that Joe had run with that crowd though, as he was a gentle man with a warm, genuine and engaging personality. Sensitive to the others, I asked Joe to come outside with me so that we could talk privately. After descending the long staircase from the second floor, we stepped into the alley next to the building.

"Well Joe, I blew it again. I haven't had anything to eat in a long time and was hoping that you might be able to loan me five dollars to buy lunch." I said.

Joe sighed and shrugged, "I wish I could Neil, but I'm flat broke! But don't worry, God will take care of you."

"You know, you're right Joe, He will. He's never let me down yet." I admitted.

Just then, I happened to look down. Between the two of us at our feet was a puddle of water. Lying right in the middle of the puddle was a five dollar bill! In the early 1980s in America, that was enough for a nice large meal, one big enough to fill me up and exactly what I was hoping to borrow! Joe and I rejoiced in the

Lord's goodness. A small miracle? Yes, but just the miracle I needed and exactly when I needed it! How great is His love for us! By the way, for many years I had bad posture and regularly had my head down, and though I'd found hundreds of pennies and a number of nickels, dimes and quarters on the ground, I've never found more than coins before or since!

# CHAPTER 32

Twelve-step recovery programs were my life blood for about six years. But one often life endangering crisis still followed on the heels of another, because when I drank and used, all caution and reason went immediately to the wind. For example, down the street from the where I lived for a while (during a short-lived break from the streets) was a bar that played great classic Rock and Roll and even had live bands of Fridays and Saturdays. The fact that it was in a terrible part of town and that a notorious motorcycle gang hung out there didn't deter me for a moment, nor did it keep me from bellying up to the bar and loudly and obnoxiously introducing myself to all the gang members. Addressing them as if they were old friends and regularly insulting and cursing them as part of my endearing schtick ("Yuck, yuck, just kidding old pal!") as usual common sense abandoned had me. Generally, these guys were the type that would kill their mothers if the price was right, and here I was playing with them! Years later while eating with a friend who knew that part of town very well, I learned that people were murdered in that bar on a regular basis before they finally closed it down! Another time I walked down Martin Luther King Boulevard in Dallas at three in the morning looking for drugs ... with no money. This was a very dangerous part of town and I was the only white guy within a couple of miles—it was like playing Russian roulette!

Illustrating the great lengths to which Jesus went to keep me alive long enough to tell this story, was something I learned when I returned to the Buena Vida Group years later after living in California. There for "Birthday Night" to celebrate the third anniversary of my sobriety date, after the meeting in the cheerful socializing which followed, an old friend greeted me. With wonder in his voice Bernie said, "I remember one time when I gave you a ride to a house over on Northwest Highway. When you walked up the sidewalk towards the house, they started shooting at you ... and you knocked on the door anyway!"

"Ha!" I replied, "They were probably my friends and were just trying to scare me!"

The fact that I walked up to the house and knocked on the door through a hail of gunfire clearly shows that, however sane I may have been while sober and clean, I was completely crazy while under the influence! Though I rarely passed out during eighteen years of extremely heavy drinking, a blackout was not too uncommon. Up to that moment I'd never heard that story before in my life, but knowing the guy pretty well I have no doubt that it was true. Considering my many other experiences with both the good guys and the bad guys wanting me to go away, the amazing truth of the matter was that the folks inside of that house were probably aiming to kill me, and the Lord, having a different plan for my life, kept the bullets from their purpose.

Given the many examples of my incredibly risky behavior, and combined with the wisdom I was hearing in the Twelve step meetings and other workings of the Holy Spirit, one night I came to another key turning point in my life. It was my first day "back" after my latest fall, and since this was the most recent in a long string of "slips" I was afraid and aching for a change. Walking home from the Buena Vida Group that night to the nice, clean, new efficiency apartment that God had blessed me with, I was full of self-loathing and felt quite unsettled as well. It occurred to me that now more than ever, I needed to take stock and do whatever was necessary to change.

"Neil" I said to myself, "You're as healthy as a horse and as strong as a bull, but the way you act when you drink or get high, one more drink or one more drug could be your last. You could easily get your head shot off!"

As I walked, I reasoned, "What is the answer? Who has the answer?"

Then, "I know that God has the answer."

Then, "Well, what are you going to do about it?"

"I'd better get to know Him!"

That night, I resolved to put into practice something I'd learned at Twelve Step meetings—to pray every morning asking God to help me to stay sober and clean that day. Since Christ is the center of my life, I also resolved to ask Him to help me to be the man of God that He called me to be each day as well. Every night I would thank Him for the day, no matter how bad it may have been—after all, it could have been worse—I could be dead!

"So, what else are you going to do Neil?" I asked myself pressing the point. My life hung in the balance!

Every night before bed I determined to read a chapter of the New Testament NO MATTER WHAT! My determination was rock solid and I knew that it had come from the Lord Himself. After entering my apartment, I got down on my knees to talk to God. Something new *had* begun. With a new confidence I thanked Him and read my New Testament before going to sleep. By His grace, I have rarely missed that regime since I made that promise to myself over 33thirty-three years ago.

The results were indisputable: my three-year pattern of slipping off the wagon every two to four to 6 weeks was broken! Although I didn't start attending church for a number of years, nor was I doing much else differently, simply by putting forth this small effort, I only stumbled back into drugs and booze five times during next three years.

One of the greatest ploys of the enemy is to puff us up with pride—to trick us into thinking of ourselves more highly than we ought to. "Pride goes before destruction, and arrogance before failure." (Proverbs 16:18 Complete Jewish Bible). Pride, the sin of satan, Adam and Eve, the Pharisees and countless men and women throughout the ages, seems to be the easiest trap for us frail and helpless human beings to fall into. After all, who wants to feel frail and helpless? The latest twist which has appealed to us recently is the doctrine of humanism which places people at the pinnacle of the universe rather than God. If satan can flatter and cajole us into thinking we are something when we are nothing, he can rob from us the innate knowledge which is inside all of us, that without God we are fatally flawed ... that we need God to redeem us. The lie which he has told over and over again since his first success in the Garden of Eden is that, "If you will only do this (fill in the blank) you will be like God!" Or, as one very famous false preacher stated once, "I'm not saying that you are like God, I'm saying you ARE God!" The recording of him spewing those venomous words sent shivers down my spine when I heard it. In his very intonation and the hellish guttural sound of his voice, the brutish, raw evil of the enemy was grotesquely manifest. The fact that this preacher and others like him have had very successful sway over thousands of people who profess to be evangelical Christians (and have collected many millions of dollars from them along the way) is a testimony not only to the cleverness and evil genius of the arch enemy of our souls, but also to our great weakness in this area as demonstrated by the power that his appeals have to us. "Pride goes before destruction, and arrogance before failure." How quick we are to believe flattery or any type of lie that would tell us how great we are!

In post-World War II America, before the school textbooks were changed to belittle our once great country and to teach young kids what bad folks we Americans are ... before they began brainwashing our children to prepare them to forsake any pride in our nation or our national heritage (so that they will submit to a one world government one da), we were actually taught that America was a powerful, kind and generous nation ... a friend to the world! Those were very special times that will likely never return. Some of that breast beating though, helped fuel the self-pride trip that the devil wants to put us on. In my generation we were taught to venerate our forefathers who braved the elements and all of the other dangers of the new, raw unsettled continent which they met and conquered, and who pushed on to success no matter what. "Rugged Individualism" was the mantra! The pioneer, the trailblazer, the mountain man! These were the characters that set a child's heart to beating fast and set the imagination soaring. The heroic soldiers, the explorers, the mighty men and women of the earlier days of our country who grimly set their jaws at peril, disdained the doubts or the warnings of lesser, more feeble folk to turn back, and courageously faced danger or any other obstacles and simply forged ahead in spite of anything, were held up high. It could be summed up as the "John Wayne" philosophy. A very famous song from my childhood came to a crescendo with the phrase, "I did it all, and I stood tall, and did it my way!" It was a compliment in those days (and probably in too many circles today) to say, "He is his own man." and "He is the captain of his own ship." Big boys don't cry …. take it like a man … anything that conveyed a bold (cold?) indifference to suffering or pain, either physical or emotional, was considered by many to the real hallmark of a true man.

Taking all that in to consideration, it understandable that I and many of my contemporaries grew up striving for that cool, distant, independent "Lone Ranger" persona. Our minds were fed regularly to cultivate that image, not only to the observing world, but within ourselves as well … after all, if we didn't believe it, who would? Being acutely aware of our numerous faults and fears, many like me pushed ourselves harder and harder, becoming harder and harder in the process as we angrily chastised ourselves for our weaknesses and failures. To help along the process of becoming self-reliant and an island unto ourselves, the wounds and trials that were inflicted on us by other people and difficult events and circumstances scarred us, putting the finishing touches on the hardening transformation. The resulting person (apart from the redeeming influence of God) was a mess! The most serious consequence of this indoctrination is that it prepared us to be diametrically opposed to the truth: the Bible teaches that self-run lives produce only one set of results, all bad.

Praise God though, that what the world, the devil and we ourselves have inflicted upon ourselves, Jesus will lovingly correct for all who come to Him. "I will praise You, for You have answered me, and have become my salvation. The stone which the builders rejected (Jesus) has become the chief cornerstone. This was the Lord's doing; It is marvelous in our eyes." (Psalm 118:21-23) and

" ... and whoever falls on this stone will be broken ... " (Matthew 21:44a). He is faithful to His word and will break us, then remake, refine and remold us into the people we should and want to be, as He promised.

Some of the lessons about who I really was (rather than the false image that I had learned) were very hard. Very late one night while walking hurriedly toward wherever I would sleep that night, my solitary trek was interrupted when I heard a crackling sound ahead and off to my right. As I turned to look, the flames leaping from the corner of the roof of a house caused me to freeze in my path. Smoke was billowing up churning and boiling as it intermixed with tongues of fire. It took a moment or two for me to realize what I was seeing. Many times in front of our cozy fireplace in Pleasantville I sat gazing as the flames danced along the logs, snapping and jumping at their work. A number of campfires and bonfires had shared their magic with me, and never burned so long that I did not wish them to burn longer. But this was out of place ... I was in the middle of a city teaming with hundreds of thousands of people. In the dead of this dark night without another soul stirring nearby as far as I could tell, this house, somebody's home was burning furiously. I realized that in all likelihood the house was full of people, sound asleep, who were about to perish. All the Hardy Boys books, all the war books and movies I'd read or seen, every novel or real life story that I'd ever known about brave heroes did not move me from that spot.

"Surely", I thought to myself, "surely someone is aware of this and the fire department is on the way. Surely the people inside are awake and rushing to leave right now!"

I imagined myself running to the house, and with no regard for peril to my own life, searching from room to room making sure everyone was safely out. Yet for a few moments I was merely transfixed by the flames. It was so quiet that time of night that the loudness of the fire seemed surreal, and the sparks rocketing upwards so unlikely. Then I came to myself, and realized that I was probably the only one on the planet that knew about this—that I must take action or someone would die. Fear seized me … sick, ugly cowardice … and then shame as I realized that I was no hero at all. Turning my back on the tragedy, I continued on my journey. How I slept that night I don't know.

On another occasion while crossing town on foot on New Year's Eve, my journey took me through an exceptionally seamy and dangerous neighborhood. A staccato series of blood curdling screams suddenly split the air around me while walking past an apartment building at about midnight. Looking up, I saw what appeared to be a lookout standing at the entrance of the building, stationed there to warn the others if the police arrived. The screams—those of young woman or girls continued, and I surmised that they likely had been lured to a New Year's Eve party by these monsters, who at the stroke of midnight were raping them all. I kept walking.

"They are gang members, no doubt," I reasoned. "If I stop at the first phone I see and call the cops, someone will snitch me off to them. They'll come after me. I walk through this part of town all the time."

Instead of acting as the hero I had once imagined myself, I just kept walking as those animals had their way.

Very harsh lessons to learn the sad truth, that apart from Christ I am not a hero at all … and lessons that I'll never forget.

Mercifully, that is a class I did not need to repeat too many times. Twice I had come face to face with the fact that I was not brave or selfless or fearless or vastly different than the most timid weakling imaginable. Not a cut above the masses, not ubermensch, not my own man, not someone to be looked up to ... but without the love and empowerment of Jesus, just a small, weak, scared man. A popular myth today says that man is inherently good and simply by cultivating that good, the whole world will soon see how noble he or she can be. Formerly I had believed myself to be a bold, strong champion of justice, a man of pure ideals and a voice for the weak and disenfranchised. Indeed, in much less dangerous circumstances I had sometimes proven those characteristics out. When my life was on the line though, my nobility vanished like a mist in the bright sunlight. Many experiences since then have confirmed to me that any goodness I demonstrate does not find its genesis in my mortal self, but in the Lord who alone is the fountain of all goodness and holiness. Today I know that every good gift and every perfect gift comes down from the Father of Lights (James 1:17) and if I ever do anything worthy of being called a hero, it will be my Heavenly Father who empowered me to do it and who deserves all the glory! Thank God that He burst my bubble so completely. The revelation that " ... in me (that is in my flesh) dwells no good thing." (Romans 7:18) is a lesson which is quite bitter to learn and which unfortunately I've needed to repeat because of my inordinately resilient ego. Whenever I begin to be deluded into thinking that I am somebody, the many sad, humiliating experiences from my past serve to remind me of my true, unredeemed nature apart from Christ.

Another common lie of humanism is that, "I can do anything if I put my mind to it." An illustration of how hollow that statement is involves a nice young man who lived at the boarding house where I sometimes rented a room in East Dallas years ago. Pete was a slim guy, about five foot eight and at the most 120 pounds, more likely closer to 110. He was barely old enough to be out on his own, and we older guys took him under our wing, chatting with him during meals and allowing him to hang around with us as well. Once he made the incredible statement that if he wanted to, he could play football for the Dallas Cowboys. I am not so gentle at times, neither had the Lord had a hold of me for very long by then, so I turned and stated in an incredulous voice, "There is no WAY you'll ever play for the Cowboys! You might grow a little bit more, but even if you did and worked out day and night, you'll never be big enough to play pro football!"

"My dad said that I could do anything I put my mind to!" Pete protested.

Reasoning with Pete for several minutes, nothing could dissuade him from the belief that all it takes is enough will power and all mountains can be moved. I'm glad he had such faith in his dad, but if he ever did play for the Cowboys, it would be a miracle of God and not through the power of positive thinking, his dad's belief in him, or his own efforts.

# CHAPTER 33

After being kicked out of Salem Christian Commune several times by now, I stayed away for a while. Though it seemed more like home than almost anywhere else, returning once again to a place where my bad reputation preceded me was getting old. Some of the leaders and long term members had developed resentments against me which didn't make it easier. More than a year had passed since my last foray west, yet I felt called to go back. After writing a letter to the leaders there stating that although I was living in the "buckle of the Bible Belt" I felt that the Lord wanted me back at Salem, I received a terse reply saying essentially that if Texas was such a fine place I should probably stay there! A short time later I decided to go anyway feeling as if the Lord was leading me—and after all, though they had kicked me out several times already, the Pastor had overruled them each time and let me back in.

As usual I began my journey penniless, hungry and exhausted ... my standard operating procedure was to completely deplete myself and all my resources before turning over a new leaf. Hitchhiking westward, the trip of over 1600 miles found me more burned out than usual, and when I finally arrived at Salem it was raining torrentially. Soaked to the bone, the rain let up for a bit as I walked up to the main house. After the cold reception which I expected, I appealed to speak to Pastor Jacob but was told that he was away on business and that I could not stay. Feeling like a balloon with all the air let out, the rain began again in earnest as I walked back to the highway.

"Had I misunderstood the Lord?" I thought. "Should I return to Dallas?"

Having just come all the way from Texas on little sleep or food and dreading another 1500 mile trek the hard way, I stood beside the road with my thumb out musing over my prospects of getting a ride at night and was feeling as low as I had in a long time.

Almost immediately a small pickup truck pulled over and the driver let me in. To my relief, the guy had some very high grade marijuana which he shared with me. By the time he dropped me at the main north—south highway I felt quite a bit a better. I do not at all condone drug or alcohol usage but think that sometimes it may be heaven sent. Close to the point of despair, I needed something to lift me out of the mire. "Give strong drink unto him that is ready to perish, and wine to those that be heavy of hearts." (Prov. 31:6) Though not wine, the pot brought me back from deep despondency.

What happened next was truly amazing. From where the ride dropped me off I would have had to backtrack and cross an overpass to get to the southbound highway onramp, a distance of about 100 yards. Considering the weight of my luggage and the weariness of my body, instead of going the long way I took a shortcut across the highway. The road was below grade as it passed through town and there were steep embankments on either side of the highway covered with ice plants. The ice plant is a smooth spongy air plant which was planted as ground cover along the sides of many California highways—when you step on it, it squashes into a liquid. Descending the steep slope with a heavy suitcase in either hand and rapidly gaining momentum, there was no chance of getting a firm foothold on the slippery ice plants. Only as I approached the edge of highway with all my weight moving downhill at quite a clip, did I think to look for traffic. Terror shot through me as I had already taken a giant step into the air and was about to step directly in front of a speeding car! To my astonishment, it seemed as if a hand grabbed my foot propelling it, me and my luggage right back up onto the edge of the embankment! If someone had been watching it must have looked like a video being run in reverse. Dazed, I stood quite a while glued to the ground, drinking in what had just happened. According the laws of physics, the combined inertial force generated by me and the luggage should have carried me right into the path of the speeding car—even titanic strength would have required a fulcrum of some type to brace against in order to reverse my direction—the car should have mangled me beyond hope. As I stood there trembling and marveling, it occurred to me that I was now completely straight and stone cold sober just as instantly as I had been saved from death ... and that God or an angel doing His bidding must have saved my life!

After another minute or two of taking stock, I cautiously crossed the highway and realized that instead of going back to Texas, I should go to the Rescue Mission in Santa Barbara. The smartest bums in the world live in Santa Barbara, California which is undoubtedly one of the prettiest spots in America. Nestled against the foothills of the coastal mountains on the east, with the Pacific Ocean on the west, the landscape in the area is rich and green thanks to its climate, location and to years of careful grooming, making it home to some of the most favored people on the planet. Thanks to its God given beauty and its proximity to Los Angeles it is also home to some of the wealthiest people on earth (who pay for the landscaping). The local bums, now euphemistically called homeless or street people, are allowed to share this paradise with the beautiful people thanks to the egalitarian nature of our great country. In the 1970s and 80s when I was living on streets, if you hit someone up for some money (which the street people call panhandling and others call begging or something less kind) you were liable to net some change fished out of your benefactor's pocket. In Santa Barbara due to the relative affluence of its citizens you were liable to get a dollar bill, a bounty back in those days! State Street, one of the main streets in town, ran right through prime the downtown shopping district and ended amidst the high end hotels on the beach, and was prime panhandling territory. The objective of panhandling was to procure enough money for head candy (booze or drugs—not food) and go to the beach or some quiet tree shaded park and enjoy the day. In almost any direction there were plenty of establishments to buy the coveted wine, beer or liquor and an ample variety of drug dealers nearby as well.

Santa Barbara was also home to one of the best Christian Rescue Missions in the country. Mr. Pope who ran the mission was a kind gentle man with great compassion for the guy on the street. If a man wanted to change his life, the mission would afford an opportunity to do so. I say guy on the street, because in those days (and I suspect now as well) most homeless were men. Whatever brought a man to the streets, Mr. Pope, his wife, and his kind Christ-like brothers and sisters across America and around the world offer a helping hand to all, ministering lovingly. These precious men and women will not only go the extra mile, but joyfully help carry the load. The Santa Barbara Mission was very clean and well kept. The typical overnight residents were the local street people, and the drifters passing through town on the coast highway. In those days there were still quite a few hippies crisscrossing the country using their thumbs as transportation, and many of us gravitated to the pleasant climate of California. When I arrived at the mission this time, instead of just staying for a couple of nutritious meals, a shower and a good night's sleep, I asked to join the staff of the Mission. Joining the staff is a face saving term which describes going into their Christ centered rehabilitation program. Staff members cooked the food, washed the dishes, and cleaned the sheets, floors, toilets etc. There was also maintenance to do on the building and other odd jobs. Best of all were the daily Bible studies and nightly worship services. The Bible studies were just for the staff and were taught by Mr. Pope or local pastors and elders, and were held in the chapel after our morning work was finished. Although I was somewhat familiar with the Bible by now, I was hungry to learn more, and these times were pleasant and refreshing.

Every evening, when our "overnight guests" arrived we would join them in the chapel for a rousing song service, followed by preaching. Everyone was invited to call out one of their favorite hymns, and I'll never forget how I was touched by many of the beautiful old songs of worship. Grateful for the hospitality and blessings of the Santa Barbara Rescue Mission during my brief overnight stays in the past, my time on the staff holds a number of special memories for me, like the local businessman Cedric, whose giant, warm smile was a welcome addition to our Bible Study which he taught sometimes. One day while on a pass downtown I happened upon him at a local coffee shop where he was meeting with the local chapter of the Full Gospel Business Men's Fellowship. He made such an impression upon me that years later when directed to join a networking group by my new boss, I began attending, and since have been greatly blessed by my association with these godly men and women. In addition to getting to know and learn from Cedric, Mr. Pope and the other Bible teachers, a fine young man named Peter who did not have a troubled background joined the staff one day and brought some unique lessons with him. The Lord directed him to leave his well-paying job in Los Angeles and come join the mission staff with us bums, and he was a shining example of God's love to us. From the standpoint of the world the fellow was right where I wanted to be, yet he gave it up to come to the mission! What a fascinating thought ... he cared so much for the Lord that he was willing to obey Him even when he received orders that were unpleasant and contrary to common sense. Because of this I spent some time getting to know him and one day he shared a fascinating spiritual insight with me. One school of thought says that someone who belongs to Christ cannot be demon possessed since the Holy Spirit cones to live within each person who has surrendered to Jesus, because a demon spirit cannot co-exist in the same body with God's Spirit. Peter told me that one day the Lord opened his eyes to see into the heavenly realm, and he saw a small, grotesque creature hanging onto his flesh which the Spirit revealed was a demon. It was not in him, but no doubt fighting to retain influence over him. This I believe is how demonic strongholds work: each demon has a special assignment to drag us in to or keep us in servitude to some specific type of sin, and those strongholds can only be destroyed by God Himself. "For though we walk in the flesh, we do not war according to the flesh. For the weapons of our warfare are not carnal but mighty in God for pulling down strongholds" (2 Corinthians 10:3-4). Those days at the mission were a restful, refreshing break from my usual exhausting and danger filled life. My angst remained though, and satan used the chains that held me tightly to booze and drugs to drag me back into the abyss again. Burning with sin and shame, one night I gathered my meager belongings, climbed down the fire escape and headed back to the streets for another death defying dance with debauchery.

# CHAPTER 34

Dallas was often my destination of choice when traveling, because my Dad was there and the economy was always strong … jobs were easy to find. Another gracious Christian outreach, the Union Gospel Mission in Dallas, was usually my first stop. Mr. Sullivan who ran the mission was a bit more dry than Mr. Pope but also had a warm heart for the poor people he worked with from day to day. Since there was so much work to be had in Dallas back then, my stays there were usually rather short and geared towards using the place as a launching pad to get off the streets. Working day labor for a week or so while staying at the mission, as long as I didn't drink up all the profits (which I often did) I could save enough money to rent a room and once again try to get a toehold on normalcy. Occasionally there was not enough work to go around as there was always a big crowd of guys in the day labor places, and I learned that there were actually places that would buy blood from people! It's likely that most people are unaware of this and would be appalled to learn about it as I was at first, but the prospect of going a whole day with no money (or booze or drugs) compelled me to check into it anyway. The process is, they take a pint of blood from you, centrifuge it and extract the plasma, then return the other blood components to the donor. Pretty ghoulish it seemed, but I could not see wasting a whole day without doing anything, so off I went. Despite the solace of knowing that the plasma would be used to help sick folks, this was a new low for me. Along with the humiliation of being arrested for public intoxication on a regular basis and the concomitant jail time, and my regular stays at rescue missions, the bottom kept getting lower for me. The spark of life was in me now because I had the Lord, but even as young and vigorous as I was, the brutal routine of drinking, drugs abuse and as many cigarettes as I could get my hands on was hammering me into the ground.

One of the first times I managed to claw my way up and off the streets, I discovered Jack Johnson's Boarding House. Jack owned a few of houses in what at one time had been a rather nice East Dallas neighborhood, and rented them out on a weekly or monthly basis. The price was very reasonable and came with three meals a day as well, with bagged lunches for the working clientele. There were some pensioners there as well a smattering of other types, including young men like me who were trying to better themselves. Like me though, many of them were strung out and just a half of a step ahead of the cops, so it was not a very good place to "rehab." It was all too easy to find a drinking or drugging buddy, or drinks or drugs ... or one or both would find me. Like many urban neighborhoods, as it decayed physically it decayed morally as well, and the people who profit from moral decline were ready to meet all the needs of their cheerless customers ... and whet their appetites too. Even so it was a step up from the rescue mission, and the first time I sat down to dinner after work with the other guys who had just gotten off, the feeling of being a productive citizen was a welcome change. It was refreshingly different to put in a good day's work day in and day out, to pay rent regularly and come back to the same place each night to sleep.

More than once, negative people expressed their opinion to me that the reason I remained a slave to my habitual sin was that I didn't want to be free badly enough … that if I simply made up my mind, it would happen. Apart from my firm belief that salvation and victory over sin is by grace and grace alone, another reason why I disagree with that whole line of reasoning is based upon my personal experience fighting the battle. While at the boarding house one year I made a serious effort to get free. Having secured a job at a company which made doors for the burgeoning Dallas construction market, I made it for about three weeks clean and sober just praying, working hard, and taking one day at a time. The Rolling Stones were scheduled to play at the Cotton Bowl in a few weeks, and more than once I turned down offers to join some of the guys to see the concert—I knew that I'd end up smoking dope and the whole thing would be shot. It was a Friday which was our pay day each week, and on the way home I stopped at the 7-Eleven to buy a Snickers bar to reward myself for a hard week's work. Ask any addict or alcoholic … if you are really hard up, withdrawing physically or just mentally from booze or drugs, you'll never find the stuff. But try and stop and old "friends" or total strangers will come out of the woodwork to offer you your old medicine! Such was the case that day … in triplicate! While standing in line to pay for the innocuous candy bar, one of my drinking buddies from the boarding house appeared in the line behind me.

"Neil! How are you?" Francois exclaimed.

"Okay man, how are you?"

"Great!" he said, "We have a bunch of beer out in my dad's van in the parking lot. Why don't you join us!"

Mind you, this guy, his dad Pierre and our other friend who was

324

with them, regularly allowed me to buy the beer as they were often penniless. Now Francois was EXCITED to invite me to drink for free!

"No thanks guy, I appreciate it but not today!" I said, kindly but firmly.

The line to pay to the cashier was long that day though and he wouldn't be deterred, asking two more times. Finally, he said, "Are you SURE, Neil?"

Well, the line was just too long that day allowing for the final invitation ... I caved, and disaster ensued. Like a plot from a bad "B" movie my fall was swift and catastrophic. After consuming as much of their beer as they'd allow, I immediately purchased an ounce of weed and proceeded to party all through the night. Sometime during the night, I learned that the Rolling Stones concert was the next day and purchased a ticket from someone that had an extra one. Making my way over to Fair Park many hours before the concert began, I met a new group of people to continue the party with, and set about to seriously prepare for the big event that afternoon. They shared their whiskey with me and I contributed pot to the party. It's hard to say how long that we sat by the reflecting pool next to the Automobile Building, but after a while my new friends decided it was time to head into the Cotton Bowl for the concert and left me with the remaining whiskey. Being an accommodating chap, I took it and nursed the bottle (well, more like chugged it) and finished it after walking to a spot not far from the entrance to the stadium. Just then someone came along and asked me if I wanted to buy a ticket to the concert. Explaining that I already had one, they told me theirs was on the floor near the stage.

"Great, I'll take it!" I said, forking over the last of my hard earned paycheck.

Walking over to the gate, I handed the ticket taker my pass and began the ascent to the stadium. Suddenly remembering that I'd left my coat on the wall I'd been sitting on, I ran back down the stairs alarming the security guards, crossed the plaza and picked up my coat … just as a Dallas Police Department squad car was approaching. As usual I had roused the officer's curiosity! Discovering me to be in an inebriated state, they searched me and found the pot. The end result of my attempt to stop drinking and using on my own? Within 24 hours I bought two tickets to the big concert yet never got to see a minute of it, would be one of eight people out of 80,000 who attended the concert that day to be arrested … and was broke and homeless by the time they let me out of jail. As the disclaimer on a TV commercial used to say, "Don't try this at home!"

# CHAPTER 35

Occasionally I would begin a hitchhiking trip, not because of any particular crisis, but simply because it was a beautiful day and seemed like a nice day to travel. So it was when I set out from Dallas to visit the cattle ranch in East Texas where I'd worked as a teenager. Without a map, and considering the fact that I wasn't paying much attention on my first trip there, I kind of felt my way along this time asking strangers for directions. Since it was fairly large, no doubt Lone Star Ranch would be familiar to the locals— not quite—instead of there I ended up at the town of Lone Star, Texas! Now I was stuck way off the beaten path in small country town at sunset. Though unsure of which direction to take, after heading as far as I could to the eastern end of the road which bisected town, I stuck out my thumb. A ride did not materialize quickly, and after standing for an hour or so I sat down to rest on the curb in front of the town drug store, one of a handful of stores in "downtown." Things didn't look good as traffic was pretty thin and getting thinner as the night drew on. As I contemplated my next move, a sheriff's car pulled up.

"Uh oh" I thought to myself, "He probably won't like my kind ... a drifter *and* a Yankee!"

After the deputy gave me the third degree and was satisfied that

I wasn't a bad guy, he told me that the drug store I was sitting in front of had been robbed six times in the last few months. Boy had I picked a spot to rest! To my relief he let me go (well, he told me to get out of town) so I walked to the edge of town and stuck out my thumb again.

When I stumbled in to Jefferson, Texas that night, it happened to be the first night of the Jefferson Pilgrimage Rodeo. The rodeo grounds were right off the main highway, and I was feeling pretty expansive when I volunteered to enter the bull riding competition. After all, I'd ridden a bull when I worked as a cowboy at the ranch a while back … these critters were all the same! Good thing I didn't have a cowboy hat which was required—I didn't have the entry fee either but that would have been easier to borrow than a hat, so I gave up and went in search of a beer. Instead, I found a young lady who invited me home to her mom and dad's house who were out of town at the time. The Lord protected me from inflicting emotional harm on her, because the young lady's friend called her up and talked her into kicking me out. Leaving another town in the dark, I pushed on to the Lone Star Ranch spending another sleepless night under the stars.

To my relief I finally reached the ranch around noon the next day and the long driveway to the ranch house gave me time to reminisce about my summer there nearly 10 years before. Noticing a gigantic Brahma bull in the pasture along the road, I guessed that it was Luke, my old friend from the morning feedings … he now stood about seven feet tall at the shoulders. Walking up to the fence nearest to the bull, I called to him by name as he stood about twenty five yards away in the midst of some grazing cows. He lifted his head and looked at me when I called, but didn't move. When he didn't show any signs of friendliness after I spoke kindly to him, I wisely discarded the idea of jumping the fence to go pet him. Approaching the ranch house, I noticed that not much appeared to have changed except that the two Lincoln Continentals were gone and in their place was a small pickup truck. After knocking on the doors of the house several times, I searched around for signs of life. "Hello!" I yelled repeatedly. Well, I'd come too far to find no one and was very tired and not inclined to give up easily. Hoping for and half expecting some of the nice Southern hospitality I'd known years ago, for some reason I felt that I deserved a welcome back, like a favorite son returning home. After all, I had cared for the ranch and had invested myself in it (for three whole months). Sensing that Jerry and Judy no longer ran the place, I knew that somebody must be nearby. Besides Jerry and I there were three other hands who worked the ranch back then. After taking a short nap under a tree, eying the pickup truck for a minute and noticing the keys were in it, I jumped in to search for someone.

Crisscrossing the beautiful pastures and piney woods which made up the Lone Star Ranch for a half an hour, not a tractor, a truck, or a mounted horse were to be seen anywhere. It was kind of fun tearing around on the sandy roads, but I finally gave up and returned to the main house. Parking the truck, I decided to sit and wait awhile and settled under a shade tree to pass the time. A few minutes later a man on a tractor drove up in the nearest pasture, climbed down and walked over to me. Greeting me in an East Texas twang, he seemed a little distressed and asked why I'd been driving the truck. My homecoming story didn't impress him much, because not only did he not offer any creature comforts, but later I learned that he had ratted on me to the ranch owner who was inclined to press charges against me for grand theft auto. So much for a happy homecoming! After the short conversation I was back down the road, another bubble burst, another romantic picture down the drain.

As nostalgic trips sometimes turn out, so far this was a bust—where to go from there? East Texas is a relatively remote spot to begin a cross country trip from, and as I calculated where to go next it struck me that South Bend Indiana had a lot to offer. That was quite a stretch because I had spent some of the very the darkest days of my life in that locale. Not given to careful thought at that time, away I went anyway. In the back of my mind I probably realized that there were not many places left where I was known and still welcome ... I had to have *some* destination. The trip to north was tough, though the Lord blessed me with a good night's sleep and some food on the way. It was about 10:00 PM as I waited for a ride by the side of the road in Tennessee and my hopes were waning when a guy pulled over and stopped. Speaking with a thick Southern accent, he seemed like a nice guy and had a good sense of humor. Though a little inebriated he seemed to be able to drive alright. As he later slowed the car to exit, he said that he would be stopping to spend the night at a motel in Nashville and offered to let me sleep on the floor—what a break! The next morning when we woke up, he invited me to breakfast. The chicken fried Southern accent he displayed the night before was completely gone! After breakfast he dropped me at the northbound ramp to the Interstate and we parted ways ... both of us chuckling about his overnight transformation.

Well aware of the ongoing years of suffering I'd have to endure, the Lord planned some serene and promising interludes to sustain and refresh me in the interim. Times of rest, mountaintop experiences, and other gentle blessings from His hand were carefully interspersed during the hard years before Jesus delivered me from the damnable slavery which held me. Standing along a pretty stretch of highway outside Louisville, Kentucky later that day was one of those times. It was an absolutely beautiful day, and as I often did to pass the time while hitchhiking waiting for the next ride, I began singing. On the sunlight flooded highway that day praise songs to Jesus rolled off my lips as I glorified God and thanked Him for His marvelous creation. The Bible compares the sun to a strong man rejoicing to run a race … the strong man was high in the sky that day radiantly lighting up the countryside, and as the melodies rose from my lips, my spirit rose with the words of the songs. An old World War I rallying song came to mind and the Lord gave me joyful new words to that melody which I sang over and over:

"Praise the Lord and pass the love to Johnny, praise the Lord and pass the love to me, praise the Lord pass the love to Mary, praise the Lord and pass the love to me. The Lord is good He takes away our sins, the Lord is good, He's good to you and me, the Lord is good so pass the love to Jesus … the Lord is good so pass the love you see!"

I sang the song over and over as the Lord gave me several variations on the melody and words to augment the beauty of the "new song" which He put on my lips. As I sang out His praises, my soul and the notes of the song seemed to rise to heaven on the warm breeze of that lovely day. Glad to be alive (a sharp contrast to my last trip to Indiana) I arrived in South Bend later that day with my head held high. By the time I reached town though, due to prolonged effects of addiction and lack of sleep and food, my grip on reality was tenuous. Feeling pretty full of myself and confident in my ability to do almost anything, it seemed fortuitous when I met a street alcoholic who needed rehabilitation, and I was just the man to help him! After hailing a taxi to take him for help (how I would pay the fare I hadn't considered) we made a beeline for Notre Dame University. I suppose it's a magnet for almost everyone who comes to South Bend, and on that day it was for me. As we drove towards the campus, the drunk, thinking me a lunatic, asked the driver to stop and abandoned me. That didn't hinder me in my mission though; I intended to find a solution, and then relocate the fellow and help him. My thought was that since Notre Dame was a Catholic establishment, I should be able to find some individual or department on campus which would help me in such a just cause. Another reason to expect help was the fact that my dad was an executive with a company which was recently one of the largest employers in South Bend and a key donor to the school. Drawing upon my past experience here, it seemed logical to look up Joe Blackwell, who was involved on the marketing side of the school's great athletic programs, and who had acted as the school's liaison to visiting VIPs who hoped to take in a football or basketball game.

Having learned that Billy Graham was scheduled to hold a crusade at the school in the near future, I just knew that Billy would help me if I could get a hold of him. We were both born again after all, and I had once attended school with his son (for two whole weeks) so surely, he would be inclined to help me … it was just a matter of talking to him! Joe Blackwell was startled by my request to help me get in touch with Billy Graham, but being a kind man (and no doubt remembering who my dad was) within about 15 to twenty minutes he handed me the phone and I spoke briefly with one of the Lord's greatest ambassadors! Billy was very kind and cordial to me, yet he told me that I was not going about this the right way. Years later in 2002 during his second Crusade at Texas Stadium in Dallas, I had the privilege of counseling people who had answered his invitation to come to Christ. Standing a short distance from him as he sat at the podium, I stopped for a minute and looked as he gazed out upon the hundreds of spiritually thirsty people standing before him … his face framed a broad smile and his eyes were sparkling with joy, peace and love reflecting the God he so faithfully served.

The nice people who bought our house when we moved back to New York years before still owned it, and they were kind enough to let me stay with them, though the rest of my time in South Bend was not very good. It was a strange visit to say the least. Bordering on psychosis the whole time, I saw my hosts only once after they welcomed me into the house the first day. I was very lonely. The second day there I came up with some money and decided to throw a party and use beer as bait to lure participants. Our old house sat on one of the main streets in town, and after making a sign reading "Notre Dame Beer Bash" I posted it, the beer and myself on the grass between the sidewalk and the street right in front of the house. (I'd gone from trying to rehabilitate a drunk to being one!) Waving and beckoning to the passing cars then pointing at the case of beer at my feet for at least an hour, no one even slowed down to look. Interestingly not one police car came by to shorten my party either. Eventually I gave up and went back to the room and polished the beer off. Later that night in confusion I locked myself out of the house. Now quite late, ringing the doorbell repeatedly and knocking as I might, no one came down to open the door for me. Trying the same tactic at the next door neighbor's house (the old folks who lived there must have been in their late 80s or early 90s by then!) when they didn't answer, I tried throwing pebbles at the upstairs windows but also to no avail. By God's mercy the cops didn't come and haul me away. With the dawn of a new day, the compound effects of the booze, more exhaustion and less food caused my thoughts and behavior to become even more erratic, but thankfully the Lord led me to leave town before getting into any trouble.

My route back to Texas took me through Champagne, Illinois which I heard from the locals used to be where

Al Capone and the Chicago Mafia hung out in during the summer when it was too hot in the city. Although penniless, after mooching a few beers at a local bar I became acquainted with one of the patrons and was invited over to his house to drink some more free booze. The guy (purported by someone in the bar to be Mafia himself) disappeared after pouring me a generous drink and left me to play pool on a table which sat where the dining room table does in most houses. He reappeared after a while and said that he had to go, and I was off into the night, alone again.

Eventually I made it to the Mississippi River at Quincy, Illinois and met a Vietnam Veteran in a wheelchair at a bar called Mutt and Jeff's. He was good company and it was nice to have someone to talk to for more than a few minutes. Gladly I took him up on his offer to sleep on his couch that night and I slept well. That was really good news because, besides desperately needing a good night's sleep, before meeting him I'd left my sleeping bag and the rest of my belongings unattended and someone had stolen them. The next day I set out in better spirits, and it was a beautiful sunny day as I approached the Mississippi River heading towards Hannibal, Missouri the birthplace of one of my favorite authors Mark Twain. When I was a lad, my mom had purchased a complete set of his works at a garage sale for $11 and I devoured them. My imagination lit up as I looked out across the river at the lush meadows near Hannibal, envisioning Tom Sawyer and Huck Finn running along the banks of the river, "With a little more sleep and some provisions" I thought, "I'd build a raft and float the river to New Orleans!" Alas I had neither, so instead stuck to concrete with my thumb, setting out as a twentieth century vagabond headed for

Texas.

Wandering off the main road while making my way through Kansas turned out okay—the rolling farmland of eastern Kansas was a beautiful sight to behold. Growing weary and scouring my memory for a friend I could stay with a while, as I closed in on Oklahoma my pal Adam West came to mind. Adam and I had become acquainted in New York, and though only neighbors for nine months or so, we had become fast friends. Glad to hear from me when I called ahead, he assured me of a warm welcome. Upon arriving at a rest stop on the Will Rogers Turnpike in northwest Oklahoma still a long way from Tulsa where Adam lived, since night was falling, I phoned him about my dilemma. Kind fellow that he is, after carefully describing my location to him he volunteered to come and pick me up.

The rest stop, although fully equipped with a restaurant and a gas station, was on a fairly isolated stretch of highway and the whole facility closed down shortly before night fall. After waiting by the closed building for a while it occurred to me that I might be mistaken for a prowler, so I walked over and sat down on the grassy strip of land between the highway and the parking lot of the rest area. Having been on the road for a while and consistently short on food and sleep, as I watched vigilantly for Adam to come, it wasn't too long until I allowed myself to lie down "just for a minute." Before you know it, I awoke to see a State Trooper car pulling onto the shoulder of the highway behind a dark Chevy coupe. A very distraught Adam and the Trooper approached me, and my friend seemed both relieved and shaken to the core at the same time. After explaining to the Trooper what I was doing and how I had arrived at that location, Adam and I were soon heading back to Tulsa. Not too fast though. While nervously glancing in the rear view mirror,

Adam explained,

"I jumped into the car and raced out to get you as soon as you called. With your directions, I found the rest stop okay, but after driving around the area for a while and not finding you, I assumed you'd gone missing and had turned around to head back to Tulsa. In the meantime, while you were sleeping alongside the highway, some passerby noticed you there and called the police to report a *body* alongside the highway! The State Trooper heard the report of the body just as I came barreling along at about 90 miles an hour heading away from the "scene of the crime"!"

I'm sure the Trooper became even more interested in Adam, when he explained that he indeed had just come from the rest area in question, and couldn't find his old friend! The cop cordially suggested that he and Adam go back and have a look around to see if they could find me, and that's where I came into the picture … much to Adam's relief, not as a corpse! If all of that wasn't enough to make my poor friend nervous, the fact that he had an ounce of marijuana in his pocket the whole time didn't help matters. They didn't just slap your wrist for that back in those days.

Things improved considerably after that. Adam lived at home with his mom in an upscale section of Tulsa and was attending a local college. His mom, a lovely Christian woman, welcomed me warmly to their spacious home. Once again, like waking up briefly from a bad dream, I went to sleep that night in a clean, comfortable bed in a large well-appointed house in a really nice part of town. After a good meal and some sleep, Adam and I talked easily and had fifty questions for each other as we caught up on the time that had passed since we'd last seen each other. During this period of my life, because of my often very sinful lifestyle I was usually pretty quiet about my recent experience with and faith in God, but I opened up about Jesus when Adam asked a question, and was grieved to learn that he didn't share his mother's enthusiasm or belief in the Lord. Shenanigans were in the works for the both of us soon, and after smoking some pot Adam and I had a pretty good wrestling match. He was a stocky guy and a good challenge and it was great fun. Afterward he asked if I'd like to go out to the country and visit Rose Fairchild, an old friend who we'd both met in New York. "Heck yeah!" I exclaimed, "There's nothing I like better than going to the country!"

Oklahoma in the summertime is a beautiful place, and as we drove into the countryside outside of Tulsa, I rejoiced in the lovely world that God created. Adam was in the local vernacular, sweet on Rose, and he drove with particular purpose over the straight country roads as we headed towards the Fairchild ranch. Rose's dad raised and sold thoroughbred race horses, and their house was nestled up to the edge of a forest in a setting that spoke of ease and comfort. Adjacent to their front yard was a long rectangular fenced corral of about forty acres which looked like a manicured lawn liberally interspersed with oak trees. We jumped out of the car and knocked on the door and Rose answered. She was as pretty as ever and glad to see us, though on further observation she seemed to be a little sad and pre-occupied. When Adam asked if he could make us both a drink and Rose agreed in a hesitant way with downcast eyes, and I understood why she was sad. Our initial visit with Rose was rather brief and after exchanging a few sentences, Adam asked Rose if he could show me the horses. She nodded, and drinks in hand we ambled out to the corral.

Soon Adam was leading the most magnificent horse I'd ever seen close up, to the tack room—a thoroughbred stallion. "You ride first, and then I'll ride." He said with a grin. We had been drinking earlier too, and although our glasses were not yet empty, it must have been comical to watch us attempt to put a saddle on that massive beast. The saddle (probably meant for a horse the size of a pony) never should have been on that stallion's back. Sweating, grunting and groaning, between the two of us we finally managed to do it, and I grabbed the reins, climbed on and gave the stallion a quick kick in the ribs and a "Yah!" The handsome steed shot off into the corral at lightning speed. After slowing him to a walk for twenty-five or thirty yards, I wheeled him around to head back to Adam for a "lookey here" pass. Whether I was ham handed on his sensitive mouth with the bridle or maybe it was the tightness of the girth belt around his midsection, before taking too many steps the horse reared up on his hind legs and the girth belt broke! Grasping for the reins, his mane, his neck, whatever I could, the saddle slid out from under me. Managing to hold on, after calming the horse and assuring Adam of my excellent horsemanship skills, I launched off bareback to finish my ride.

A drunken man on a thoroughbred stallion even with the proper equipment would have been a risky adventure, but a man's reason is the first thing to go when he drinks, so gleefully I galloped off. It was only by the grace of God that I didn't get my head hung up in tree like King David's son Absalom did, or get it knocked right off! Though animals and I have always gotten along well, I'm not much of a horseman—the only two gaits I am comfortable with are a walk and a gallop. A thoroughbred can run at forty to sixty miles per hour depending upon who you ask, and on that beautiful sunny day in the bucolic countryside of Oklahoma, galloping seemed the thing to do. With no speedometer or radar gun to confirm the speed, it seemed as if we were flying as that sleek, formidable beast raced to end of the corral. Patting and rubbing him on the neck then walking him a bit, we turned around to head back to where Adam was standing by the stable. Kicking him even harder as we streaked the length of the corral, I was amazed at the incredible speed, ease and smoothness with which the stallion ate up the turf. He must have felt like we were getting a little too close to the fence at the end of the corral, and suddenly without warning the big horse took half a dozen halting steps and then came to a dead stop. As we went from *super*-fast to zero in a moment's notice, I instinctively grabbed the stallion's mane and hung on for dear life. The whole weight of my body was thrust upon his neck, and that caused the head of the mighty horse to bow completely down so that his nose was pointing at the ground if not under his belly, back toward his hind end … and my face was inches away from the Oklahoma grass underneath his feet. Again, by some unexplainable circumstance I managed to hang on. As he lifted his head, I scooched back and settled into where the saddle should have been, and spoke soothing words to him as I patted his neck. Adam, stood gawking at me with his mouth hanging open. As we sidled over to him, I had an "Awe shucks, weren't nothin' to it!" expression on my face.

For some reason Adam decided not to ride, and shortly after putting the horse and the tack back in the barn and bidding goodbye to Rose, another wacky adventure came to a close.

# CHAPTER 36

Another time my Savior Jesus gave me a lift during the long road to sobriety happened one day when I was hanging out in downtown Dallas. While waiting for a bus, homeless again and feeling pretty hopeless, I approached the bus stop not knowing if my bus trip would net me a warm reception at the other end. A guy approached me and offered to sell me some marijuana. "Sure." I responded. As the guy walked away with the some of the very little money I had, I looked around for a spot to smoke it. Realizing that I was in the middle of downtown and a long way away from any trees or bushes which could be used for cover, I decided just to play it cool and blend in with the scores of people who were walking and waiting around. Pretending to smoke the pot like it was a cigarette, I learned that my supposed relief from misery was a bust—although there may have been some pot in the joint the guy sold me, it was mostly seeds. The smoke I inhaled was harsh and bitter and didn't do much to improve my mood, especially when the seeds popped and my hand and face were burned a couple of times.

As the reality of this latest bad turn of events sunk in adding anger to my hopelessness, loud noise off in the distance caught my attention. Just north of me was a parade! Hundreds and hundreds of people were marching west on

Elm Street through the middle of downtown Dallas singing and carrying banners! Dumbstruck by the sight I stared at the procession and racked my brain to figure out what the occasion was. It wasn't the Fourth of July or Memorial Day ... or any other holiday for that matter. What could it be?

Half running, half walking the two blocks that separated me from this magnetic phenomenon, I began to make out the words of the song they were singing. They were singing praise songs to Jesus! The people were not marching in ranks like a military parade, but were just walking along in small klatches with big smiles on their faces. Some were carrying or waving flags or banners, some waving their hands at the people watching them from the sidewalks and some were just wrapped up in walking and singing praise songs. It felt as if a river of love was moving west through Dallas that day, and without thinking about it I joined the parade. It was a river—of the Lord's love! The scripture says that God inhabits the praises of His people (Psalm 22:3) and surely He was there that day! Wafted along on the joy which surrounded me, I was almost instantly transformed from an empty, exhausted, frustrated and angry young man into a joy filled one who was greatly blessed by my God's unmerited grace and favor. The exuberant crowd walked along celebrating for another quarter mile or so until we all came to an open square where a platform had been set up for a speaker. David Albritton, an evangelist, took the podium and began to speak shortly after all of the people arrived. His talk was inspiring, though I was almost giddy from the phenomenal experience and was not as focused on his talk as I should have been. Still somewhat baffled by the whole thing, I asked the people around me,

"What is this? Why were you marching?"

"We're from Christ for the Nations." One of the young people around me answered.

"What is Christ for the Nations? What is this about? Why the parade?" I sputtered as the words rushed out of me.

Explaining that Christ for the Nations was a local Bible school they took turns trying to convey exactly what this was. While trying to get my arms around it, I continued to ask questions. Finally, one of the folks, summed it up succinctly by saying, "This is about Jesus! The march, the songs, it's all about Jesus! We love Him and we're celebrating!"

I grappled with that for a moment and turned to listen to the speaker for a while longer. It was probably something David Albritton said, but surely the Holy Spirit had touched me as I turned to the people around me and confessed to them my sad predicament. Admitting my bondage to alcohol and drugs and the terrible consequences it had led to, they just kept smiling and encouraged me. One of them asked if they could pray with me. "Of course!" I exclaimed. After a beautiful of prayer time during which they prayed for my deliverance from booze and drugs, I felt as if their prayers (and mine of longstanding) were close to being answered. I told them, and we all rejoiced in the goodness of God. One of them told me that they knew of a Christian rehab program where I could live. This buoyed my spirits even more, and with rejoicing we sang some more worship songs.

Then it happened ... a pivot point in my life. A fork in the road which I wasn't expecting. A young lady who was standing beside me noticed the cigarette package in my front shirt pocket.

"You could be set free from those too!" she said in innocent faith.

I froze. This was getting too close to home. "No. No I don't think it's the right time for that."

Some of the others joined in encouraging me that the Lord wanted to break those chains too. Well, I must have had one powerful demon hanging on to me or it was just my own prideful self-willed flesh, because I dug my heels in and wouldn't budge. They gave up and went back to worshipping, but when I tried to sing again it wasn't the same. My awareness of the sweet, glorious presence of God which I'd been experiencing since seeing and joining the parade was gone—I was cold and lifeless again. When the rally was over, they took me to a little church building in East Dallas that was in the process of being converted for use as a Teen Challenge Center. Before leaving they assured me that the minister would be by shortly, if not that day then surely the next. The day wore on and no minister. Grateful for a night's sleep on an old couch, after awakening the next morning hungry and waiting for what seemed like forever for the pastor to appear, I left and went back to the streets, the expected relief vanishing like mist. Hindsight is not always twenty-twenty, but I cannot help but think that had I cooperated with the Holy Spirit that day and yielded up the cigarettes, I could have ended my time in the pit sooner than I did.

# CHAPTER 37

Actions like smoking pot on a public street or a movie theater, or walking into the worst bars in the worst parts of town all over the country and walking out again alive were representative of the many circumstances in which the Lord protected me from my own stupidity during those years. Though my life and freedom had hung by a thread many, many times, the Lord in His awesome love and power saw me safely through numerous incidents which should have ended in prison or death for me. My history with street drugs was a case in point. Back in those days they would have called me a garbage head—that is, I would take anything to get high, it didn't matter what. Although I likely did just about every illegal drug known to man at that time in an attempt to get high, the Lord protected me from the needle. Don't let anyone ever tell you that the things we watch on TV or in the movies don't have an effect on us—why else would advertisers pay millions upon millions of dollars for commercial time every day? When I was a kid growing up just outside of New York City there was an anti-drug commercial on TV that showed a guy sitting by the window in a darkened room in a New York tenement building with a latex tube around his arm and clenched in his teeth, about to inject himself with a hypodermic needle. The scene sent chills down my spine as a kid, and years later even though I would do almost anything when stoned or drunk, the memory of that commercial held me in check most of the time when the thought of doing a needle drug occurred to me.

Once when I met a biker at a convenience store on the California coast, after talking a few minutes he asked me if I wanted to get high.

"Yeah, sure man." I said.

Then he warned me that the drug was heroin.

"No problem!" I proclaimed. Actually sober and clean that day, apparently my brain was out to lunch. When we got to his house and he brought the stuff out though, he refused to let me have any since I intended to snort the stuff up my nose like cocaine instead of shooting it.

"I'm not gonna waste good dope man!" he said in disgust.

Sorely disappointed that I missed out on a high, that may have been on my mind a few years later in Dallas. Having just swallowed some LSD and having spent my last money on some beer, I ran into a guy in the parking lot of the beer store. Always preferring to party with others rather than alone, we worked out a deal: my beer to drink and his speed to shoot. "Great!" I exclaimed as we drove away into the darkness.

He was from way over on the other side of Dallas, so I suggested that we go see a girl I knew nearby. Fiona was at home when we arrived, but since her roommate had guests inside already, we stood out in the street leaning against the guy's car talking with her for about twenty minutes. Fiona had to go inside for a minute and when she did, I said the guy, "Hey man let's go do that speed!"

No sooner had the words left my lips then a car pulled up alongside us and a lady started talking with him ... an old friend who just happened to be in the same neighborhood many miles from where he lived. A minute later, he jumped into the car and said that he was going with her.

"Wait! I thought we were going to shoot the speed!" I objected.

"Sorry." he said, and away they went. The Lord took him away.

Considering the crowd that I ran into on the streets, and the hunger that the enemy has to destroy people, it's seems rather unlikely that only one other time did the opportunity to use needle drugs present itself to me. A third temptation to shoot drugs occurred right before the Lord set me free. Clean and sober for about nine months, I fell off the wagon again in Salinas, California, where Janis Joplin's Bobby McGee split from his girl. On the back end of week long run I was broke, tired and dying for the next high. Stumbling upon a really sleazy hotel in the worst part of town, I remembered hearing that it was a drug house. Without a nickel to my name and without knowing anyone in the building, I ventured in. This action alone might have well been the death of me, as extreme violence was not uncommon in this type of place. My plan was to knock on doors and ask for drugs (as if some dealer was just going to pity me and give me some!). Unexpectedly, the first door I knocked on was opened by a guy I knew from jail. Not unusual to find a former jailbird in a place like this, but quite a coincidence to find an acquaintance at the first door I knocked on.

"Can I come in?" I asked.

"Sure" he said through the chained door.

He unchained the door and let me in, chaining it again behind me. The small apartment was a quite a scene. On the bed and slumped in chairs unconscious were three or four pretty young ladies, really not more than girls. My "friend" who was almost completely covered with tattoos sat back down at a desk with all the apparatus to prepare and shoot drugs in front of him. To all appearances the guy was a pimp and these were his off-duty prostitutes, spending their leisure time passed out on drugs.

I asked him if he had my drug of choice, which was pot. "No, only H." he responded, meaning heroin.

Desperate to get high to escape the hell I'd once again created for myself, after thinking for a split second I asked, "Can I have a shot?"

"No" he said. Ready to risk an overdose, a deadly infection of HIV or Hepatitis C or slow death by addiction I pleaded with him two more times, finally offering to bring money back for the favor.

My pleas fell on deaf ears and I left to wander into the night. Once again Jesus' loving hands ushered me safely away from a potential death sentence.

# CHAPTER 38

Besides the draw of Salem Christian Commune and the great California scenery and climate, I discovered another reason to like the Golden State. After blowing into town one time at a very lovely spot on the Central Coast and unsure of what I would do for food and shelter that night, I asked another homeless guy what the deal was around there.

"You can go down to the Department of Social Services, and they'll give you vouchers for food and a hotel room." he said.

"You've got to be kidding me!" I exclaimed. "Just like that?"

"Yup!"

Sure enough, a few hours later I walked out of the county building with the necessary paperwork, and before long I was checking in to a hotel room with a bag full of groceries to boot! Granted this was not the Hilton, but in this upper middle class town hundreds of miles from any big city, there was not anything vaguely resembling a bad part of town. This welfare hotel which I came to call "The Dark Hotel" not only because of its distinctive lack of lighting but because of the deep, dark spiritual shadow that hung over the place, was actually fairly well kept up. Situated at the foot of a mountain and next to a station where passenger trains still stopped along the coastal route, the hotel was housed in a lovely old three or four-story building in what was probably a fine establishment at one time when railroads were the lifeline of the country. The room I was given was on the third floor and overlooked a lovely little park bedecked with the usual beautiful trees and ever blooming flowering shrubs which are so common in California. The weather there is so often pleasant that I spent many hours with my window wide open looking out on the lovely park and surrounding neighborhood. More than once I marveled that a penniless bum like me could hitchhike into town and end up well fed and living indoors in short order.

Of course I was required to register with the state employment commission and to prove on a regular basis that I was actively looking for work—and I did want to work! The Dark Hotel was a pleasant break from the streets and I was grateful to be able to take advantage of the opportunity several times as I struggled to break free from the treacherous and life draining cycle of drug and alcohol abuse. The town was not far from Salem, and since it was also one of the loveliest spots I'd seen during my wanderings back and forth across America, I returned there again and again over the years. During one of these trips I met Yoyo. After attending a Twelve-Step meeting which happened to meet across the street from hotel, someone there told me about a halfway house called Middle House. Homeless again and always open for anything that might help me get sober and clean, I made an appointment with the manager as soon as possible. Middle House turned out to be another great gift from my Heavenly Father. He knew how battered and bruised I was and how a really good, clean and nice place to live would help me. The house was situated in a beautiful, crisp, clean residential neighborhood perched on the slopes of a mountain overlooking town. Washed in sunlight and surrounded by flowers and trees, the appearance of the place was in stark contrast to slimy, dirty, sin filled places I was much more accustomed to in those days.

When I made it to the address on the paper in my hand, the beauty of the setting made me unsure if I had the right place. When I knocked on the door and no one answered, I was a little afraid to venture around back thinking that I might be arrested for trespassing or suspicion of burglary if someone spotted me. Taking a few tentative steps down the driveway in that direction, someone came out of a building behind the main house. When I stated my purpose, he acknowledged that this was the right place, but told me that he'd resigned as manager and would soon be leaving, so I would have to interview with the new manager when he took over in a few days. "Drats!" I thought, "Another night on the streets!" The wait was worth it though. When I met the new manager a few days later, it was the beginning of my friendship with one of the kindest, nicest men that I've ever known. Robert Hedrick who was known by everyone as Yoyo, was a gem of a person. He was one of the most gentle, humble, self-effacing men I've ever met. One of the endearing things about him was that he tried to put on a rough exterior, which I'm certain fooled nobody! My first conversation with him was short and to the point. Refreshingly, he took me at face value (an uncommon thing in those days and something that I did not often deserve yet either) and took me into the program. To my delight that meant a room of my own in the dormitory behind the main house. Up until that point, a room of my own was with extremely rare exception, almost unheard of since leaving home. The whole place, including my room was clean and well kept, and combined with the great people that the Lord brought into my life at that time, my ten months or so at Middle House were some of my happiest in years. Yoyo made a great friend and sometimes confidant, and with him as our "dad" and us younger guys his prodigal sons come home (he made us all feel like that) the sense of having a home and belonging somewhere was a really nice change.

With all its beauty the Central Coast of California is a great place to heal, and as I walked the streets of this lovely town nestled in a coastal valley between the towering mountains and the sea, the Lord was continuing to love me back to health. Though much larger in population than my hometown of Pleasantville, it had a really nice small town feel. The parts of town that I frequented were all in easy walking distance of Middle House, and strolling through the well kept neighborhoods surrounded by the lovely vistas and gardens, it was pleasure just being there. A job came quickly as the Lord has so often done for me over the years, and between work, Twelve-Step meetings and relaxing in my room reading or writing an occasional letter back home, I settled into a comfortable rhythm. Work, home, dinner, a meeting, a walk into town on the weekend, a trip to the beach … it was a gentle and a nice routine. Comfortable had not been the standard for me for a long, long time and it was a very welcome change. Most of my life for quite some time had consisted of one harrowing and unpredictable disaster or incident following on the heels of another. It was great to live what may have seemed to some a humdrum life for a while.

I'll never forget an experience I had when walking through downtown one lovely evening on the way to a Twelve-Step meeting. While enjoying the walk and rejoicing in life and in God's glorious creation around me, my attention was drawn to some people on the sidewalk across the street when it hit me … for the first time that I could remember in a long, long time I felt like just another guy walking down the street. Most, if not all of my life up until that point I'd felt different—different from all those around me and not in a good way. The devil had been trying to hammer the idea into my head all of my life that I was weird, wrong, unwanted and unacceptable to other people—all other people. He had me pretty much convinced during most of my life that other people could tell simply by looking at me that there was something wrong with me. To my great joy, as I walked through town on that lovely evening I didn't feel as if people were staring at and wondering about this odd fellow named Neil Leary ... I was just another guy walking down the street, minding my own business and living life! To most folks all of that is probably a given, but to me it was a fabulous, chain breaking revelation and a gift from God.

Yoyo and Middle House were a great gift as well and I always cherish my memories from those days. During that time I achieved the longest period of voluntary sobriety that I'd had yet, and I began to see a glimmer of hope that the long awaited "someday" that God had promised me on that night so long ago might soon come to pass. These were days when strength and hope began to return to me—a time when I began to regain a sense of confidence in my abilities. Though it seemed as if I'd finally made it to the Promised Land of sobriety, I wasn't quite there yet.

After being laid off my job as a plumber's helper when the project we were working on wound down, then getting stuck in a swamp of self-pity shortly after that, I discovered that my bank account had exactly $666 in it ...a sign (the devil told me) that was irrefutable evidence that I'd sold out to the world system and was lukewarm for God. That lie combined with other well paced anxieties created an ugly cauldron of emotions which led me straight to a bottle and a bag of drugs. As was typical for me, I went through the money like a hot knife through butter, or a drunken sailor as a friend of mine used to say. Demonstrating keen discernment, I handed a hundred dollar bill to a relative stranger to go buy some pot for me, only to learn minutes after he left that he was a heroin addict and that I'd never see him or my money again. Within 24 hours I dropped the last of my money (again a hundred dollar bill) on the floor of a crowded, bucket-of-blood bar. Just as I began to freak out and loose my temper looking for the culprit who picked it up, God sent a couple of guys (angels) to rescue me. Friends from the Twelve-Step group who had heard that I had started drinking again walked through the door and waltzed me out into the street ... just as easily one of the toughs in the bar could have knifed me or gunned me down. Never one to get back on track easily (though many in the group reached out and tried to help me) I was headed for a train wreck. Even Yoyo's love and patience wasn't enough. He had to ask me to leave Middle House and before long I was at the end of my rope again.

After climbing through a window at Middle House one night in order to crash on the couch and get some desperately needed sleep, Yoyo was kind enough to not turn me over to the cops for unlawful entry, but I knew it was only a matter of time before I'd have to leave this peaceful paradise. Once gain I was wearing out my welcome.

Diagnosed with liver damage at the age of twenty-two and now twenty-eight, my week or so of hard drinking was having a very dangerous effect on me which I didn't realize yet. When I ran into my dear friend Dwight one day, he handed me a bag of marijuana on the condition that I only smoke the grass and not drink anymore. He wouldn't explain why he did it but I knew it was a great sacrifice. Dwight was also was battling addiction, and addicts generally part with loved ones and all earthly possessions before parting with their medicine. I was deeply touched, and have never seen Dwight again.

A few days later while hitchhiking towards Northern California and standing in front of the Black Oak Inn in Paso Robles panhandling, the Lord sent a guy from another Twelve-Step group to rescue me. Realizing my condition, he let me spend the night at his house before bringing me to the meeting hall the next day. While shaving that morning before leaving his house, I looked into the mirror and found out why Dwight had given me the pot. My eyes looked like a couple of old ivory cue balls, colored a sickening, jaundice yellow. In just a week or so of drinking, my liver was shutting down ... a few more days may have killed me.

At the meeting hall I ran into a beautiful lady named Helen who used to attend Twelve-Step meetings at Middle House, and caught a ride with her and her friend to Monterey. I'd been through Monterey more than once, but don't recollect stopping for anything but necessities. Having worn out my welcome in the paradise to the south, I ended up in yet another utopian spot. Nestled against the coastal mountains next to Carmel and just north of Big Sur, it is a magnificent place of tall dark green pines and rugged hills overlooking beautiful Monterey Bay. The capital of old Alta California under both Spain and Mexico, it is steeped in history, charm and natural beauty. On a sunny day the area is one of the most beautiful I've ever seen. The tall, luxuriant pine trees which are named after the bay and peninsula, framed by the deep blue sky and the cool green ocean, and the perfectly mild air which brushed my cheeks made it hard to imagine wanting to be elsewhere. The foggy nights there have an otherworldly feeling to them which are very beautiful in their own way. The earthbound clouds swallow up most of the extraneous noise and bring a profound hush on the landscape. The deep, dark silence is dramatically contrasted by the mournful sound of barking sea lions in the bay and the lonely wailing of the foghorn warning mariners away from the rocky coast, which seems to call from a different time, far, far away.

The day I arrived in Monterey this time however, I was unable to enjoy very much. Quite downcast after my most recent fall from grace, the beauty was lost on me. The sun was not penetrating my sin blackened soul. Battle weary and broken, I stood at a corner not far from downtown and wept openly, uncaring as to whether I was noticed by anyone passing by. After getting a hold of myself, I found my way to a local Twelve-Step meeting hall. Enter Glenn Harmer. Bud, the only name I ever heard anyone call him, was a throwback to another time, a better time. A commercial fisherman by trade, he was every bit as rugged and tough as the coastline he fished off of for many years, but his ready smile and occasionally sparkling blue eyes belied a very warm, caring and loving heart under the flinty exterior. God had no doubt prepared us to meet, because although a loner by nature in those days, I was seriously in need of a good friend and found one in Bud.

Bud, who was about sixty years old at the time, was a great man, and with his solid grasp on life and on sobriety he had helped a number of guys get back on their feet. He must have noticed the lost, hopeless look in my eyes when I walked into the hall that day, and immediately introduced himself and took me under his wing. After talking for an hour or so and learning that I was homeless, he offered let me sleep in his van. Used to living on fishing boats, he had not had a traditional place to live for some time. The old converted Ford Econoline camper van that he lived in was as rustic looking as Bud was ... they both looked like they had just come off of a movie set. That was fitting and was all part of what endeared me to him. I've always had a nostalgic bent and seem to prefer things, people and memories from an America that is now gone. In

Bud's background were a lot of the things that made our country great. Reared in a cold water flat with his mother and sister, he had an austere upbringing in the days before almost everyone in the USA had plenty. Unlike most of my heroes from those days, he had not served in the military because of a minor yet disqualifying health problem. In spite of his poor formal education due to the fact that he quit school early to help earn money for the family, he was a brilliant, self-taught man. Early on he told me that if I couldn't find him at the Twelve Step hall he'd probably be in the library. Sure enough, many times I found him there with his nose buried in a book. He had one of the hungriest intellects I've ever known … if he was curious about any subject he'd head for a book and find his answer.

Whether it's peculiar to people with a history of substance abuse or not I don't know, but most of the folks I met in the recovery groups liked to hang out in coffee shops either eating or drinking coffee (and back in those days smoking cigarettes) and talking, talking, talking. The whole bunch of us seem to have an awful lot to say if me, Bud and most of the others I've met are any indication. They also for the most part, seem to be an unusually bright bunch and Bud certainly fell into that category. When he and I weren't sitting in a Twelve-Step meeting or about town on some errand, we'd likely be sitting in a coffee shop talking. Bud, my patron at the time and my elder did most of the talking, but I didn't mind. He was absolutely brilliant! I am no slouch, but on almost any subject we came upon, the guy had genuine and extensive knowledge about it that kept me asking more questions about the subject and occasionally adding to our shared knowledge. It was during one of these talks that I learned that a cousin of his was the founder of one of the nation's top aerospace and defense companies, Northrop

Aviation … it appears that brilliance ran in the family.

At the time Bud had no driver license, not because of anything criminal but because of a technicality, and since at the moment I had one, I served as his driver. Newly sober, just hanging with Bud each day was a good job for me. He was not rolling in cash, but was kind enough to feed me when he ate as payment for driving. Bud was a very wise man and forthright in his speech, actions and approach to life. For someone like me who had been living a life of convoluted deception, he was the perfect mentor and I was honored that he would have me along. Over the weeks that I was blessed to live with him, I grew to love and admire him like few others I've known.

When Bud wasn't talking I was, and I've never been shy about talking about myself. Since Bud knew a lot about me in a short time, this made it difficult for me to talk to him about Jesus due to the track record that I brought to the table. Still, I longed for Bud to know my Savior and brought Jesus into the conversation as often as possible. It was kind of like how I felt about my Dad—both are such fine men with many admirable traits and it seemed such a terrible shame that men of their caliber were missing it. Because of my great love for them, the fact that they did not know God, the One Great One worth knowing and the fountain of all truth and goodness and holiness, within me were engendered the same feelings that many of us get when we see some great athlete, leader or scientist struck down in their prime by accident or disease … what a waste! If only Bud and Dad were on the winning team so that they could use their great hearts and gifts to the glory of God!

One fateful day I stumbled upon a job working as a stage hand for a promotional company which was putting on a concert at the Monterey County Fairgrounds. I really wanted to bring in some money so that I could buy Bud lunch for a change. The first day Jermaine Jackson, formerly of The Jackson Five and Michael and Janet's brother, was to perform, then Jefferson Starship the next day. The Jackson Five were a very big name when I was younger, and after all the equipment was in place on the stage, I sought out a security guard and asked him which direction Jermaine would come onto the stage from so that I could talk to him for a moment before the show began. Poised at the top of a short spiral staircase, when he appeared I said, "Hey Jermaine! Did you bring any of your brothers with you?"

"It only takes one of us!" he replied.

Standing in the wings, I saw a first rate concert as all the musicians played flawlessly and sang and danced in perfect unison! Having a backstage pass was an exciting opportunity, but I should have anticipated the temptations that invariably accompany concerts. Without planning to, I found some pot, and after smoking a joint nearly skewered a guy with the forklift while loading equipment onto the stage—thank Jesus for preventing that! One of the few conditions for staying with Bud was that I stay clean and sober, so by the time I'd finished that particular party, I no longer had a place to sleep.

Bud and I ran into each other off and on over the next few of years, but we only spent one more day together when we went to visit a mutual friend in the hospital. After being nearly beaten to death after falling off the wagon (drinking again) and being pulled back from the brink of death in the Monterey area, Sam had been moved to a facility in San Francisco for extensive neurological rehabilitation ... another grim wake up call for me. As we visited Sam, although he was glad to see us, he had no idea who we were and no recollection of meeting us before even though we had lived at the same halfway house, and he lived with Bud for a while too. Bud and I didn't cross paths again in this world, but to my great joy (mixed with sorrow) a few years later while visiting Monterey I happened upon a mutual friend and asked about Bud. Had he seen him? Did he know where he was? The fellow told me that Bud had finally left Monterey, something he had talked about doing, and went to live in a town in the northern part of the state where some old friends had settled. He became very ill there and died. The one question I had to know the answer to was, "Did Bud come to know Jesus as his Savior?" YES! In fact, he had also been reconciled to his sister who for years had been trying to introduce him to Jesus. The last time our friend saw Bud, he was holding a Bible in his hand. As I walked away waves of joy washed over me and bittersweet tears flowed down my cheeks.

# CHAPTER 39

The Lord kept drawing me closer to Him and I kept plodding along attempting to stay on the path. Praying as often as I remembered to, reading my Bible every day, working and going to almost every of Twelve-Step meeting I could get to, and focusing on the goal, expecting a miracle. After my stint with Bud, someone steered me to a local treatment program / halfway house in Salinas called Sun Street Center, and with God's help I fought my way back to normalcy again. One day while sitting in the chow hall during some down time, I overheard a disgusting stream of language coming from some guys sitting nearby. As filth flowed out of their mouths which included references to women in the crudest of terms, my skin crawled and I felt as if I'd been slimed. Walking over to another building where I could be alone, in a huff I reflected upon this angrily and said to the Lord,

"Why Lord! Why do I have to listen to stuff like this? It makes me sick!"

While I continued to fume about this, the Lord wordlessly spoke to me,

"Neil, you used to talk exactly like that ... after you became a Christian."

While I was marveling about this He went on, " ... and almost every time you opened your mouth, you used My Name in vain."

Stunned, I said to Him, "Yes Lord! What happened? I don't go to church, I hardly ever pray ... what happened?"

The Lord showed me that is was His Word, the Bible that had changed me. Since I had vowed to myself to read the New Testament at least one chapter a day, each day, a couple of years before, the change had happened. The Lord reminded me that His word " ... is living and powerful, and sharper than any two edged sword" (Hebrews 4:12). He showed me that it wasn't because He made me so smart or that I understand almost everything that I read and rarely forget anything—the transformation had happened simply because of the power of His Word. As the scripture says," That He might sanctify and cleanse it (His church) with the washing of water by the word," (Ephesians 5:26) A tremendous revelation, this experience solidified my resolve to read the Bible daily for the rest of my life. Over the years I've continually seen incontrovertible evidence of the Bible's powerful ability—in concert with the Holy Spirit—to make us less sinful and more like Christ.

As I struggled with this new way of life, rather than running into a bag of dope or a bottle of booze to hide, but instead learning to face life on life's terms with His help, I often still looked at things from my old, flawed perspective. In answer to my prayers the Lord sent another Christian to Sun Street Center to help me. Harvey was a pleasant man in contrast to some of the current crowd. A tall, white haired guy who seemingly always had a smile on his face, he was a bright light in the sometimes dismal place. Shortly after meeting Harvey and discovering that he also belonged to Jesus, I walked back onto the campus one afternoon in a sour mood, having failed at an attempt to find work that day. When I came upon Harvey sitting on the back porch out in the sun, I vented my frustration.

After listening to me rant for a while he said with a smile.

"You don't get it, do you?"

"Get what!" I bellowed.

"Ephesians chapter six, verse twelve."

"What does that say?" I cried in exasperation.

"For we wrestle not against flesh and blood, but against principalities, against powers, against the rulers of the darkness of this world, against spiritual wickedness in high places."

"Oh!" I gasped with relief, "Of course! Can you repeat that?"

Harvey patiently repeated the verse, and again three or four times over the next few weeks as the Lord used him to hammer the idea into my head. After a while before Harvey could admonish me, I'd repeat the verse to him, and have quoted it many times to myself and others since then.

Prior to learning that great lesson, I spent way too much time with my eyes on people and the circumstances of this world rather than looking to my Heavenly Father for strength and direction. By realizing that the difficult people and other roadblocks along life's way are most often born of the enemy of our souls and not merely of people or random chance, it transformed my understanding of the battle from an "us and them" struggle to a heaven versus hell war .... much bigger than me and certainly not a case of the big bad world picking on poor little me! Rather than looking at the world through my own eyes, but attempting to gain God's perspective, the reason and focus of the predicament shifts away from me, and to the much greater conflict, a very noble one in which I am not a victim to be pitied but a warrior who is privileged to participate ... on the right and winning side! This true understanding of the universe knocks the self-pitying, angry, victim mentality right on its ear! This was a vital turning point for me, and once again God used words from His Bible to calibrate the compass of my life ever closer to true north. Yet even after all these years, unless I am vigilant, all too often the old trap of mistaking people for the enemy catches me, so it remains very important to maintain a heavenly perspective and not lose focus of the true, big picture.

Shortly after this while walking down the street in Salinas one beautiful sunny day, the Lord spoke to me,

"Neil, it's time you become part of what I'm doing in this world. I'm coming back soon and there is a lot of work to be done. I need you to grow up in Me. You need to become a useful, active part of the church, My body here on this earth."

He showed me that yes, He does wonderful work with people One on one as He did with me in bringing me to salvation and later, by baptizing me with His Holy Spirit with the evidence of speaking in tongues—both of these priceless gifts were given to me while I was alone. That day God showed me however, that most often He uses people to do His work on this earth. While that was evident to me, this fact made me rather uncomfortable. The Lone Ranger mentality was fully entrenched in me and it was very hard to once again trust people and let them get close to me again. Yet God was saying that in order to become part of what He's doing here on this earth, I'd have to join the rest of His team—His church. Opening myself up for hurt by growing close to and dependent upon others was something I had avoided like the plague for many years now. His direction to me however was unmistakable, and after a little while I visited a church. My first experience was much like my previous forays. After sitting through about half an hour of the worship service, I stepped out to use the restroom. Emerging from there I saw an usher or deacon nervously glancing around looking for me, likely considering me a security risk. "Well by golly, wait until they get to know me!" I thought to myself indignantly as I walked out never to return.

The Lord was pleased with my meager effort and was determined to help the process along, so a friend told me about Joy Fellowship. After dragging my feet for a few weeks, I went. Pleasantly it turned out to be something I hadn't seen since Salem Christian Commune ... a lot of sincere and enthusiastic people coming together, alive and burning with love for Christ! The worship services were really exciting and I could feel the Holy Spirit come and meet us as we praised our Wonderful Lord. The worship wasn't just ten or fifteen minutes either, but the music, singing and words of praise lasted thirty to forty-five minutes. At each service it felt as if I was being recharged and empowered to face all that life and the enemy—could throw at me. The preaching was Bible based and relevant to our everyday lives, and people were being healed emotionally and physically, set free from sin and filled with joy ... this is the way the Lord meant church to be! The truth that God is alive and powerful and actively working in mankind every day was being broadcast unmistakably through this church. "This is how He *meant* for us to live!" I exclaimed to myself. The first couple of months were pure bliss, and I basked in what was surely the next exiting stage in my new life.

Then it came one Sunday afternoon right after worship as I prepared to shake a few hands, exchange pleasantries and make a hasty exit, the Lord gave me my next marching orders:

"Neil, I want you to let these people know who you are! I want them to become your family!"

I froze. "Let them know who I am!" I thought. "Oh yeah, I'm Jack Armstrong, the All-American Boy. Once I tell them my past, they'll be looking sideways at me every time they see me!" Yet I knew that it was the Lord who had spoken to me.

It took me several weeks to get up my courage, but finally I located a home meeting (an off campus mid-week service of Joy Fellowship) fairly close to where I lived, and on the appointed night I headed out. Walking was my main mode of transportation in those days, and being unfamiliar with that part of town I left early. Although close to the bad part of town, the neighborhood that the house was in was well kept and had a cozy air of prosperity to it. As I approached the area I became uneasy, realizing that my appointment with destiny wasn't far off. Even though I am generally good with directions, somehow the first house I came to wasn't it. The house was completely dark, and after looking around the side of the house for another entry or any signs of life, I noticed that down the driveway over the garage there was a second story apartment. Thinking that may be where the meeting was, I started that way to explore when a sense that I was trespassing came over me, and after a glance I turned and walked quickly away. Two houses away was the correct house, yet looking at my watch and discovering that it was fifteen minutes until starting time, I decided to take a walk … certainly I didn't want to be the first one there and draw attention to myself! The night was warm and still, and as I strolled through the neighborhood to pass the time, the tidy little houses seemed to glow with wellbeing. It had been a little while since I'd lived in a nice neighborhood, and I drank it all in like a thirsty man.

Then something happened that highlighted just how important it was to become part of His church in order to begin the work that God had for me. The events that transpired in the next few minutes abundantly demonstrated to me the truth that the we are in a war, and it is spiritual and not carnal in nature—and that demon spirits conspired to keep me from the meeting that night. Since satan is a defeated foe, often all he has to work with is smoke and mirrors since he can only cross boundaries when our Holy Father lets him. Abba is protective of His children, so it seems that more often than not, mind games are all that the enemy has to work with. He is an expert at that though, and fear and doubt seem to be his favorite weapons. That night He wielded the fear club with frightening accuracy and effectiveness. As I walked along enjoying the night, I looked at my watch and noticed that it was about time for the meeting to start and turned to head back to the host's house. Just then, my finely tuned ear picked up the sound of a finely tuned, high performance automobile engine—every nerve in my body tingled. After years of running from the police, I knew the sound of a police cruiser as a mother knows the sound of her child's voice. Out of the corner of my eye I noticed that indeed it was a patrol car, and it was paused in the middle of the street just behind me and to my right. It then proceeded to slowly follow me as I walked down the sidewalk.

"Someone has committed a serious crime in this neighborhood—they'll arrest me and I'll be framed! With my record no one will believe my innocence!" the demons (no doubt) shouted into my ear, mimicking my own voice.

Paranoia? Not likely, since not only did the cop continue to slowly follow me, pacing me step for step, but he then turned his search light on me, even shining it in my face as I walked toward the house. Every fiber in my being was saying, "Run!" but I knew that I must not … that was exactly what the cop was expecting (and the devil was hoping) that I would do. Though I was still young and strong, something told me that this time I'd be caught and that my final destination would be the penitentiary. Trembling with fear I continued walking, then turned left onto the sidewalk leading to up to the house where the meeting was to be held. Climbing the two steps of the porch I knocked on the door. The few seconds I waited seemed like hours as the policeman stopped to see what would happen. A somewhat perplexed looking man opened the door, yet after I stated my purpose, he let me in. Flooded with relief, the police cruiser pulled away as I stepped through the door. No wonder the man looked puzzled—besides seeing my police escort, I was probably as white as a ghost!

My little walk didn't keep me from being the first one there, and as I hadn't met these folks at the church yet, I waited quite awkwardly for a few minutes, fending off their questions with nebulous answers before more people arrived. Still quite shaken up by the police scare, I was unready to let my guard down yet. The meeting finally started and it was outstanding. We sang quite a few beautiful worship songs and the Spirit of God came and blessed us. As the meeting was nearing an end the Holy Spirit repeated,

"Let these people know who you are."

Again, fear came upon me. "Lord, I am a terrible sinner! These folks are all clean cut, have good lives, and probably all live in nice houses like this. They will feel very uncomfortable and even afraid for their children if they know where I come from!"

Still the Spirit continued to urge me. Finally, when it seemed like the meeting was about to break up, I opened my mouth and began to speak. Instead of looks of horror and rejection though, I saw looks of concern and tenderness. The first one to speak was the owner of the house, who told me that he used to be a drug dealer and that they all had sins in their past ... that I shouldn't feel uneasy about mine. Several others echoed his thoughts, and one by one they all came and hugged me! Of course the enemy tried to keep me away! That night was not only an illustration of the spiritual war we are all in, but of the truth that often, if not every time, when we attempt to do what God wants us to do we will experience resistance from the enemy of our souls, the devil. The importance of Christians being plugged in to the Body of Christ (the local church) was also brought into focus … the enemy had gone to great lengths to keep me from breaking through that night!

Not long from then, these small group meetings were to be the beginning of my healing and final deliverance from drugs and alcohol. When I began to attend these meetings regularly, time and again my precious new family would gather around me and comfort me, minister to me, and often lay hands on me in prayer. One night I was prophesied over, as two of my new friends echoed the words of the prophets speaking directly to my impoverished soul, "I will restore to you the years that the locust has eaten" (Joel 2:25), and "I will give you a new heart and put a new spirit within you; I will take the heart of stone out of your flesh and give you a heart of flesh" (Ezekiel 36:26). As they spoke these words, my heart indeed began to melt within me … only the Lord could know how cold and hard I'd had grown during my many years of wallowing in the filthy pit of sin. Only the Lord knew how bankrupt, desolate and tormented my soul had become as I unknowingly, then knowingly sold myself to the devil in pursuit of pleasure and the vain attempt to escape the pain. In the days prior to this my heart had become so cold that if my mother had walked into the room and dropped dead on the floor in front of me, I would not have been able to shed a tear. Since the night I became an atheist until that day, I could remember crying only three or four times. After becoming a Christian, twice I wept uncontrollably before God begging Him to set me free from addiction and sin, but except for those and a couple of times before, my heart was stone cold, seared by sin and pain as with a hot iron.

Now the Lord was promising to restore my life to me as He did to Lazarus ... and to heal my scarred, tortured heart!

The next 6 or eight months were both joyful and trying. Like a teenager growing up, this time was very exciting yet scary as well. In one of the many substance abuse classes at one of the many treatment centers I was blessed to be admitted to, we learned that an alcoholic or addict stops growing emotionally at the age they begin to drink and use. By that standard I wasn't even a teenager yet, but about twelve years old ... with a long way to go to grow up! The days were especially exhilarating because during this time I also grew in understanding the truths of the Bible. Praying in faith in a way I had never done before and actually expecting answers to my prayers was an exhilarating thing. As a joint heir with Christ as Paul taught us in his letter to the Romans (8:17) and as a member of God's royal priesthood which Peter taught us (I Peter 2:9) the world became an exciting adventure! Our Lord showed me early on that I should pray with the understanding "... that if we ask anything according to His will, He hears us. And if we know that He hears us, whatever we ask, we know that we have the petitions that we have asked of Him" (I John 5:14-15). Armed with these truths and other scriptures, we as followers of Christ have been commissioned as a part of God's army on this earth. By His grace we have the privilege of being His active agents through which His Kingdom Power and Light overcomes sin and death, and the dark forces and plans of the enemy!

With that understanding, a couple of experiences further expanded my understanding of our God and His ways, and became an important part of my ongoing lessons in faith. Once a big fan of author John Steinbeck, before I knew the Lord, I'd read a number of his books. After coming to the Lord, while living in Salinas—

Steinbeck's home town—I read his book "East of Eden" and decided it would be my last. East of Eden the Bible tells us, was where Adam and Eve ended up after being ejected from the Garden of Eden for rebelling against God. Some of Steinbeck's book of that name graphically depicts some of the terrible depths that fallen men and women go to in sin … a subject I knew all too well. Radically changed since I was now, as the Bible teaches, a new person (2 Corinthians 5:17), gratefully my appetite for the things of the world was now spoiled and the book left me feeling dirty and went unfinished. As I walked the streets of Salinas one day, I happened upon a beautiful old clapboard building that had been a church at one time, but had been converted into a restaurant named "East of Eden" no doubt hoping to lure Steinbeck fans.

"Errrr!" I said aloud.

"What a travesty!" I thought.

"A place where once the God of heaven was worshiped has been tagged with that name!"

I prayed, "Lord, PLEASE shut that place down and turn it back into a church!"

The building sits on Pajaro Street near downtown, and every time I passed it, I'd beg the Lord to wipe away the aberration. A few years later after moving away I discovered that the Lord had answered my prayer! The building is once again being used to glorify God. A new congregation, The Harvestlands Church, where a number of my old friends from Joy Fellowship attend, is now putting the old building to use the way its builders intended! The tainted name is gone. Not only an outstanding example of what a prayer of faith can accomplish, it was also an object lesson contradicting a false notion that I had lived with up to that point: that only "holy" people were good enough for God to listen to. In the religion of my birth only a very small group of people elected by the church leaders after their death are called "saints" and really have God's ear. This elite group also had the privilege of going straight to heaven when they died. The rest of us would languish away our whole lives at some distance from Him, our prayers apparently for the most part falling upon deaf ears, and after dying (if fortunate enough to miss hell) were condemned to untold years in Purgatory, a place " ... like hell, but only temporary ..." where we had to suffer for our sins until we were purged of them. Only then would we be worthy to stand in His presence. In their theology the Blood of Jesus Christ is not sufficient to atone for our sins ... our blood needs to flow too!

Through the experience of God answering my prayers, some of which like this one were extraordinary, I was learning the remarkable extent of God's love for me and was experiencing first hand His generosity as illustrated in Jesus' statement, "If you then, being evil, know how to give good gifts to your children, how much more will your Father who is in heaven give good things to those who ask Him" (Matthew 7:11). The scripture also says that, "The effective, fervent prayer of a righteous man avails much" (James 5:16b).

Ah but there was the rub I thought ... I am NOT a righteous man! But thank God the Bible also says, "For He made Him who knew no sin (Jesus) to be sin for us, that we might become the righteousness of God in Him" (2 Corinthians 5:21). Because of what Jesus did for me on the cross, ALL of my sins from birth until death were atoned for with our Holy God and my prayers are heard in His throne room just as easily as those of the "holiest of saints." As the apostle Peter understood, "... of a truth I perceive that God is no respecter of persons" (Acts 10:34 King James Version). In fact, the

Bible refers to all believers as saints, and after reading it through carefully and prayerfully many times, I have found absolutely no Biblical basis for the doctrine of Jesus' death being only a partial atonement for our sins (and that we must suffer to pay the rest of the price) or for the doctrine which teaches that our good works are partially responsible for our salvation. As an old hymn says, "Jesus paid it all, all to Him I owe; Sin had left a crimson stain, He washed it white as snow!"

With the naiveté and enthusiasm of a new believer and thanks to some very good grounding in God's Word at Salem Christian Commune, Joy Fellowship and others, I was developing the habit of asking God for exactly what I or others need AND expecting Him to answer in the affirmative as long as my petition is not in conflict with His wise and perfect will. The truth is that as long as our petitions meet those criteria and I am living the way He wants me to " ... as best as I know how" as Cliff Barrows so often said, that God will eventually answer ... either yes, no, or not now, but He will always answer.

Another fantastic answer to prayer similar to my "East of Eden" experience, yet even more dramatic occurred not too long after that. One of my favorite things to do for years was to go home to visit my mother in New York, which I was privileged to do a number of times usually during the Christmas or Thanksgiving seasons. While there, a trip to New York City was likely on the top of our agenda. To see the city at its finest decked out in Christmas decorations and bustling with even more people than usual is always a treat. One year mom had purchased tickets to a Broadway show, and as we rode the train into the city the usual sense of excited anticipation filled the railcar. The glitz and glitter, the feeling of excitement and luxury which are tantamount with a trip to New York and

Broadway, all served to build the magic we felt as we settled in to our cushioned seats and awaited the opening curtain. As I thumbed through the Playbill though, and came upon the biography of the play's leading man, I was sadly disappointed to see that the editors made it a point to highlight the fact that the star was living in sin with another man. The spell was broken, and as the play commenced it turned out to be laced with a series of one tawdry sexual innuendo after another. Squirming in my chair, I fought the urge to get up and walk out. Since my mom had bought the tickets as a Christmas present, I was careful not to reveal my thoughts by any expression of disgust or pain. What could I do! Fervently I began to pray, "Lord, if this is what Broadway has to produce these days, PLEASE Lord, shut this place down. PLEASE Lord, shut this place down and replace it with something that will glorify your Name rather than this filth!" The more I prayed the better I felt. Finally, I prayed, "Oh please Lord, shut this place down and turn it in to a church!" As I continued to pray and praise Him, I felt the Holy Spirit lift me up, and as I communed with the Lord, I hardly noticed as the rest of the play whizzed by.

A couple of years later while again visiting my mom, I decided to visit Pastor David Wilkerson's church in Manhattan. David's early experience in New York City was the focus of the 1970 movie "The Cross and the Switchblade" starring Pat Boone as David Wilkerson and Erik Estrada as Nicky Cruz, and was viewed by an estimated fifty-million people in over thirty languages in 150 countries according to World Film Crusade. The events upon which the movie was based led to the founding of Teen Challenge (later called "Adult & Teen Challenge"), the extremely successful Christian drug treatment program. David was close to my friend and mentor James Thomas, and I'd heard that the Lord had called him from East Texas back to New York City to start a church. Calling ahead before flying to New York and noting the service times and the address of the Times Square Church, I knew it would be one of the highlights of my trip. As I waited for the train in the comfortably familiar surroundings of the station in Pleasantville, memories of many Christmas trips into the city put me in a festive mood. The old dark green railroad coaches with "New York Central" stenciled in gold lettering above the windows, and the upholstered benches which flipped back and forth smartly so that you could face forward both going to and coming from the city had long since been replaced. The sterile, stainless steel Metro North cars with plastic seats just weren't the same, yet the feelings were. Quickly picking up steam after leaving the station, the landscape blurred by as we passed one rustic little town after another until the suburbs gave way to the urban sprawl of the New York metropolitan area and then the borough of the Bronx. After crossing a bridge and going through one fairly long tunnel (which as a kid always fooled me into thinking we had reached Grand Central) then exploding into daylight for a while longer, the train burrowed into the belly of Manhattan. Finally, creaking and creeping, the train rumbled through the long tunnel to a stop. Like a giant anaconda disgorging itself the train released its thick stream of its passengers, and we all hurried up the ramp into the historic, cavernous expanse of Grand Central Terminal. New York City seemed like a giant organism teeming with life, and as I stepped out into the cold December air the great city seemed more alive than ever.

Checking the address in my notes, I made my way to Times Square. At first, I was a bit disappointed that the building was not directly on Times Square. When I found the place though, my disappointment evaporated—the Times Square Church met in The

Mark Hellinger Theater, the same theater where my mom and I had seen that nasty play a few of years before! The crowd pressing in through the doors was alive with God's Spirit! Blacks, Whites, Hispanics and Asians were all packing into the old theater to worship God! The service was great and after it was over, I hurried to get in line to talk with David Wilkerson. Not only did I want to thank him for Teen Challenge and how his friend and former student James Thomas had been such a blessing to me, but I couldn't wait to tell him how I'd prayed for the Mark Hellinger Theater to be shut down and to be re-opened for God's glory. With a line of people behind me still waiting to talk with him, I briefly related the story and David threw his head back and laughed. He said that the play my mother and I had seen "Legs Diamond" was the last one to be performed in the building. It was a tremendous failure, lost a vast amount of money, and caused the theater to shut down! God then handed it over to David Wilkerson and Times Square Church, and as of this writing over 25 years later, the church is still thriving on that spot. Once again, my prayer was answered, though not at all because of my righteousness which doesn't exist apart from Jesus. I am anything but a "saint" according to the commonly accepted definition.

No matter how fervently I pray ("The effective, fervent prayer of a righteous man avails much" James 5:16b), unless it is "according to His will" (I John 5:14, 15) it isn't going to happen. The "name it and claim it" doctrine of some contemporary prosperity preachers is nothing but a big lie, most often perpetrated to line their own pockets with money, and even worse, undermines the faith of any whose prayers are not answered as they are taught to expect.

# CHAPTER 40

My time at Sun Street Center was productive and once again I'd strung together months of sober and clean time. Yet having that and a good job under my belt didn't mean I was quite ready to put my old life behind me yet. It wasn't God's time yet either though, since no one can simply will their sin away—if we could do that, Jesus' death on the cross was unnecessary! Tired of walking or riding my bicycle everywhere, and immature in my walk with the Lord, I lied about my job history to convince an auto dealer to sell me a new pickup truck on credit. Justifying my lies by telling myself that I was a new man—the old Neil was dead and gone, the new Neil was trustworthy—for hours I sat in the dealer's credit office sticking to my story. Of course, the very fact that I was willing to lie even though I had hours to think about it while waiting for the credit approval, was proof that the old man was far from dead. Once I entered this realm of "let's pretend", the truth (from God's Holy Spirit) like the hounds of heaven whispered to me, preventing me from sweeping my shameful actions under the rug. Since I refused to listen and repent, the enemy clobbered me with feelings of guilt and eventually hopelessness, until I once again submitted to the demons and ran for some medication for my tortured soul. As surely as ever, that false oasis disappeared shortly after I reached it, but it was too late for me to escape without the usual disastrous crashing and burning. How I actually got started that time I don't recall, but it was a madcap two weeks in which I was arrested three times for drunk driving. The circumstances of the first two Driving Under the Influence charges escape me, but the third one came after I narrowly missed running over a prostitute who was standing on the sidewalk in Salinas' small red light district. To the detriment of the general population they let me go from jail each time within a day or two pending a court date, and I was left to contemplate my dim future, which simply inclined me to drink and drug even more.

The last time, they released a few of us at the same time, and with my first few breaths of fresh free air I remembered my truck and decided to go get it. Nothing to it, except that it was now in the auto pound and I was penniless, but a little thing like that wasn't going to stop me. One of the other newly released inmates came along with me as we sallied forth with high hopes. Without any money, the desk man at the towing company yard had little sympathy for me, and after trying my best to persuade him, my new pal and I left. Just then, a brilliant idea hit me and I turned to him and said, "Wait here!"

The auto salvage yard and pound was situated next to a mobile home park. A six or seven foot high wooden fence surrounded the pound, and my thought was that if I could just find my truck I'd start it with my spare key and away I'd go. Making my way into the rather well kept mobile home park, I encountered an older man out in his yard. Being the friendly sort I greeted him, and after some pleasantries told him of my plan to liberate my truck.

"I'm going to drive it right over this fence!" I proudly proclaimed.

Though I often talked my way into big trouble, this time I

shared my plan with the right guy, because instead giving me a look of disgust and calling the police, he said, "You don't need to do that, there is an open gate in the back. Just drive out!"

Thanking my new friend, after looking this way and that I jumped the fence. It was a big yard, but I was happily surprised to see that the truck was parked right up against the fence not far from where I landed. On the other side of the lot about fifty yards away were a couple of Doberman Pinschers asleep in the sun. As nervous as a hippie in a barber shop, I climbed into the truck and turned the ignition key. As the engine roared to life (I was kind of wishing it would purr instead) quickly putting it in gear without waiting a minute or to two allow the oil to circulate through the engine, I backed it out. Thankfully there was no one in sight and the dogs slept on as I drove through the back gate and made my way around the front to where my pal was waiting for me. "Jump in!" I yelled, and off we went on a new adventure.

We hadn't gone a mile before we came upon a guy hitchhiking. He was a young guy with a multi-colored Mohawk haircut, black leather and clothes, and metal rings and studs sticking out of his body from various places. When he learned we were headed for Los Angeles he wanted to come. Since the truck was a compact with room for only two in the cab, he jumped in the bed and away we went. Typical of my crazy escapades I don't recollect a tremendous amount about our trip south except that we bought some beer, picked up another guy in Santa Barbara and that I was going around 100-miles-an-hour most of the time. With a load of four men, the hilly terrain, and the breakneck speed at which we were traveling, we almost worked the little engine to death. For some reason I thought to check the oil when we stopped for gas (not a typical thought while drunk) and discovered that the tremendous heat generated by the prolonged high speed drive had evidently vaporized almost all the oil ... had I driven much longer the engine would have been cooked! After adding a couple of quarts of oil we continued on our journey and ended up at Knott's Berry Farm ... and almost landed in jail. With the bed of the truck full of empty beer cans and our colorful friend, we drew the attention of the security guards as we pulled into the parking lot. It turns out that our young friend was younger than he told us, and the dark image of jail bars began to play on the screen of my mind for a while, but thank God they let us go. Broke and deflated, we returned to Santa Barbara, then Salinas shortly thereafter, none-the-wiser for our efforts.

With court dates approaching and the prospect of prison again hanging over me, I concocted a scheme to befriend a bi-lingual Mexican American and enlist him to accompany me to Mexico as a translator so that I could sell my truck on the black market. The plan was to take the proceeds and head to the South Seas never to return. As the poet said, "the best laid schemes of mice and men often go astray." He didn't mention poorly made ones, and as you can imagine the outcome wasn't good. Francisco, who I met in a coffee shop in Castroville was up to the job, and after tanking up in Pacific Grove on a cocktail of Yukon Jack (a flavored whiskey drink) and milk since my stomach was now hurting, we set sail for Mexico. Feeling expansive as the South Seas was my ultimate destination, I decided take the scenic route out of town, and a nice oceanfront drive through Pebble Beach seemed to be in order.

In the strange alcoholic reality that I was living in, everything in the world was bright and I was on my way to a sensational new life in the South Pacific! Feeling like a tourist on vacation, we cruised along enjoying the scenery. Shortly after passing The Lodge at Pebble Beach and enjoying the view a little too much, I failed to watch the road. Francisco yelled out just before we plowed into a Mercedes 500 SL stopped at the intersection in front of us. With my truck making an unpleasant whining sound, I backed up and then pulled beside the Mercedes.

The driver, a lady who must have been eighty or eighty-five years old said "Oh, oh" and looked stunned but unhurt.

If my new friend hadn't shouted just before impact causing me to slam on the breaks, which in turn made the front of my truck nose down causing the radiator and other "softer" parts of the small truck to absorb the force of the collision rather than the bumper slamming into her car, I may have killed her.

Just as I was taking all of this in, a car with the windows rolled down crossed the intersection and stopped in front of us blocking our way, and a young lady in the front passenger seat called out, "Don't worry ma'am, we'll call the police right away!" and drove off.

That and the fact that the truck didn't seem as if it would make it to Mexico, inspired me to pull into the driveway of the nearest mansion and park. "Quick", I motioned to Francisco, "This way!" We sprinted across the elite golf course and then walked nonchalantly up to The Lodge.

By God's grace, the doorman who greeted us decked out in a very formal outfit akin those worn by doormen at high end hotels in New York City, was a friend of mine. After I breathlessly told him the story, he took us inside and told us to sit down, " … and don't say a word and don't move!"

After a few nervous minutes of waiting, he reappeared and said that some friends of his were getting off of work, and to just sit tight for a few more minutes. Sure enough, within a short time my friend ushered us out to a waiting car and away we went … safely right through the guarded gates of one of the most exclusive communities on the planet, and on to freedom.

The wreck was likely God's way of preserving my life—had I made it to Tijuana as planned, the local criminals probably would have simply killed me for the truck. Sensing the end of the party, I turned tail and headed back to Sun Street Center. They took me back in, but I was simply waiting for the axe to fall … my court date for the three drunk driving charges was approaching, and my old fear of the penitentiary, like an ever present specter hung over my head. Prior to the slip I had about ten months of sobriety under my belt and my dad had given me some frequent flier miles to come home to mark my first year of sobriety. The airplane tickets in my pocket kept calling to me. At that time, without paying a penny you could change the destination or departure dates for that type of ticket with merely a phone call. Three times I walked to the pay phone outside the chow hall to call the airline, planning on booking a flight to the east coast to escape prosecution. Again, the Lord interceded on my behalf, for on each attempt to do so I froze up. Once I dialed the number, but couldn't talk, the other two times my hands began to shake and I couldn't even dial the phone. Praying hard and asking a brother in Christ to pray with me, and knowing that I should stay and face the music, in the end the Lord kept me from the terrible mistake.

Not long after that I was tested further—something else came to light which made a prison sentence even more likely. One day the Program Director at Sun Street called me out of class and said that a Highway Patrolman was there and had asked for me by name. The law stated that the Director did not have to disclose whether or not I was there, but by now I was resolved to face any and all consequences which were coming, so I met with him. The Patrolman, a somber older gentleman, said that they had found my truck in the Pebble Beach driveway and in the glove compartment were copies of the three recent Driving Under the Influence citations. The guy knew that I was in very hot water already and didn't ask too many questions. Committed to following Jesus and obeying His Word as best as I could, I admitted driving the truck that day but didn't volunteer to incriminate myself any further than that. He left saying he would continue his investigation. Any new charges on top of the three cases already against me increased the likelihood of a trip to the penitentiary. Once again fear rose up in me like a nightmare, yet praying fervently in the days leading up to the date for my appearance in court, the Lord preserved my resolve.

When the day arrived, to my great relief I missed the going to prison again. My sentence was six months in the county jail, which didn't exactly delight me, but beat the alternative. Almost every other trip to jail prior to that had been hell on earth. Remaining silent in the face of injustice of any kind is not easy for me, and given the segment of society that ends up behind bars, any justice that does transpire usually occurs outside the jail and not in it. What normally happened was that I'd intercede when some bully was taking advantage of a weaker inmate or in some other way stand up to a bully, and he would jump me. Thank God He gave me a very thick skull and a strong body to carry it on, so I was never hurt badly. Violence and I don't mix well though, so jail time meant that extreme stress was the rule, day and night. While being booked in, I told the jailer that I was in imminent danger of taking my own or someone else's life. That landed me in solitary confinement which was my plan ... although lonely and boring, it would be safe there. For two or three weeks I had my own little world, out of the cell only once a day to shower. After watching me for a while though, one day they decided that I wasn't crazy after all and sent me to the main jail. "Yikes!" I thought, "Here we go again!"

While being processed through the area where they issued clothes for the main jail population, the cold glances of the trustees didn't do anything to make me feel more comfortable. My change from the orange jumpsuit which designated high risk prisoners, to the standard jail uniform must have caused extra scrutiny. From that point on though, the whole experience would be quite different. Along with my time in Santa Barbara, this was to be the best jail time I ever did in my life! (Sounds like an oxymoron doesn't it?) Within just a few days I learned that they had Christian meetings almost every day of the week, and beginning that day I attended every one. Next, another of the believing prisoners helped me get assigned as a trustee to the work crew that he was on. Much to my surprise Monday through Friday for about 45 hours a week I rode around outside the walls of the jail working on a county work detail—I only had to bear the jail environment a few waking hours a day, and on weekends. The prayer and worship meetings, Bible Studies and godly counseling we were receiving made it seem more like a Bible college than a jail. When I wasn't working or in a meeting my head was buried in the Bible or a biography of one of the saints of the church. Although impossible to forget that it was a jail because of the lack of freedom, and the presence of the normal constraints and routines found in such institutions, this place seemed to have much less of the heavy, raw feeling of evil that hung over most of the other jails I'd been in. The guys in the bunks next to mine shot heroin every night and I heard other stories, but didn't see or experience much of the usual stuff myself and was very grateful for that.

Rev. James Thomas the local Teen Challenge pastor, was a bright beacon of light there. James brought several meetings to our section of the jail each week and counseled one on one with anyone who requested it. Later I learned that he spent about fifty hours a week in the jail. A hard-boiled New Yorker, James, who along with Mary his wife had been delivered from heroin addiction through David Wilkerson's original Teen Challenge program in New York City, was the perfect teacher for me. Typical of a native of Manhattan he saw most things as black and white, wasn't shy about speaking his mind, but didn't say much that was frivolous or unnecessary either. James told us the truth about God and the Bible, and as a good friend, without apology he let us know what we'd need to do to change our lives. Most importantly he taught us to refer to the Bible for guidance in every aspect of our lives and as the final authority on every question. He was as sold out for Jesus as much as anyone I've ever known, and seemed to be 100% dedicated to His cause. What my Dad would call "a regular guy", James didn't have his head in the clouds … he was one of us, and a nice guy who really cared for the people he ministered to. Since he was so on fire for the Lord and so ardent in his dedication to what was right, he constantly challenged us not to be halfhearted in our commitment to God. Our Lord used James Thomas to teach me that the only way to seek my God and to thrive in my walk with Him was to give myself completely to the Lord every day. We learned that lukewarm Christians not only let the Lord down, but themselves and all those who love and depend upon them as well. When we live life with our allegiance divided between God and the world (that is, anything which we allow to contend with God for preeminence) the joy and peace and power go out of our lives and we bring trouble upon our heads—and end up drawing ourselves and others away from the Lord rather than towards Him.

My time learning from James Thomas and the other kind Christians who ministered there made this particular stint in jail seem to end rather quickly, even taking into account that I served only four months of the 6 because of "good behavior." My kind sister Pam and her husband Duncan had arranged for our mom and me to fly to England to visit them immediately after I was to be released. That combined with my new closer relationship with the Lord put me in a buoyant mood when I was given an eight-hour pass to go to town a few days before being released. The pass was designed to allow the inmate the opportunity to find a job and a place to live. Since my friend Jeff had already agreed to rent a room to me and as I was set to leave for England three days after I got out of jail, my trip into town was purely a delight, simply savoring a taste of freedom and visiting friends before my release. The pass was just about over when I stopped in to say hello at Sun Street Center prior to going to back to the jail. After chatting with a number of folks and about to head out, the lady at the front desk handed me some mail which they had been holding for me. My countenance fell when I discovered that one of the letters was a warrant for my arrest for the hit and run in Pebble Beach! Having all but forgotten about it since they had me in jail for four months and I hadn't heard a word, it was a shock. More than one inquiry about it to the guards at the jail had turned nothing up and it appeared that they had dropped the charges. Like the talons of a vulture, fear seized me again … if the old lady who was driving the Mercedes had one hair on her head hurt, besides another drunk driving offense, a charge of felony hit and run could be filed against me! The terror of the penitentiary loomed black over my head again. Trudging back to the jail like a robot, part of me wanted to turn and

RUN in the opposite direction. My legs just kept moving though …
I had come too far now … I knew that I must play this thing out.
It's unlikely I would have made it though unless the Lord had
inspired me to begin singing hymns. As I sang, I was strengthened
in my spirit enough to walk back to the place which may well have
led to the end of my freedom, and my life.

Once inside and back in my jail clothes, I made a beeline to the
command center and handed the letter notifying me of the arrest
warrant to the jailer on duty. The guard listened to my plea and said
he'd try to get me to court as soon as possible since I was due to be
released in three days. Knowing how slowly things move in jail, my
hopes were dim. Given the best possible outcome it seemed rather
unlikely that I'd get to court in time to be released before my plane
left for England … at worst, it meant a trip to prison and an early
death. Immediately I began praying and asked my brothers in Christ
to pray with me. In answer, the very next day I was called to the
command center and they told me that I'd be taken to court the next
morning! Earlier in my stay, one of the other inmates who came
from another part of the state told me that the judicial system in
Monterey County was one of the toughest in California … there was
not one lenient judge on the bench. As they loaded us up for the trip
to the courthouse in Monterey, I prayed and prayed. Even though
I'd experienced God's tremendous grace again and again
throughout my life, I was as nervous as a balloon in a pin factory as
we were ushered into the courtroom. When they introduced me to
my public defender who was rather young, I thought, "Great, where
is Perry Mason when you need him!"

The Lord had picked this one just for me though, because the
advice the attorney gave me (twice) was, "Just keep your mouth
shut. Let me do the talking!"

Only God could have known what I needed at that moment … the attorney had just met me.

A ray of light shown when a black robed man walked in to the courtroom with a big smile on his face and said, "My name is Traffic Magistrate Johnson. Judge Martin is out sick today and I'm filling in for him!" When my case was called, the District Attorney presented the charges against me, and my attorney responded tersely after stifling my attempt to speak. I was so paralyzed by the tension I don't remember exactly what the DA recommended as a punishment. Within a few seconds (which seemed like hours) the judge pronounced, "90 days in jail (pause) … time served."

The DA jumped to his feet and said, "Your Honor, aren't you even going to require restitution in this case?" (meaning that I pay to repair the damaged Mercedes).

"No I'm not." replied the judge, "In my experience you people don't follow up on these things."

With a tap of his gavel I was free! The trip back to the county jail to await my release was spent praising God all the way. Like a fairy tale, within a few days I went from being an inmate to flying overseas on vacation.

# CHAPTER 41

Dawn was just breaking as we descended over the southern tip of Ireland and the black fingers of the Emerald Isle jutted into the sea below, as we prepared for landing in London. I longed just to jump out and parachute to my ancestral homeland and explore the place which I had often dreamed about, but that would have to wait for another day. We had uncommonly good weather during our stay in England as it only rained one day out of eight, and it was sunny and in the 60s and 70s the whole time. Though it was February, flowers were blooming in St. James Park! My poor sister Pam who had recently moved there from sunny Southern California and had yet to acclimate to the ever present rain and fog kept exclaiming, "It's never like this!" A sense of awe accompanied me as things I had read about came alive before me. Being from an area of America which is rich in history dating back to the Revolutionary War, the antiquity of the Old World was an order of magnitude greater and was very impressive. Stepping off the tour boat which had just moored on the River Thames, as I stood on a huge block of stone which was part of the foundation of fortress Londinium and had been laid by the Romans 2000 years earlier, the gravity of it blew me away. On the weekend we drove to the city of Bath, and I marveled as we walked through an ancient building built around natural hot springs in which Roman soldiers had once soaked their weary bodies. Equally impressive to me as an avid student of more recent history, was the Imperial War Museum where artifacts pertaining to World Wars I and II and the British Empire at its height were on display. In awe I stood gazing at a small room filled with the furnishings of Winston Churchill's bunker command office. The trip was a restful break and it was so nice to spend time with my family ... but struggles awaited back in the U.S.

For every step I took forward the enemy came roaring back attempting to put an end to me once and for all. Unrelentingly he worked away at me, and being fully acquainted with my weaknesses again found a way to trip me up. The goose hung high for a couple of months, but eventually I felt it necessary to celebrate my birthday with alcohol and drugs. Shortly after that party began, I was arrested again when a taxi driver whom I failed to pay delivered me to the Police Station. Uncharacteristically, they released me shortly after arresting me upon my promise to appear in court the following Tuesday. It hadn't been long since I'd received five years probation for the three drunk driving convictions, and the possibility of showing my face before a judge again terrified me. If the judge ruled that I had violated my probation and sent me to prison, I'd be dead ... there was no way I'd go. Still in the middle of a drinking and drugging binge, logic did not prevail this time, and I decided to flee the state. Concocting a plan to hitchhike to Interstate eighty in San Francisco and then to the east coast to hide in the mountains for the rest of my life, off I went.

San Francisco was as far as I got. Within a week and after five close brushes with death my trip ended. The first place I landed was Civic Center Park in front of the San Francisco City Hall. One morning, after hanging out with the local talent for a couple of days mooching their booze and drugs, I decided to head over to Haight Ashbury to see if I could get some drugs there. Eying the people walking on the street for a few minutes, I hoped to find a kindred spirit but did not. Dropping into a couple of bars with the same thought ended up being a wash as well since the crowds were thin, and there wasn't an easy opening to invite myself for a free drink. Without sleep for quite some time, when a guy invited me to crash at his place after hearing my sad story (contingent upon his roommates' approval) I felt a sense of relief. A few minutes later though after lying down on the hardwood floor of the clean well-kept second story apartment where he left me, he came back and said that it was a no go. Off into the night I walked as so many times before … aimless, just walking to walk. Where should I go? I was very hungry and very, very tired … craving food, a drink, a drug, and desperate for some sleep. As I walked along the deserted streets of a residential neighborhood late into the night, an intense rage rose up in me which was unfamiliar. The thought crossed my mind to rob somebody to get what I wanted. The story of some teenagers in Dallas I'd heard about years before came to mind: they would to hit people over the head with a brick, rifle through their pockets, and watch them twitch as they died. Appalled at the time, but now in desperation and with anger burning in my chest, for a moment I was almost ready to smash someone too. Now treading on very dangerous ground, a cold chill went down my spine as I came back to myself and walked on, shaken to the bone and very afraid that I could have contemplated such a savage act even for a second. Thankfully I happened upon some woods. Realizing that they were on the grounds of The Presidio which was still an active US Army base at the time, I pondered for a minute as to whether I should risk detection and arrest by crawling in there to sleep, yet exhaustion won out. After settling comfortably into a soft pile of leaves and brush and about sleep, I realized the brush was full of needle sharp burrs, the kind that stick to you! Disgusted and once again angry, for an hour I sat picking the burrs off of my clothes before getting back on the street and moving on.

It was mid-morning by the time I made it back to Haight Ashbury and a generous street person offered to share his booze—I was sedated for a little while. After sleeping in the bushes that night though, another sorry scene unfolded the next day. As I made my way down to the end of Haight Street and ventured in to Golden Gate Park, I thought, "This is it!" Ground zero for the hippie movement two decades before, it was still a hangout for druggies.

Just inside the park entrance there must have been a hundred people sitting around in groups, some on blankets, most just on the grass. Some were playing Frisbee or throwing a ball, some playing guitars, and many looked like throwbacks to the 60s—I knew with some persistence I'd get my prize—drugs.

After reconnoitering for a minute, I settled on one klatch of folks and asked a guy named Sam if he could score five dollars' worth of pot for me.

"Yeah." he said, but then went on talking to his pals. He was doing me a favor and I didn't know him, so for fifteen minutes or so I just hung out, expecting he'd get up to score for me in a few minutes. When he didn't, I got up and walked around checking out the scene. When I came back and sat down, I asked Sam if he was going to cop for me.

He stopped his conversation long enough to turn and say, "Yeah, just a minute." Then jumped back right in the conversation where he left off. Figuring he meant what he said, I stuck around.

From their conversation I learned that I'd stumbled upon a

group of Hells Angels without their colors on.

Acting out of character I kept my mouth shut for a while and waited, at least for a short time. I knew enough to tread lightly around these guys. Lamentably my exercise of wisdom was transient, because after getting up a second time and meandering around for a while, my well known impulsiveness and impatience and kicked in, and from about twenty yards away I shouted, "Hey Sam! When are you going to get that nickel bag for me?"

Sam rose to his feet in a fury with blood in his eyes. One of his chums jumped up to trying to calm him down. No doubt there were narcs in the crowd which accounted for Sam becoming infuriated at me for bringing attention to him, but also causing his friend to try to keep Sam in check—it would have been messy if he cut me open like a mackerel in front of the police! Again displaying an incredible lack of sense, I just stood there and watched the whole scene play out.

"See no evil, hear no evil, speak no evil!" Sam hissed between his teeth.

That's the street version of, "Dead men tell no tales." and Sam was itching to quiet me down permanently. His pal reached to restrain him and spoke in to his ear (probably alerting him to a nearby undercover cop) and thankfully Sam sat back down. Only then did I walk away. But for the grace of God they would have carried me away that day for my last ride.

Having escaped my first appointment with death, as sanity returned to me briefly it seemed wise to avoid Golden Gate Park for a while so I headed back to Civic Center Park near downtown. As I stood talking with someone the next day, two tall thin guys who claimed to be in the Coast Guard were a few steps away practicing martial arts. The next thing I knew, one of them kicked me in the jaw knocking me to the ground. In bars all across America men had tried to shut me up by punching me in the mouth, but none successfully. This time, my jaw was broken ... had it not given way absorbing the force of the blow it could easily have broken my neck. Twice now within a day my life could have been snuffed out, yet it was spared. Taking stock of the situation I soon found a hospital. After waiting a long, long time to be seen I got tired of waiting and faked unconsciousness, collapsing to the floor. Once safely on a gurney being fussed over by medical folks I revived. They diagnosed me with a broken jaw and gave me some medication for the pain, but then kicked me out without treating the jaw because I had no insurance. Someone on the street suggested another hospital where they would treat me, and about eleven o'clock that night my jaws were wired shut with stainless steel wires. It was daylight by the time I headed back towards downtown and within a few hours I was mixing the liquid codeine pain medicine they'd given me with cheap wine. By mid-afternoon an overwhelming feeling of nausea hit me and I remembered the story a friend had told me about having his jaws wired shut ... the doctor had warned him not to drink, because if he vomited, he would aspirate the vomit and die! Having remembered the warning earlier but choosing to ignore it (!) I had stolen an expensive pair of wire cutters from the oral surgeon who wired me up anticipating such a circumstance. Ashamed, I later returned them to the doctor but pleaded with him to give me something to cut the wires with just in case. Though disgusted, he was kind enough gave me an inexpensive pair of wire strippers that had a small area on the end to cut wire. The nausea wasn't going away but getting worse, so I solicited help from a storefront charity to get to the hospital. Knowing I was about to vomit any minute, fear crept over me as death approached. As I became more scared and agitated, the charity eventually gave me money for a taxi cab, yet by the time the cab came night had begun to fall and I was very close to throwing up. Urging the cabbie to step on it and realizing that we wouldn't get there in time, rolling down the window in anticipation of getting sick, I broke into a cold sweat and with shaking hands I started cutting the four wires which held my mouth shut. One, two, three ... but I couldn't quite get the last! As strong as stainless steel is, even with only one wire intact in the back right side of my jaw, my mouth was still clenched tightly shut. Desperately I clipped away at the last wire. Whether I had scored it enough to weaken it or the Lord did a miracle I don't know, but a second before I vomited, the wire broke and I was able to vomit out the window of the cab without aspirating it. Three times now I had narrowly missed dying.

At the hospital they wired my jaws shut again and sent me away with stern warnings not to drink again while I was wired up. Acting out of character I managed to avoid booze for a while, but of course needed to anesthetize myself in some way. When on a run I never stopped until hitting the wall ... hard. The casual observer would have noticed that I'd hit the wall hard several times already, but it took a lot for a hardhead like me to give up and for the time being there was more stupidity left in me. There was more to it than that though, because true to what I'd learned about spiritual warfare since becoming a Christian, unaware of it at the time, strong spiritual forces were driving me like an ox to the slaughter. During my years as an addict and alcoholic, although often deluded into thinking that I was running the show, in fact I was like a marionette, dancing to the devil's tune ... being led like a dog on a leash. To my shame and dismay he played me like arcade game for years, like a cat toying with a mouse before having him for dinner.

In pursuit of the next high and still displaying an inordinate amount of foolishness, back I headed to Golden Gate Park for drugs in spite of the fact that Sam and his friends frequented the place. Without any money this time, my plan was to rely on an old scheme to get some for free. The idea was to find buyers who were looking for dealers, then act as a middleman so I could share the drugs with the buyers (who of course were always grateful when I returned with the goods). The plan worked, and the college kids who were my hosts for the day even wanted to purchase my two favorite drugs, marijuana and LSD. With their money in my pocket, I ventured in to the park and returned shortly with the dope. Before you know it, we had all swallowed some LSD and were driving to Ocean Beach near the end of the park to party. There were four of us in the compact car, and once we arrived at the turnout parking area overlooking the Pacific Ocean, the financier of the deal pulled out the pot and started rolling a joint. Surprise! Within about thirty seconds we were surrounded by four plain clothes police officers with their guns drawn and pointed at our heads. One false move and we would have been dead, dead, dead! Thank God nobody moved. Angrily and nervously they ordered us out of the car and frisked us. After questioning us thoroughly, in disgust they us let us go after warning us and pouring our dope down the sewer. It turns out that they were expecting to bust a major drug transaction at the same location and time, and we had blown their cover ... and could have lost our heads! Brush with death number four.

Shaken and feeling defeated, I decided to abandon my plan to run from the law. My plan wasn't working and it didn't even look like I'd get out of San Francisco alive! Heading back to Salinas to face the music finally seemed like a better thing to do ... the right thing and certainly safer. Unlike the travel modes I knew as a kid,

Lost Boy Found

traveling in style now meant Greyhound Bus Lines. I made my way to the station and when I got there, my eyes lit upon the Traveler's Aid office—as far as I can remember that was the only time I've seen one. After rehearsing part of my sad story, they agreed to buy me a bus ticket back to Salinas. For some reason though it couldn't happen until the next day, so they arranged for a room in a hotel for the night and sent me away with five dollars in my pocket for food. The room was in a "hotel" in the Tenderloin section of San Francisco, one of the roughest neighborhoods in the country. Knocking on the door of the manager's office, he directed me to a room without any problem, but the looks of the place gave me the creeps. Any place indoors beats living on the streets though, so I climbed the stairs to the room. Stepping onto the landing and heading down the hallway, just before reaching the room I looked to my right and noticed that someone's door was open. My jaw dropped as I looked in and realized that a beautiful woman lay naked on a bed about five feet away from me. It seemed to be way too good to be true, and it was.

"Do you know where I can get some pot?" I asked.

"No. How much money do you have?"

"Five dollars." I said, "But you just said that you didn't know where I could get any?"

"Crack." she said, "I can get some crack."

"Let's go!"

In a flash, she was fully dressed and we were out in the street headed for the crack house. She walked fast, so fast I had trouble keeping up with her. When we got to the house, a two or three-story brownstone, she went inside while I waited impatiently on the street. She must have been in there for fifteen minutes and I began to wonder if she would come out. When I noticed that virtually everyone walking up and down the crowded street was of a different race, with some giving me hostile looks, my discomfort increased a notch. Suddenly the woman came out of the door, rushed past me and started running down the street. I gave chase, but she was a lady with a mission and she was fast! Staying up with her but not gaining much, after about two blocks, as if it was prearranged, she ran into a bus which was waiting at the curb. As soon as she was inside the doors closed and it sped away. Panting, stunned and deflated, I stared as it disappeared around the next corner. As I walked back to the hotel, it occurred to me that as a white guy chasing a woman of a different race through the streets of a ghetto, her ghetto, I could *easily* have taken a bullet or knife in the back from one of her friends, or a fellow gang member. Back at the hotel I found her stoned out in her room unable or unwilling to talk or explain. Indignantly I went and complained to the manager about the incident … as if I were staying at the Hilton!

five times! Five times in the last week my life could have and likely would have been ended but for the mercies of God. Flopping into the bed at the fleabag hotel that night, hungry, exhausted, morally bankrupt and in total despair, it wasn't so much sleep that overtook me that night but numbness.

Scared of what might await me back in Salinas but also with a sense that I must go, that it was only thing to do, a sense of relief came over me when I climbed into the seat on the southbound Greyhound bus the next day. It was wrong and stupid to plan a life as a fugitive from the law. What kind of life would it have been to always be looking over my shoulder? My life had come way too close to ending in my attempt to flee, and yet I was still alive.

Maybe, just maybe God still had a use for me …. maybe there was still hope.

# CHAPTER 42

As the bus lumbered around the corner and approached the station in Salinas, my sense of moral bankruptcy settled in firmly. Before being born again, the multitudes of sins that I had committed and my incredibly filthy lifestyle had hardened me to the point of complete callousness. After finding the Lord and attempting to know Him for almost ten years now (and with increasing fervor in the last three) I had begun to soften and became reacquainted with shame. In fact, because my past guilt had been washed away completely by God's grace and I knew the joy of forgiveness for the unforgiveable, I felt shame in a way that I had never known before … as if I'd bitten the Hand that fed me. Because of that sense of condemnation, I stepped off the bus with no intention of contacting anyone that I knew. Having wallowed in filth again I couldn't face the church people. After talking to them about Jesus then falling down hard twice, I couldn't face the people in the Twelve-Step recovery group either … how weak and helpless my God would seem to them! Devastated, I left the Greyhound Station and headed south on Main Street. Within a few steps I ran into Merle Haggard. No, not the Country Western singer, but a black man by the same name that I'd met in jail. Though completely defeated (and forgetting my recent experience almost dying because of drinking with my jaws wired shut) I asked if Merle had enough money for a bottle. He did, so we went to the nearest liquor store and bought some rot gut wine. Unlike typical streetwise drunks, we walked around behind the liquor store and sat on a stump and began to drink. No drunk in their right mind would have done that. This was not a hidden alley behind the store, but a spot which could be seen from over fifty yards from several different directions. The store sat at the convergence of three streets, not a quarter mile from the police station—it seemed that neither one of us even cared any more. Throughout my entire drinking career with almost no exceptions, I was a "happy drunk" … laughing, joking and talking a lot (which accounted for many punches in the mouth). That day as Merle and I drank, we sat there and bemoaned our ill spent lives. We rehearsed many of the wrongs we'd done to ourselves, our families and others as we swilled the poison down. When the subject of our parents came up, both of us began to cry. Oh, if our cellmates in jail could have seen us then … a couple of rough tough cream puffs! In fact, we were completely broken men.

Besides the bottle, nothing would go as usual this day. Even though we sat there for at least twenty minutes no police cruiser came by, which was fortunate since we didn't make any attempt to hide the wine. When it was gone, somewhat inebriated but with very little of our pain deadened, we walked back north toward the bad part of town. Out of cigarettes, we approached a group of people in the parking lot of an apartment complex to ask for "spare change." They wouldn't give us money, but offered us food instead. Failing in our mission, we both stayed a while for some food and conversation. It turned out that the people were Christians and even knew some folks that I did. After sharing a little of our stories with them, they shared Jesus with us. As the conversation drew on, Merle decided to move on. Eventually the last of the people had to go too, and I headed in the same direction that Merle had gone. The strong pull of nicotine drove me on, and noticing a car pulling up to an ATM machine at a bank, I approached the car. Instead of asking for money for food, or some other concocted excuse, I told the truth,

"Ma'am, can you spare a couple of dollars so I could get some cigarettes?"

"Yes ... here." The pleasant lady said as she handed me a five dollar bill. "God bless you."

"Are you a Christian?" I asked.

"Yes." She said with a smile.

I thanked her, and she drove off as I pondered the fact that twice within an hour Christians had crossed my path.

After buying a pack of smokes I turned and headed back south to the nice part of town. I'd had enough of the bad part of town for the day ... and for a young lifetime. There was a nice clean bowling alley on Main Street that had a bar in it. Planning on drinking some more, even though I'd only be able to buy one or two draft beers there, drinking in an alley just wasn't appetizing to me at that point. The bar restaurant was nice place (as bars go) and faced the bowling lanes so that the patrons could watch the bowlers through large plate glass windows which lined the upper half of the wall facing the alleys. Walking in, as my eyes adjusted to the dim light, a man sitting at a small table just inside the door came into focus.

"Robbie! What are you doing here?" I said incredulously. Robbie was a guy from my church.

"I'm just sitting here having a Coke." he said.

"In a bar?" I said.

"I used to work here" Robbie stammered, "I'm just sitting here having a Coke and watching the bowlers! What are YOU doing here

Neil?" he asked. Robbie knew of my battle with booze.

"I came to get a beer."

Tears welled up in Robbie's eyes, and his lip began to quiver. "Please don't get a beer Neil. Please!" he pleaded.

I lump came into my throat, and tears welled up in my eyes too … "Okay Robbie, I won't. I'll go call someone and get some help."

Three times in less than ninety minutes, God had sent His people to me on a rescue mission. Almost ten years after beginning to pray for deliverance from the wretched slavery which seemingly held me in a death grip, the miracle had begun.

Lost Boy Found

*Part 4*
## "LAZARUS. COME FORTH!"

# CHAPTER 43

"Then Jesus said to them plainly, 'Lazarus is dead' ... Now
when He had said these things, He cried with a loud voice,
'Lazarus, come forth!' And he who had died came out bound hand
and foot with graveclothes, and his face was wrapped with a cloth.
Jesus said to them, 'Loose him, and let him go.' "
John11:14 and 43-44
"I once was lost but now am found, was blind but now I see"
Amazing Grace, John Newton

In the midst of my shame, guilt and complete brokenness the
Lord reached out to me that glorious day and sent His children my
way as signs of His great love for me. After assuring Robbie again
that I wouldn't buy a drink I called my friend Jeff who also attended
Joy Fellowship and who had previously rented me a room in his
house. Hopefully he would take me back in temporarily until I could
get back on my feet.

"I'm sorry Neil, but when you left in the middle of the night
and didn't come back it scared my mom. I have an old sleeping bag
I can bring you though, and if you sleep in the bushes tonight, I'll
pick you up tomorrow morning and we can go to the prayer meeting
at the church. There's a guy there who may help you." Jeff said.

It was all I needed to hear. Jeff picked me up from the bowling alley in a little while, and for the first time in weeks, though in the bushes, I slept like a baby underneath the Lord's beautiful, starry sky. The day dawned bright, cool and full of promise. Faithfully Jeff came, and the morning prayer meeting at Joy Fellowship was indeed a joy.

As the small group was breaking up, I nudged him, "Are you going to introduce me to the guy who may help me out?"

He called Jim over, a man I knew casually from the home fellowship that met at Jeff's house, and in a few minutes he and I were off to the doughnut shop for a talk.

Jim asked me a few questions then put forth a proposal: if I was to stay clean and sober, and go to church every Sunday and to morning prayer with him every week day, I could stay at his place.

"Sure! I can do that!" At the moment it didn't even occur to me that in the past I'd been unable to keep that promise to myself or anyone else, yet ...

The six or eight weeks living with my new friend Jim were like awakening from a long sleep. Everything seemed new! Not being a morning person, I bridled a bit at the early start to the day, but prayer first thing in the morning was a prescription straight from the Great Physician Himself. What a tremendous way to begin the day! My spirit grew in leaps and bounds under the bright, nurturing Light of God's Holy Spirit. Jim and I became close friends, and the Lord told me that he and I were brothers. Yes everyone, man and woman, who belong to Christ are my spiritual brothers and sisters because we have our Heavenly Father in common, but the Lord showed me specifically that I was supposed to be just like Jim's birth brother. Jim is one of the nicest men the Lord ever created, with a tremendous giving and generous heart and as transparent as glass in his dealings with others. He had only seen his father for a few days when he was a boy, and he passed away not long after that. He was very close to his dear mother who had worked with him in his business for years, yet she had died young too. As far as he knows, Jim has few blood relatives left on the earth, and I was to be his brother in the same way that Jesus from the cross commanded the apostle John to be a son to His mother Mary. In the years since then God has continued to prove this special bond between us ... some friendships wane with distance and time, but ours has remained rich and rewarding.

It seems that between my incredible appetite and equally strong desire to talk, my jaws muscles had become so powerful that I kept stretching the stainless steel wires stabilizing my broken jaw. Having been warned by the doctor after my jaw had to be rewired a third time that I could possibly die if the bones didn't mend soon, work of any type was off limits for me until he gave the word. This left me a lot of time to think, pray, and read my Bible. Jim's place is on about three acres of land along the Salinas River near a break in the coastal mountains which are astride Carmel Valley to the south and west and the Salinas Valley to the east. It was an idyllic place to begin of my newly emancipated life. As the days and weeks passed, the realization was dawning on me that the chains which bound me to alcohol and drugs were broken forever! Gone was the constantly present sense of unease, which was no doubt a tool which the enemy used for all those years to drive me from one drink or drug to another.

A deep peace and a new sense of freedom pervaded my soul. The no work order didn't sit well with Jim though—he is a tireless worker and life just isn't complete for him unless there is plenty of it going around. The tension between us began to build up, and combined with the fact that we both have very strong personalities, we got on each other's nerves to the point where he asked me to leave. There were no hard feelings between us and we both knew that the Lord would take care of me ... just as in many other things God's ways are not our ways.

Something (I soon realized was the Holy Spirit) prompted me to call a lady who, like Jim had been a member of our weekday home church fellowship group that met at our friend Jeff's house. Like Jim, Louise and I had only been casual acquaintances before this, and the fact that she was a sixty-year-old lady caused me to ponder why I should call her. It seemed pretty far out to ask her if I could stay with her until I was allowed to go back to work, yet to my surprise (and to hers I later learned) she invited me to stay at her place in spite of the fact that she was about to go out of town for two weeks. Although Louise Shands—who went by Lou—was severely disabled with chronic rheumatoid arthritis, she rarely uttered a word of complaint though her pain must have been excruciating. Her knee joints were almost completely disintegrated and her legs bent inwardly, her knees almost touching each other as she walked. The prescribed pain and arthritis medicines made her sick, so she didn't take them and just bravely endured her lot. Although unable to work, the Lord had blessed her with an apartment in an almost new building in the sunny little town of Gonzales, California just south of Salinas. For two weeks I just rested in my Lord, basking in the lovely surroundings and enjoying my newfound freedom.

When Lou returned, we began the rich friendship that lasted until she went to heaven a few of years later. We became like two peas in a pod, like Mutt and Jeff, like the Odd Couple. The Lord was the center of her life too, and we would share for hours sometimes about the innumerable kindnesses that had He showed us in the past and continued to shower upon us every day. Lou laughed easily and found most of my jokes funny, although she didn't hesitate to groan at some of them. We also shared a great love for God's creation ... she is one of the few people I've ever met who, like me, could watch a sunset from the beginning all the way to the end, and was often enraptured and fascinated by the incredible beauty of His creation to the point of being touched emotionally. The Lord used Lou's life and experiences with Him to strengthen me in the faith. Her faith in His Goodness was immovable despite the many trials that she had endured.

After I got my own place we often went for coffee after our mid-week home church group meeting, and one night we were having a particularly raucous time of it laughing and cutting up. A couple of California Highway Patrolmen sitting at the booth right next to us turned their heads once to see what all the racket was. Eventually one of them got up and left, but the other guy, an older chap, gray, balding and wearing gold, wire rimmed glasses stayed on after their meal to complete some paperwork. Lou and I continued to carry on having a grand old time of it, when suddenly her demeanor changed.

"Oh my! Look at that fog!" The booth was on the outside wall of the coffee shop and windows ran for almost the full length of the eastern side of the building. Looking out, it was easy to imagine we were 30,000 feet in the air in a cloud bank.

"How will I be able to drive home tonight?" Lou exclaimed. Being older and twenty miles from home it was a real concern for her.

"Let's pray Lou, the Lord can make that go away!" I volunteered.

408

I reached across the table and took her hands, and we prayed as fervently and faithfully as we could. Returning to our conversation, about ten or fifteen minutes later Lou exclaimed,

"Look, it's gone!"

Sure enough, as far away as we could see it was clear as a bell, and the stars sparkled in the heavens above. Just then I noticed the cop in the next booth; he was looking over the top his glasses at us incredulously as we laughed and praised the Lord!

Besides blessing me with a great friend, God used Lou to teach me two very valuable lessons. Some wrongly teach that miracles, healing, signs, wonders and speaking in tongues are a thing of the past, and that those and other gifts of the Holy Spirit as described in the New Testament went away when the last Apostle died. Others (equally wrong I'm certain) teach that if believers in Jesus are not healed of all of their diseases and other physical infirmities or are not wealthy, it is because either they do not have enough faith, or they have some sin that they refuse to let go of. That the gifts of the Holy Spirit are as real and relevant for today as they ever have been is supported by New Testament scripture and ample evidence. The "God wants to heal everyone always, and intends us all to be rich" position is not supported by the scriptures or any viable evidence and does *not* take into consideration that God is sovereign, and that it is *He* who decides when to wield His power and not *us*. God is not compelled to perform miracles simply because we pray (however fervently) or fast or pronounce certain scriptures over sick or wounded people as if they were magical incantations … He is not a vending machine or an automated teller machine. That miracles are not just a thing of the misty past I already knew, but just how and when and why does God choose to perform them?

Lou was the beneficiary of His loving power as few I've

known. While still a relatively young woman, she suffered a massive stroke that required her to learn to read and write and walk and talk all over again. It also caused total kidney failure which forced her to be tethered to a dialysis machine several times a week. That routine caused her to despair of life, and eventually she pleaded with the Lord to take her home to be with Him. He did not want her just yet, and He healed her completely—after nine months! Several doctors I shared this with all confirmed what the doctors told Lou at the time: it is unheard of for someone to recover kidney function after more than 90 days of total kidney failure.

Not many years later, Lou was struck with a very serious heart problem for which surgery was required. After being prepped for surgery, while she was being wheeled to operating room, her son stopped the surgeon in the hallway and asked him what to expect.

Thinking Lou was under anesthesia already and completely unconscious (though she wasn't) the doctor replied, "She's not coming out of that operating room."

Stunned and afraid Lou looked up, and at the foot of the gurney on which she laid stood Jesus! He assured her that everything would be alright, and it was. She lived on for years to tell me and many others of the miracles, and of His love for her and for all of us. The gifts Jesus gave me through Lou's life were her witness of trusting and loving Him no matter what, and a clear understanding of the "signs, wonders and miracles" issue.

As C.S. Lewis reminded us in his great Chronicles of Narnia series, the Lion (of Judah a.k.a. Aslan) is not a tame lion. He does not always behave as we expect Him to, nor will He jump at our bidding. Though the recipient of two stunning miracles, Lou's severe arthritis was never healed as far as I know. The "word of faith" (name it and claim it) preachers would say that Lou wasn't healed of the arthritis due to a lack of faith, or unconfessed sin in her life. If that was the case with her, it certainly didn't hinder God from doing miracles the first two times. Neither can the "miracles ceased when the last apostle died" preachers explain the healings which happened twice to Louise and to many others. The theology of either one of these groups just doesn't hold water!

Upon calling her daughter to try and locate her a few years after leaving California, I discovered that she had died suddenly, perhaps of a stroke or heart attack. Knowing Lou, her faith never failed to the end. Just how and when and why does God choose to perform miracles? The answers lie solely with Him, and as in every other area of life we cannot put Him in a box.

Regarding the trip to the penitentiary which I was dreading, when my day in court for stiffing the cab driver eventually came, God's amazing grace prevailed again .... the five years' probation was never mentioned and by simply paying the cab fare the incident was closed. After leaving Lou's, a room rented from a military couple didn't last too long since they had neighbors whose cars were equipped with 2000 watt speaker systems of which they were most proud of it seemed, after midnight while I was trying to sleep. The Lord then sent Mrs. Eris into my life. Mrs. Eris was a little old lady of Irish descent whose husband had been a French professor at the local community college. She and her husband Louis built a beautiful little house near downtown Salinas back in the 1930's and they had transformed the back yard into a verdant garden in which they planted a multitude of fruits, vegetables, trees, vines, and flowering perennials from around the world, all of which thrived in the ideal Monterey County climate.

Mrs. Eris had been renting rooms in her house ever since her beloved Louis had passed away prematurely many years before.

You could tell how much she loved him because even after many years hardly a day passed when she didn't mention him. Since she was eighty-seven years old when I first rented the room, we had a little adjusting to do. Although my room was in her basement and had a separate entrance, she had generally rented to students from the college before I came along and had been used to having a kind of motherly relationship with them from the standpoint of watching the hours that they kept and that sort of thing. Though surely and completely set free from my former slave master, I was still a nocturnal creature. On Friday and Saturday nights when not working the next day I would often stay out until very late, and it bothered her. After gently reminding her a few times that I wasn't a student, but a thirty-year-old man who made my own decisions, and promising to be as quiet as possible as I came and went, we settled into a comfortable relationship. The benefit of living in her lovely home for a reasonable price was mine, and in return she had some company to occupy her sometimes and the knowledge that she wasn't alone in the house every night.

My TV watching days were all but over by then, but I would occasionally sit in the front parlor with Mrs. Eris and watch Jeopardy or we'd just chat while she watched something else. Fascinated by older people ever since I was a little boy and wanting to learn as much as possible from them, engaging my elders in conversation has been a lifelong habit for me. They have been down roads that I may not or cannot ever go down, and have seen the world we now live in as it has developed. Since they lived it, our elders know the why and the when and the how and the who of recent history whereas we likely only know a small subset of it. What we have learned from books, television, movies and the Internet is filtered through the eyes of people who may have manipulated the facts to conform to their own agendas. By talking with as many people as possible who have actually lived history, we are able to gain an alternate, deeper and richer perspective on the past, and hopefully some wisdom as well. In the same front parlor where Mrs. Eris and I often sat and talked was an old handmade wooden rocking chair which had come across the Great Plains of America in a Conestoga wagon when her father and grandparents came west. During their journey west while camping near Salt Lake City, Kit Carson had stopped by to ask if he could pass through to reach the nearby stream. Yes, she was merely the descendant of those pioneers, but how would I ever have touched that bit of history hadn't I taken the time to talk with that dear old woman. Since our elders are the ones who have gone before us, on whose accomplishments our society has been built and upon whose shoulders we stand, isn't it fitting that we give them special attention and listen to, learn from and honor them?

The first weeks and months of freedom were like a dream come true. For the first time I became fully engaged with the church, the body of Christ. "For as the body is one and has many members, but all the members of that one body, being many, are one body, so also is Christ. For by one Spirit we were all baptized into one body— whether Jews or Greeks, whether slaves or free—and have all been made to drink into one Spirit. For in fact the body is not one member but many" (1 Corinthians 12: 12-14). Joy Fellowship was vibrant and exciting and rejoining them after my deliverance I was there every time the doors opened, including the love filled mid-week home meetings. My every day was centered around the new family that the Lord had given me. Even before I moved to Mrs. Eris's the Lord had given me the task of cleaning our church auditorium and straightening the chairs in preparation for Sunday services each week. Either late Friday night or sometime on Saturday, I would turn up umpteen watts of praise music on the auditorium sound system and sing and praise my Lord while doing this simple work for Him. The Lord also blessed me with an ideal first job to start my new life as well. My friend Valerie from church, a precious woman who loves the Lord, worked for a man who lived in the beautiful hill country just to the north of town, and she recommended me for a job with him. Jake's house was at the top of one of the hills surrounded by three and a half acres of native trees and brush, and he wanted to clear the underbrush from all of it. Although he had become completely blind due to an accident while in college, he didn't like the way land looked when it was cleared by a bulldozer, so he contracted with me to do it by hand. Using a machete, a mattock and a chain saw, I labored away for months on that fabulous Central California hilltop, basking in the beauty of the Lord's breathtaking creation.

The bright sunshine and balmy breeze intermingled with the melody of the wild birdsongs made for a paradise like workplace. When not being serenaded by the birds or running the electric chain saw, I'd use the 300 feet of electrical extension cord to spend much of each day listening to giants of the faith teaching the Bible on the local Christian radio station as I worked. What a glorious Bible School God had created for me! How wise and good of our Lord to prepare such a therapeutic environment for me grow in my new freedom. First, I was reborn from the walking dead, a sinner saved by grace ... now the chains of addiction which had held me in their death grip for eighteen years had fallen away like so much wax under the blazing rays of a summer sun! While my body, which had been neglected and damaged during those years of drug and alcohol abuse was being exercised to the great benefit of my physical health, my hungry and thirsty, heart, mind and soul were being nourished on the sure Word of God, solidifying the foundation upon which my new life was being built. What a blissful time it was as my spirit was lifted up on wings like eagles along with the songbirds above the treetops of the lovely California hills!

Jake my boss was quite a man, and yet another example of how fearfully and wonderfully the Lord has made the human race. Valerie told me that he was incredibly capable for someone totally blind, but I learned firsthand that amazing is the only way to describe him. Once when the chain saw failed and I left it on his work bench where he kept his woodworking tools, upon arriving the next morning he announced that he had fixed it and admonished me to be more careful in the future! Completely sighted and somewhat mechanically inclined, it is possible after many hours I could have repaired it ... but a blind man? He worked a full time job in a distant city, yet had did the job overnight!

A month or so into the job, the Lord began dealing with me about my dire bondage to cigarettes. They were a source of great frustration to me since I'd been an athlete when younger and had always been mindful of my health. The stupidity of the habit confounded me because it does not even come close to being a joy, yet takes such a terrible toll on the human body. Having begun smoking marijuana years before smoking cigarettes, I'd always thought that people who smoked cigarettes were fools because they weren't even getting high for their trouble! Well that isn't completely true—when you first start, whether it's oxygen deprivation or the nicotine or a combination of both, you do feel a bit light headed and euphoric. Although it doesn't last very long it kept me going long enough to get hooked. Also, as any tobacco smoker can tell you, once hooked a very nice feeling of relaxation comes over you when you take the first few puffs after being without for a while. The withdrawal symptoms from nicotine set in so quickly with the accompanying restlessness and craving, that just accessing the drug again is quite comforting and gives the smoker the illusion that cigarettes are their friend. Quite to the contrary it rapes the body of health and brings many to an early grave. Over the years I had tried to quit numerous times and was only successful once. Having sworn off both cigarettes and hard liquor at the same time, and choosing strictly beer and marijuana as a better diet, I succeeded in shaking them for a while. The beer and pot both acted as tranquilizers to take the edge off of the withdrawals, but one night at the bar I became thirsty for some whiskey, and since my habit was to drink whiskey straight and chase it with a hit off of a cigarette, soon I was puffing away again.

In the years before the Lord delivered me from drugs and booze, I'd made many futile attempts to quit cigarettes. Shortly after the Jesus set me free from mind altering chemicals, the deleterious effects of the combination of both the cigarette and pot smoke on my lungs became more apparent to me, and the motivation to be free from cigarettes increased regularly. However, the wisdom in the secular alcohol and drug recovery world said that it's unwise to make any major changes in life in the first year after becoming "clean and sober." Getting married or divorced, moving, changing jobs or quitting cigarettes are all stressful events highly charged with emotion which could endanger one's sobriety and thus should be avoided—and that seemed to make good sense. Not to mention that trying to quit was a tortuous process for me. My condition would progress from mild unease to an indescribable state of agitation. Combining the withdrawal symptoms with a feeling of lightheadedness that may come from the additional amount of oxygen reaching the brain, and what seemed to be a short circuiting of my thought processes, and it was hair raising! Sometimes, after a day or two without a cigarette it seemed as if I was about to crack up. Since I'd been an athlete and had done heavy physical labor most of my life and was very strong, another concern was that someone might confront me and I might snap and break their neck!

The last two of my attempts to quit were exemplary. Having determined to quit on a Wednesday night so that the worst of the withdrawals wouldn't hit while I was working, the following Saturday morning while at the laundromat to wash my clothes at seven in the morning, the full blown symptoms were closing in on me. Anyone who knew me well and saw me up and about that early on a day off would have realized something was amiss, since by nature I'm a night person. With my brain racing around inside of my skull, I sat in the deserted Laundromat oddly enough feeling somewhat content for the moment, although physically my head felt like a ball of cotton, almost numb. While waiting for my clothes to wash and uncharacteristically leafing through an ad magazine which was lying on the table, reading about things that I would never buy, my trance was broken when two women came in with three little kids and sat right next to me. Straining to focus on my reading (which was hard enough already given my condition) the kids whirled and scampered around me, finally running one of their toys into my foot.

Rage suddenly rose up in my chest, "I'm going to drop kick the little bugger!" I thought.

Wrestling that impulse down, I walked stiffly but quickly over to the adjacent convenience store, bought a pack of cigarettes and sat down on the curb and smoked a few, restoring myself to sanity. My last attempt to quit on my own was similar and occurred when

I awoke on a Sunday morning and was completely out of smokes.

"Well" I thought nonchalantly, "I just won't smoke today." It was a beautiful morning and as I jumped on my bicycle and rode to church, I was a bit excited at the prospect ... new day, new start! Arriving after the service had already begun, slipping in the door I joined the folks on the back row. The worship song they were singing was a lively one and everyone was clapping to the melody.

After only one night without a cigarette, my nerves were already stretched to the breaking point. "These people are clapping MUCH TOO LOUDLY!" I thought. Hurrying back out the door I walked over to the Woolworths next door and bought some cigarettes ... yes, after I smoked two or three, I felt just fine.

A few weeks later I came to a crossroads. One day up on the lovely hillside where I worked, as I lit up a "last one before beginning work" cancer stick, the taste of the thing just about gagged me. It was as if for the first time I could taste all the tar, nicotine and other toxins that the filthy thing contained. The Lord was showing me the dangerous poisonous tube of death for what it was, and over the next few weeks several other signs that my smoking days were numbered popped up as well. Joy Fellowship's worship services sometimes lasted almost two hours, and regularly right after the service nicotine fits would strike and I'd make my way as quickly as possible out to the plaza next to the auditorium and torch one up. One day a kid approached me and lectured me about smoking—in turn I lectured him about addiction and we parted ways. This scene repeated itself a number of times, but the Sunday after tasting the poisons in the cigarette I said to the kid, "Don't lecture me, pray for me!" He said he would, and turned on his heels and left. The Lord continued to gently convict me of the damage the cigarettes were doing to me and my need to quit. On another Sunday morning out on the plaza not long after that, my friend Robbie from the bowling alley approached me after church while I was smoking. Reminding him of the key role he played in my deliverance from drugs and booze, I asked him to pray for emancipation from nicotine as well. He said he would. Not long after that, one morning I woke up and it felt as if there was a steel band around my chest. Fear ran through me as I thought,

"I may be tough enough to quit smoking by myself, but then again I might die from emphysema or lung cancer before I get around to it."

Then the thought crossed my mind, "Neil you have two packs of cigarettes left. That will take you through Saturday morning … after that you won't have to smoke anymore."

After trying to quit smoking so many times before and ending up angry and disappointed in myself, I didn't dwell on it long. Saturday arrived, and after my usual breakfast of a couple of cups of coffee and three or four cigarettes, I rode my bicycle to the church for my cleaning duties. Securing the bike outside the church, I smoked the last cigarette in the pack and looked at my watch—it was 10:30 A.M. Physical work has always been a pleasure to me and I appreciate cleanliness, so listening to praise music while working, the time passed quickly. Stopping only once for a short break, when I finished up I looked at my watch—it was 2:30 P.M. It had taken me four hours to finish the job. Then it occurred to me that I hadn't had a cigarette in four hours … then it occurred to me that I hadn't NEEDED a cigarette. Not even the slightest sign of withdrawals! Hours passed and I marveled that there was not even a hint of the ferocious nicotine fits that had tormented me every time before when trying to quit. I was free! In fact, I had smoked my last cigarette at about the same spot where I had asked the kid and my friend Robbie to pray for me. The tremendous miracles of my deliverance from the chains that held me to all of those deadly substances brought to mind Jesus' statement "Therefore if the Son makes you free, you shall be free indeed." (John 8:36) It's now been over thirty years since any of those poisons have entered my now healthy body.

# CHAPTER 44

My new life was sailing by in a very pleasant manner, my routine consisting of work, worship and fellowship with my new brothers and sisters in Christ. Long ago I'd forgotten how much fun, joy and freedom could be had without getting high! We spent many hours in warm camaraderie talking after worship service, over a meal or coffee or at an outing of some kind. One of the young ladies in our singles group named Lydia had a penchant for coming up with fun things for all of us to do, and we grew close to each other while growing closer to the Lord. It was during this time that the Lord taught me the inestimable value not only of prayer, but the importance of praying now rather than later. While fulfilling my duties cleaning the church auditorium, I became better acquainted with our dear Assistant Pastor Keith. Keith is one of the most gentle, soft spoken men I ever met, and almost always had a radiant smile on his face which shone with the love of God. Until the Pastor was able to trust me with a key, Keith would unlock the auditorium to let me in and lock it when the job was done, and it was during these times that I got to know and love the man. Although I had been a born again believer for about ten years by now, I was only a baby in the faith because of my continued forays into sin and my general lack of attention to the things of the Lord. Often I'd ask Keith questions and advice when we talked, and would frequently ask him to pray for some need as well. With a giant smile and his bright blue eyes looking right at mine he'd say, "Let's pray right now!" and we would. It seemed that the Holy Spirit would always come in a special way. His eager invitation to come before God's presence boldly with our every need, and quickly as soon as we felt the need, taught me the invaluable lessons to pray *now* and *often*! To reinforce the idea, my kind and good Lord sent another brother in Christ to me named Kenny. A former US Marine, Kenny was a no-nonsense kind of guy ... kind, yet down to business about life and without room for a lot of small talk. If I had a person or issue of particular concern, I knew could count on him to pray. As with Keith, the Lord taught me through him how important it was to pray NOW! Any time I cornered Kenny and asked him to pray about something, he'd respond, "Let's pray right now, before I forget." and right then and there we'd stop and bring our petitions before God's throne. We are fragile and easily distracted creatures, and the Lord who made us knows this. The enemy would love to snatch the thought from our heads before we pray, distracting us from seeking God's great power and the comfort of His freeing love in response to our prayers. If the enemy is successful in depriving us of the accompanying assurance that we and our problems are safe in God's Hands, this leaves us open to doubt and fear, two of his most useful weapons. The great gifts of praying often and "striking while the iron is hot" became powerful tools in my spiritual arsenal, and no doubt will continue to be blessings all of my life.

This time of learning about God was quite joyful: His power, His might, His boundless love for us all and His desire that we participate in His good work on this earth were great and delightful revelations to me. To think that He would use a wretch like me do

His royal business! Yet in fact God tells us that we who are called by His name are joint heirs with King Jesus His Son (Romans 8:17). The apostle Peter tells us that we are, "a royal priesthood, a holy nation" (1 Peter 2:9). The apostle Paul tells us that the Lord purposely called many of us who in the world's eyes are "least likely to succeed" to be His servants (1 Corinthians 1:26). In fact, Jesus " ... made us kings and priests to our God; And we shall reign on the earth" (Revelation 5:10). It is hard to imagine that someone like me who so often was the laughingstock and the outsider, and eventually one of the dregs of the earth would be called by the King of Kings to be His trusted servant! As the psalmist said, "Marvelous are Your works, and that my soul knows very well" (Psalm 139:14b).

In addition to my cleaning assignment the Lord opened the door for me to help in our church's nursing home ministry. At first I was hesitant to join knowing that the Lord's work is holy, as I was still adjusting to the idea that I who had been such a filthy sinner was now completely guiltless and clean because of my Savior Jesus. When first invited I felt like a convicted thief being asked to help count money at the bank even though the bankers knew of my past. What a joy it was though! A number of the old people couldn't get out of bed, and some were not even aware when we were in the room when we stopped to see them. Many were alert though and looked forward to our visits as much as we did. Our time consisted of singing hymns and worship songs, reading aloud from the Bible and sharing the good news of Jesus in any way we could. Just the fact that we were there to visit them was enough for many of the precious old timers. The Lord even sent a special friend to me, a fine old gentleman named Harry Straight. Harry looked as if he could have been a retired Marine Corp officer—with his snow white flat top haircut, his ramrod straight posture and his calm, honorable demeanor, he reminded me of everything that is good about America. Although he probably could have served in our military and surely would have done so honorably, he spent his career in the aerospace industry and had worked on the Apollo Project which landed us on the moon. Harry had a horrible case of neuritis which caused him to be in incredible pain over every inch of his body most of the time. It would subside a little sometimes, but at all times he needed to wear heavy cotton gloves because it hurt for him to touch things without them. His days largely consisted of either sitting up in his chair or laying in his bed praying, reading or watching TV (what he could stand of it). Often the pain was so intense, that he could only pray. When that happened, pray he did! He would pray for everyone he could think of including praying for our country and all of our leaders every day. Since I lived nearby, I'd occasionally visit him in between ministry times. Though we could never talk too long because of his pain, I came to know him in a way that caused me to deeply admire him and to listen carefully when he spoke. This was man of God and one who pleased his Lord! Though Harry had prayed many times for the pain to go away and his prayers had not been answered, this didn't cause his faith to waver. He told me that the pain had become so intense one day that he didn't think he could bear it—as he prayed again for relief the Lord answered and took it away! The pain didn't go away for too long, but it was a sign that he needed in order to keep going. The memory of that dear man's love for our Lord and his steadfast faithfulness in spite of his suffering will stay with me always.

Those early days of my new freedom were blissful and mostly trouble free—the Lord had blessed me with a "life vacation"—but a huge test was not far away. About nine months after Jesus set me free, I faced the enemy of our souls in a deadly battle. In what seemed a carefully planned and insidious way, the devil set in motion a plot to destroy me by exploiting techniques and lies that he had used on me successfully for years. Setting me up for weeks through various events with the purpose of building resentment in me towards my employer, one day while laboring away on that lovely hillside north of Salinas, a great feeling of revulsion came over me.

"What are you doing working as a common laborer!" A voice which I took for my own shouted (wordlessly) in my head. "You're smart enough to be president of a large corporation, and here you are toiling away in the dirt like a peon!"

Anger rose up in me as I worked, and the enemy goaded me on by saying that since I was unappreciated, underpaid and mistreated here, the best thing for me to do was to pick up all the equipment, lock it away in the garage and quit. The devil hammered away at me for over an hour and finally, with vengeance and pride welling up in me I thought, "I'll show him!"

Thank GOD at that moment the Lord interceded and showed me a small part of the future, as it might unfold. In my mind's eye He showed me how I would put the stuff away and walk down the hill in triumph. Feeling very full of myself for "showing the boss" that he couldn't mistreat ME, I would swagger down the hill like a man in charge of his own destiny. Once I was on the road in the little valley at the bottom of the hill which led to US 101, flush with a new (false) sense of power and freedom, and reveling in the beautiful day which I was now "in charge of" a sinister transition would take place. My attention would be drawn to the cars that passed by me, and I'd feel eyes staring at me from within as they went by. Another voice would begin to speak to me—the devious, cruel voice of one of the hordes of hell which seek to destroy us all. The voice would say, "Neil, what are you doing walking down the road at ten o'clock in the morning? Everyone else is working!" and "Why did you quit your job Neil? You don't have any savings. How will you live?" and then … "Is there something *wrong* with you Neil?" implying that I was mentally unstable.

The enemy would continue to work on me during the long walk out of the little valley, repeating damning lies he'd been telling me since my childhood, and at the end of the road was … a bar! In the God enabled glimpse into what may have been my future, I saw myself walk in to the bar and begin drinking, which would have been (the Spirit revealed to me) the beginning of the end of my life.

Shuddering I thought, "Lord! What shall I do!" The Lord in His grace had opened my spiritual eyes just as He had opened the eyes of Elijah's servant, allowing me to see the workings of the unseen world. The enemy had once again set me up in an attempt to destroy me. The Lord reminded me about the many, many times satan's minions had plotted and schemed against me in the past to cause me to fall back in to drug and alcohol abuse. So shaken up by the immediacy of the impending mortal danger, I cried out to the Lord again, "What shall I do!" The fact that I was so easily deceived as I had been so many times in the past, revealed that I was on very treacherous ground and needed help now! The Lord then opened my eyes to see what a beautiful day it was: the sun was shining and the birds were singing, just like many days before. Nothing was different from those happier days except what was going on inside of me. This day I was locked in a deadly battle for my life with the enemy of our souls.

Praying fervently while I worked, the same feeling of heaviness which had caused me to want to quit and walk away pressed down upon me like a stone blanket. An hour or so passed, and the assault continued, wearing me down. I cried out,

"Why Lord? Why are my prayers not helping!"

In reply the Lord reminded me of the day before when I had been singing praise songs to Him and my soul had been soaring with the birds. He then reminded me that He, inhabits the praises of His people. (Ps. 22:3), "Neil, when you praise Me, I come closer, and the devil cannot stand the heat and he flees!"

So sing I did! I sang four or five praise songs or hymns in a row as I hacked away at the vegetation around me. Within a short time, as my body rejoiced in the vigorous exercise, my soul was again ascending with the birds. Relief had come at last! After a short while though the enemy came back with a vengeance, so I began to sing again. So it went for three days on that hilltop as I fought a titanic battle for my life—finally the enemy gave up. This and other experiences taught me that praising God in the midst of terrific pain or battles, when it seems an unlikely thing to do, is a powerful weapon. Once again, the truths "For we wrestle not against flesh and blood, but against principalities, against powers, against the rulers of the darkness of this world, against spiritual wickedness in high places" (Ephesians 6:12), and, "… the weapons of our warfare are not carnal, but mighty through God to the pulling down of strong holds" (2 Corinthians 10:4) were impressed upon me. On our own, we are hopeless and helpless, BUT we can do ALL things through Christ who give us strength (Philippians 4:13). Instead of an early death like my dear sister, cousins and many of my friends and acquaintances suffered due to the ravages of alcoholism or addiction, it was granted to me until now to live for my Savior Jesus and to carry His message of love, hope, life and freedom from sin and death, to the lost and dying world around me.

It's been many years since that battle up on the hill. Numerous times since then I've been locked in warfare with the enemy of our souls—sometimes aware of it sometimes not—yet every time the outcome has been the same.

"Yet in all these things we are more than conquerors through Him who loved us." (Romans 8:37) Many of the battles were no doubt fought by angels on my behalf; during others it seemed that I was all alone, though in each dangerous skirmish one thing is indisputable: my dear Jesus has never left me nor forsaken me … and He never will (Hebrews 13:5b). Still a sinner, though by God's grace becoming more like Him all the time, I have not fallen back into the use or abuse of alcohol or drugs since then, and my life has continued to get better and better. Once a walking dead man with a sentence of physical and spiritual death hanging over me like a guillotine blade, today I live a life of joy, peace and fulfillment that few can dream of. There have been a number of mountaintops and some deep, dark valleys in the years since Jesus delivered me from that hell bound slavery, but with my eyes firmly fixed upon my Loving Savior, I continue to trudge the road to happy destiny and will join Him one day in His heavenly paradise!

"Now all things are of God, who has reconciled us to Himself through Jesus Christ, and has given us the ministry of reconciliation, that is, that God was in Christ reconciling the world to Himself, not imputing their trespasses to them, and has committed to us the word of reconciliation. Now then, we are ambassadors for Christ, as though God were pleading through us: we implore you on Christ's behalf, be reconciled to God. For He made Him (Jesus) who knew no sin to be sin for us, that we might become the righteousness of God in Him" (2 Corinthians 5:18-21).

# ACKNOWLEDGEMENTS

With all of my heart I want to thank my father, mother, sisters (one in heaven already), wife, children and dear friends for all that they put up with from me during my worst years, and for being a very important part of making me who I am! Most of all, I thank our great God and Savior who paid all of my insurmountable debt, and gave me a reason to live.

Made in the USA
Coppell, TX
02 December 2021

66932529R10236